Two Parts Textbook,
One Part Love

Also by LouAnne Johnson

School Is Not a Four-Letter Word:
How to Help Your Child Make the Grade

The Girls in the Back of the Class

My Posse Don't Do Homework

Making Waves: A Woman in This Man's Navy

Two Parts Textbook,

One Part

Love

A RECIPE FOR
SUCCESSFUL
TEACHING

LouAnne Johnson

HYPERION
New York

Library of Congress Cataloging-in-Publication Data

Johnson, LouAnne
  Two parts textbook, one part love: a recipe for successful teaching / LouAnne Johnson.—1st ed.
    p. cm.
  ISBN 0-7868-6275-0
  1. Teaching–United States–Handbooks, manuals, etc. 2. Teacher-
student relationships–United States–Handbooks, manuals, etc. 3.
Classroom management–United States–Handbooks, manuals, etc.
4. Motivation in education–United States–Handbooks, manuals,
etc. I. Title.
LB1025.3.J64   1998
371.102–dc21   97-28386
                                                         CIP

Designed by Christine Weathersbee

First Edition
10 9 8 7 6 5 4 3 2 1

Author's Note:

All of the incidents in this book are true, but student names and identities have been changed to protect their privacy. Real names of readers and teachers are included to acknowledge their generosity and graciousness in allowing me to use portions of their letters and lesson plans.

Dedication

For the wonderful teachers I was blessed to have during my own school days:

Mary Ellen Boyling, Eleonora Sandblade, Evelyn Hodak, Mary Ann Greggan, Mary Ann Clinton, James Miller, Tom Craig, Kenneth C. Brodeur, "Dr. Bob" Hunter, Marilyn Raby, Al Black, Kevin McIlvoy, Jane Allen

And for my first teachers, Bob and Shirley.

Contents

2. THE BIG D:
Discipline Is Not a Dirty Word   61

4. PSYCHOLOGY & SALES: Education Is the Product; You're the Salesperson   155

7. TIME & ENERGY SAVERS:
Tips for Making Life a Little Easier   259

12. TWENTY YEARS FROM NOW:
Your Students Will Remember You   360

Introduction

I never intended to become a high school teacher, and I certainly never expected to write books about my experiences in the classroom. Teaching high school was supposed to be a brief stop on the road to a doctoral degree and a career as a university professor and literary novelist. My well-laid plans went astray when a group of "at-risk" teenagers took me hostage and held me for five years. Those truants and troublemakers changed my life, first by needing me, then by loving me, and finally by teaching me how to be a teacher. Those students inspired me to write their stories, to tell the truth about why they weren't succeeding in school, and their truths became my book *My Posse Don't Do Homework*, which later became the movie *Dangerous Minds*. Those same students have gone on to become dental technicians, coaches, teachers, legal aides, medical assistants, data processors, college students, and parents. This book is their legacy. It contains the lessons they taught me.

If you are a teacher who believes in following the rules, always, whether they make sense or not, then do not read this book. Put it down right now! I'm warning you. I'm going to talk about outrageous concepts, such as starting each student with an A, and letting little people go to the restroom when they need to, and not punishing them when they're a few minutes late, and a hundred other ridiculous ideas that could very well lead to total anarchy in the classroom. You wouldn't want to consider such things, would you? I didn't think so.

But, if you are an idealistic, passionate person who believes that our job is not simply to teach science and history and English and math, but also to teach young people how to be the kind of people we want them to be—and that the best way to treat children is with kindness and generosity—then welcome to my book.

By the way, I didn't write this book because I think I'm the best teacher in the world or that my way of doing things is better than somebody else's. I wrote it because I have met so many teachers who said my teaching philosophy and techniques encouraged them to try their own ideas (with good success), and they asked for more suggestions. And I've received hundreds of letters from beginning teachers who wanted to know my "secret." So, here it is—the best advice I have to offer. I hope it will make you think and laugh and develop a new trust in your own good instincts.

Perhaps you will see yourself in these pages and think, "She's not so special. I do very similar things in my own classroom." That wouldn't surprise me a bit. I know I'm not the Lone Ranger. I know there are thousands of wonderful teachers in this country, and I was blessed with several of them as my own teachers. If you are one of those wonderful folks, I offer you my respect, my admiration, and my gratitude.

Do Your Homework

Things to Consider Before
You Step into the Classroom

You have a college degree. You know your subject. You have your credential. And you know all about lesson plans, curriculum guides and the latest theories of education. So, why are you nervous about your first day? Because you aren't stupid. You know that teaching is a scary business. Not only are you responsible for effectively educating children, but you are legally responsible for their safety, although a good number of them seem intent on self-destruction. And you are aware that our current system of education is an elaborate game—one that works only if our students agree to participate. If your students decide not to play school, you will have to convince them that it is worth their time and energy to cooperate with you before you can teach them anything.

Whether you have detailed instructions about how you are to accomplish your classroom goals, with curriculum guides that list specific readings and activities to be completed

I

during a given time period, or the freedom and responsibility of creating your own curriculum, your first—and most important task—is to grab your students by their brains so quickly that they forget they are supposed to hate school. In Chapter 6, "Good Morning, Class," I'll suggest some specific, practical suggestions for grabbing your students, but right now, I'd like to focus on your personal philosophy of teaching and your attitude towards your students. If you consider the ideas and issues suggested in this chapter before you step into your classroom, I believe they will make your job more enjoyable, your students more comfortable, and your teaching more effective.

You're the Star of the Show

The standard classroom is a miniature theater: it holds a small captive audience and an even smaller stage. But you are the star of the show, and when you're standing on that stage, your audience can seem overwhelmingly large. The brighter your spotlight, the faster you'll draw your audience into the show. Later on, you may choose to share the spotlight with your students, but you will need to take center stage until your students have learned their roles. I don't mean that you should be the dictator and they the unquestioning subjects, but you have a job to do and specific goals to accomplish, and it is your responsibility to lead your group toward those goals. It is their role to follow, although it is perfectly acceptable for them to suggest changes in the script.

1. *Choose your teacher persona.*

Since your students will take their cues from you, it's very important that you decide before you step onto your stage how you will portray your role. I don't mean that you should strut and posture grandly or pretend to be something you are not. But your students are going to decide what kind of person you are from the first moment they see you. They will look at your clothes, your hair, your skin color.

They will note your posture, the length of your stride, the tone of your voice, your expression as you observe other students, and the look in your eyes. They will decide whether you seem crabby or nice or tough or easy or scared or confident. All of this will happen within the first few minutes of your first class—long before you begin your first lesson. And once your students decide who you are, it will be difficult for you to convince them to change their perceptions. It can be done, but it demands so much time and energy that if you goof and get started on the wrong foot (as I have done more than once), you may be inclined to simply cope with the status quo and hope things will improve over time. But coping and hoping are not good substitutes for confidence and leadership.

What kind of image do you want to project to your students? How do you want them to see you: As the scientific expert? The hip dude who knows algebra inside out? The toughest but best chemistry teacher on earth? The drill sergeant grammarian? The stand-up comic who happens to know all about history? The serious student of literature? The hard-boiled journalist? The tough but tender coach?

2. *Be yourself.*

Whatever persona you choose should be one that is natural for you, one that you can maintain for the entire school year. I am not advising you to put on a mask or try to change your personality, but to consider how to make the best use, as a teacher, of your own unique personality. Here's how I think of myself as a teacher: I am strict but flexible, inclined to use humor instead of threats, intolerant of rude behavior, passionate about my subject, and willing to meet students halfway.

It took me a while to perfect my drill sergeant/stand-up comic/counselor persona, and I made many changes along the way. My first year, I tried too hard to be cool and it caused discipline problems. I joked around a lot because I wanted the kids to like me, to think of me as an older friend. What I didn't realize at that time was that they don't need more friends. They have plenty of friends—friends who offer them dope and cigarettes and plagiarized research papers, friends who pierce their navels and wear T-shirts with death masks on them, friends who think heavy metal is great music and Ripple is fine wine. What my students needed was for me to be a teacher, an adult who would accept my responsibility as their guide and a leader who sometimes had to be the bad guy in order to help them.

My second teaching year, I took the advice of a veteran teacher who said, "Don't smile until after Christmas." I decided to be the drill sergeant who could stare a student to death. I couldn't do it (I'm a smiling kind of woman), so my message was inconsistent and the students responded by misbehaving half of the time.

My third year, I sat down and figured out what were my biggest strengths and biggest weaknesses. Then I combined my three strongest assets and came up with a combination that worked for me, so I kept it. Now, I make a few important rules that cannot be broken, I take the time to know each student personally, and I use humor whenever possible to make my point.

3. Dress for the part.

In my search for my most effective persona, I discovered an interesting student response to my clothing. They perceive some outfits as more serious than others, and they behave accordingly. If the lesson for the day requires creativity, spontaneity, and lots of student input, I wear more informal clothing; jeans and a sweater, perhaps. On days when I want to limit the amount of spontaneity, during an important exam or a lesson that will serve as an important building block for future lessons, I wear a suit.

Using clothes to project an image is basic psychology, and we see it all around us. Corporate executives are often very adept at "power dressing." The makers of TV commercials, especially commercials for health products, often dress their announcers in white lab coats that give the impression of medical authority, so we will be more inclined to believe them when they tell us that we'll have fewer gastrointestinal disturbances or sinus headaches. "Difficult" students often use clothing—leather jackets and ripped jeans, for instance—to advertise their contempt for authority and send a clear challenge to adults, a warning to stay their distance. Some adults heed the message, while others answer the challenge. In either case, those students have used clothing to provoke adults into specific behaviors. Teachers can take advantage of the same psychology to influence student behavior.

4. Don't let students direct your performance.

You probably will decide to make changes to your persona after you've had a chance to test it in action, but you will be making those changes for the purpose of achieving specific goals—and not simply responding to your students' reactions. There is a tremendous difference in the way they will perceive a change in your behavior, depending upon the reason for the change. When you choose to alter your own actions in order to create a different reaction from your students, your choice indicates self-control and power. When you repeatedly change your behavior in response to their actions, it gives them the clear signal that they are in charge of you and can dictate your behavior.

Let me give you an example. One year, I followed the school policy of forbidding any food or drink in my classroom, end of discussion. My fourth-period students, who were assigned to the second lunch period, often begged for permission to eat snacks and promised to be neat. I said no. But fourth period didn't end until thirty minutes past noon, and the kids were hungry. I could hear their tummies growling. Sometimes my own stomach joined the chorus. So, I sneaked snacks between bells, and they sneaked food when I wasn't looking. When they left my room, I'd find stray potato chips in the aisles, candy wrappers balled up and stuffed behind the dictionaries, little gobs of peanut butter and jelly smeared on the edges of the desks. No matter how hard I tried, I couldn't seem to catch them in the act, or prevent them from eating. I could have punished the entire class, but I've always hated being punished for other people's mistakes.

So I reconsidered my options. I could continue to ban food in my room, then waste a lot of time and energy trying to catch them eating, threaten and punish the culprits when I caught them, and waste even more time and energy cleaning up after the ones I couldn't catch. No matter what I did, I wasn't going to stop them from eating. I knew they weren't being deliberately defiant; they were truly hungry. As it was, they were the ones who were deciding what would go on in my classroom and I was coping with their decision. But if I decided to change the rule and add some reasonable restrictions, then I would once again be in charge. One day, I announced that I thought the no-food rule was unreasonable and that I would permit food to be eaten in my classroom under the following conditions:

1. *All drinks would be consumed before class began, and cans or bottles deposited in the trash can so we wouldn't have spills and ruined books and papers.*

2. *If the principal entered the room, no chewing would occur.*

3. *No crumbs, scraps, or wrappers were to be left on the floor, in the desks, or between the pages of books— they were responsible for appointing a clean-up team to police the room every day as soon as the bell rang.*

4. *If I found one potato chip or one candy wrapper on the floor, the deal was off forever and the culprits have to stay after school until they were twenty-one years old.*

By deciding to change the rules and take control of the situation, I altered the entire dynamics of that class and learned a good lesson in the process. Not only did my students follow the new food rules, they were so impressed by my willingness to compromise and trust them, they returned the favor by cooperating with me on classroom assignments and exercises. They didn't interpret the relaxed rule as a sign of weakness on my part, as I had feared they might, but saw it as a sign of strength, instead.

5. Rehearse your role.

After you have a clear idea of your persona, figure out what you need to do in order to project that particular image. Practice on your friends and family, talk to yourself in the mirror, ask a friend to videotape you walking into a room and introducing yourself. Try to see yourself as your students will see you. If you don't like the picture, ask for help—from your college professors, veteran teachers, administrators, family and friends. Visit the self-help section of your local bookstore and page through the books on developing confidence and leadership skills.

What Are You Really Teaching?

Once, during my first year in the classroom, I confessed to my master teacher, Hal Gray, that I was afraid I wasn't teaching my students enough. I explained that I believed students should reach a minimum standard to achieve a passing grade, but I wasn't sure where to set the minimum standard for my different English classes.

"Minimum standard of what?" Hal asked me. "Commas? Spelling? Vocabulary? Should a kid know four ways to use a comma and the correct spelling of four hundred words? Should he know what defenestration means? What if he doesn't know that word, but knows a thousand other ones? What is the standard? I'm not talking about the district's objectives. I'm talking about your own standards. What is it you expect those kids to know when they leave your class?"

I thought about Hal's question for a few minutes, but couldn't come up with an answer. "I don't know," I admitted. "But I worry about whether I'm really teaching them anything."

"All teachers wonder whether they're really teaching anything," Hal told me. "I used to wonder it myself, hundreds of
years ago when I was your age. But then I learned something
important. You aren't teaching English. What are you teaching? you may ask. You're teaching kids how to analyze information, relate it to other information they know, put it
together, take it apart, and give it back to you in the form that
you request it. It doesn't matter what the class is, we all teach
the same things. We just use different terms. You use commas
and adjectives, biology teachers use chromosomes and chloro-
phyll, math teachers use imaginary numbers and triangles.
And you're also teaching an optional agenda—you're teaching your kids to believe in themselves. So don't worry about
whether you're teaching them grammar. You're teaching
those kids. Trust me, you're teaching them."

1. What is your "optional agenda"?

After I had a chance to think about Hal's comments, I realized that what he called the "optional agenda" is the most
important factor in teaching—more important than school
district objectives, because it is your optional agenda that
answers Hal's all-important question: *What do you want your
students to know when they leave your class?*

What did I want my students to know? Naturally, as an
English teacher, I wanted my students to have improved
reading and writing skills, bigger vocabularies, increased
comprehension of abstract ideas, better thinking skills and
an appreciation for literature. So, I designed specific lessons
for vocabulary building and literary analysis and composing
logical arguments—hundreds of different lessons over the
years, tailored for different levels of student ability. After my
discussion with Hal, when I spread out my various lesson
plans and looked for common areas among them, my own
"optional agenda" became clear. In almost every case, my
lessons were framed within larger lessons. One composition
assignment, for example, urged students to write about a
time they had faced a problem and overcome it. A short
story unit included fictional accounts of people dealing with

challenges such as divorce, death of a loved one, peer pressure, and prejudice. The poetry I selected for special attention involved pursuing your dreams, standing up for your principles, admitting your errors.

My answer to Hal's question is the same today as it was then: I want my students to have better academic skills, but I also want them to have a strong sense of their own ethical standards, an unquenchable thirst for knowledge, a desire to succeed according to their own definition of success, and the strength of character to treat all people with basic human dignity and respect.

2. *What you are is what you teach.*

What is important to you as a person will shape your own personal teaching philosophy. Even if you don't intentionally try to include your beliefs and attitudes in your lessons, they will be there, hidden within the context of the reading assignments you select, in the methods you use to determine who passes and who fails, in the tone of your voice when you address certain students, and in a thousand other subtle clues. Every day, you will be teaching your students what you think is important.

Take a moment to recall your own elementary and secondary school teachers. I would bet my gigantic teacher's salary that you are not thinking of algebraic formulae or prepositional phrases. More likely, you remember a compliment that sent your spirit soaring or a humiliation that still makes your cheeks burn. I remember my second-grade teacher using masking tape to attach my glasses to my face because I kept taking them off when other kids teased me about wearing them. What she taught me was how embarrassing and infuriating it is to be helpless under the control of an authority figure who misuses her power. I also remember my fifth-grade teacher assigning me to be editor of our class newspaper and encouraging me to write. What she gave me was a sense of self-respect and a desire to write good things that would make her proud of me.

As you reflect about your own school days, make a note

of the best and worst things your teachers did. Post that note somewhere in your classroom as a reminder. If your students notice and ask what it is, tell them it's there to remind you to be the best teacher you can be. I guarantee that if you should slip and commit one of the crimes on your "bad teacher" list, your students will alert you immediately.

3. Covering curriculum is not teaching.

If you are a master organizer, with a creative flair and the ability to teach your advanced, regular, and remedial students and at the same time deal with administrative interruptions, then you probably have no trouble covering all of the curriculum required for your course. If you don't spend a minute worrying about how you're going to fit everything you want to teach into one school year, then you're an uncommonly talented teacher and I would recommend that you skip this section. The rest of us worry, because it's common for teachers, especially new teachers, to fear that they can't teach everything they need to teach because there is too much material, not enough time, too much paper shuffling, and too many time-consuming administrative tasks. Instead of sharing this fear and discussing ways to become more effective teachers, most of us worry privately and fear that our colleagues will think we're ineffective or unqualified if we admit that we feel inadequate to the task of teaching all of the required materials for our course.

The question every teacher, especially beginning teachers, must face is this: *Given a conflict, where does my priority lie—in covering the material or in meeting the needs of my students?* It's easy to err in either direction. Some teachers blast their classes with impossible workloads from the moment they enter the classroom. Often, these are the teachers who boast that "Nobody earns an A in my class because I'm just too darned tough." My questions to those teachers are: *What is there to be proud of in not being able to teach students well enough that they can earn a high grade?* and *What would motivate a student to try hard if he or she knows, in advance, that an A is impossible to achieve?*

Other teachers toss aside the textbooks and spend their entire class periods chatting with students about current events, or designing fun projects that take weeks to complete, leaving their students unprepared for the following year's requirements. Those teachers may be popular, and may enjoy themselves immensely, but they are cheating their students.

It is possible, although not easy, to find a middle ground. My district supervisor gave me a big boost in the right direction when she explained her viewpoint at a meeting of Academy teachers. Working as a team, we four teachers had the task of teaching fifty at-risk teens, students who had severe attendance problems, substandard reading ability, and apathetic attitudes towards education.

"Covering curriculum is not teaching," our supervisor explained. "Nobody expects you to address the problems these kids have, bring them up to grade level, and cover your entire textbooks in one year. I advise you to select the key elements in your texts and teach those elements well. Don't worry about covering everything, just teach the most important concepts and skills, and teach your students how to learn so they can pick up the slack later." We took her advice and were amazed at how well it worked. When our students realized that we would slow down when they needed to, and spend time on areas of special interest, they repaid us by working harder at the mundane tasks in between. Our students performed as well as the "regular" students in English, history, and computers, and our math students zoomed right past the regular geometry classes, earning higher grades and completing more of the same textbook!

Those students reminded us of a lesson we sometimes forget—our students will perform to meet our expectations because they are capable of much more than we require of them.

4. *There is no such thing as a casual remark to a child.*

Sometimes I think we forget how impressionable children are. We forget how excruciating the smallest pain can be, how exhilarating the tiniest victory, and how lasting the effect of a comment from an adult they admire. One day, before class started, a group of football players were boasting about their latest gridiron glories. I noticed another boy, Sean, blush and fidget as he watched the athletes trade playful insults. A skinny youngster, all elbows and knees, Sean often dropped things or tripped over his shoelaces. When one of the ball players complimented himself on a sixty-five-yard touchdown, Sean sighed and looked out the window. I walked around the room until I stood near Sean's desk.

"I'm very proud of you, Paul," I told the touchdown scorer. "But I hope you go on to achieve great things after school, too. I'd hate for you to be one of those people who peak at age sixteen, whose lives are all downhill after high school."

"I'm cool," Paul responded with a grin. "You know the scouts are already looking at me." I was looking at Sean, who was looking at me.

"You're going to be one of those men who peak much later in life," I said softly to Sean. "I can see it in your eyes. You have a lot to look forward to." I quickly walked past so that I wouldn't embarrass him and just as quickly forgot about my remarks.

A few months later, Sean's mother, Mrs. Campbell, attended Open House at our school and stopped to see me. "I wanted to thank you for what you said to Sean," she said, as she took my hand and held it between her own. "He said you told him you knew he was going to peak late in life and he shouldn't worry about not being the best athlete or the most popular right now. You should have seen him smile when he told me. And he has been a different person ever since. You changed his life. I can't thank you enough."

I was so stunned at Mrs. Campbell's remarks that I just stood there, grinning stupidly at her, until she left the room. I had forgotten all about that day. But Sean remembered. When I recovered my composure, I hurried to my desk and made myself a note that I taped to the top of my desk as a reminder. My note read: *Be careful: Everything you say, every single day, may be recorded forever in your students' hearts.*

Physical Logistics

1. Arranging your room.

Desks and chairs. No big deal. You put them in rows, students sit in them, and you teach. Simple, right? Yes, but something as simple as the seating arrangements can have a tremendous affect on the dynamics that occur in your classroom. How your students sit will affect their attitudes and interactions, and your teaching style.

If you line up the desks so they stand in straight rows like little soldiers, with equal spacing between them, your students will immediately form an opinion about you— even before they see you. They'll expect a strict, orderly, standard-issue teaching style to match your neat, orderly rows of desks. If you place student desks in a circle, instead of rows, on the other hand, you send a message to students the second they enter your room—this isn't going to be a "normal" classroom; something interesting or unusual is going to happen. The more relaxed the desk arrangements, the more relaxed the classroom will feel.

You can take advantage of the psychology of seating by designing different seating arrangements to complement different lessons. For example, when you want students to feel less inhibited, during an informal class discussion, you might create a jumbled appearance, with desks askew. In my own classroom, I normally place desks in short rows, half on each side of the room, all facing inwards or angled forward towards the front of the room, so that I am closer to each student and can move quickly to offer help or squelch disruptive behavior. During major exams or important lessons, however, I move the desks into straight rows to let my students know that I expect them to be quiet and pay special attention.

If you place student seats in a circle, semicircle, or rows facing each other, be alert for signs of impending trouble. Most of the time, students enjoy being able to see each other, especially when we are reading a play or story— when students speak into the backs of each other's heads, as they must when seated in long straight rows, they can't hear well and they may lose important information, as well as interest in what's being read.

Sometimes, however, being able to see each other causes problems for students. A bully or gang member may "stare down" a student on the other side of the room; teens who are engaged in romantic rivalry may conduct a silent battle; and raging hormones may make it impossible for both girls and boys to concentrate when faced with so many interesting people to flirt with or observe.

Classrooms are often so crowded that your options for seating arrangements will be limited. If you have the room, I would advise against five or six long rows facing forward, six to eight desks per row, because of the physical and psychological distance such an arrangement puts between you and the students in the back of the room. With several bodies and desks separating them from you, students in the back row are more likely to duck behind their neighbors to avoid being called upon, to daydream or disrupt other students, and to fall behind in their lessons. If you must use the standard five- or six-row arrangement, I would suggest that you rotate students periodically, so that those in the back row move to the front seats and everybody else moves back one row.

Don't forget to save a seat for newly arrived students, guests, visiting students, or administrators who need to observe your teaching in order to write the required evaluations. If you don't have a spare desk to put in a corner, find a folding chair and keep it on hand so that you won't have to interrupt your lessons to find a seat for the unexpected guest. In the meantime, a spare chair comes in very handy when you have a disruptive student who needs a brief "time-out" in the back of the class.

2. Position yourself carefully.

Consider your own position in the classroom as carefully as you consider that of your students. If you stand behind a podium or teach while seated behind your desk, you'll place a psychological barrier between you and your students. (It is tempting, I know, to hide behind a podium or desk, so your nervousness and/or fear won't be so obvious to your students—but hiding won't help you overcome these problems.) You need to be able to move freely around your classroom, between student desks, so that you can reach anyone who requires help or attention. Make sure that you can see every student, and every student can see you.

For maximum efficiency, place your desk where it won't be in the way during lessons, and place file cabinets or bookshelves nearby. Otherwise, you'll find yourself trotting back and forth, wasting time and losing your students' attention, while you search for necessary materials. Keeping books and files near your desk also will discourage curious students from exploring while you are busy assisting other students.

If your classroom has windows, or a window in the door, you might consider covering the bottom portion with posters or construction paper, to discourage roaming students from peering inside to distract (unfortunately, sometimes to threaten) your students. Reducing outside visibility also helps you maintain some privacy when you are working before or after school, busily grading papers or planning lessons, and you don't have the time or inclination to chat with friendly visitors, either student or staff. If you place your desk near the door, in full view of windows, you won't be able to hide for a moment of peace when you feel the need.

3. Seating charts—pros and cons.

Should you assign student seats? A good question. Some teachers swear by seating charts; they make it easier to take roll, faster for students to take seats, and simpler to assign group activities. Assigned seats allow you to place shy or talkative students along a wall, or in the back of the room, to create a buffer zone around them, for their protection or that of other students. Seating charts also create a sense of comfort for students who need the security of a routine; they like structure and dislike having to make decisions. Even if you don't assign seats, those students will come to class early so they can sit in the same seat every day—and they will become agitated if other students sit in "their" seats.

In spite of all their advantages, I think seating charts create too many problems. Students who have poor vision or hearing may end up in the back of the room and be too embarrassed to say anything. Remedial students who need extra attention may be too far away for you to notice. And some students simply feel more comfortable sitting at the edge of the classroom, instead of in the middle where they are exposed and more vulnerable to intimidation or distraction. Imagine if you were required to sit directly in front of the principal at every staff meeting, or in the back row where you couldn't hear or see clearly. At one high school, our principal expected the undivided attention of every teacher for the entire meeting. After two or three meetings, at which teachers ignored the principal's pointed stares and continued grading papers or whispering to each other, the principal removed all of the tables from the library and set up folding chairs directly in front of his podium. Half the staff stopped coming to meetings, and those who did sat with arms folded across their chests, insulted and indignant. Students often respond in the same way when they perceive that they are being ordered about unfairly; they resent the implication that they can't be trusted to select their own seats and behave themselves.

Seating charts also prevent teachers from observing actions that reveal student personalities. A sharp teacher can learn a lot from watching where students choose to sit when they first enter a classroom. Students who opt for the front row tend to be either ace students or shy ones who need the comfort of being close to the teacher. Students who head straight for the back row may be potential troublemakers or kids with apathetic attitudes—but they also may be scared of some other student in the class, or trying to avoid taunts or unwanted romantic overtures from others. (You would be surprised to know how many boys choose the back row to avoid flirtatious girls.) If you do decide to use a seating chart, I would recommend waiting until you have a sense of your students' personalities, so you can split up the nonstop talkers, for example, or seat students with poor study skills near those with good study skills in the hope that their goodness will "rub off."

I do use seating charts occasionally, when I have a class that needs the extra control. But I begin the year by allowing open seating, asking students to move when necessary. I remind them that choosing their own seats is a privilege and one that they must earn by cooperating with me. When I do assign seats, I announce that anybody who has a serious problem with their assignment may come to discuss it with me after school—not before or after class. If a student is concerned enough to stay after school, I will change the seating arrangement.

4. Avoid "ethnic seating."

Without realizing it, I once made the mistake, as many teachers do, of assuming that students would feel more comfortable if I seated them near other students who shared the same ethnicity or native language—and I wasn't even aware of my assumption until a student pointed it out. When a new Hispanic student arrived in midterm, I seated her next to three other Spanish-speaking girls, all good students, because I thought they would be most likely to make her feel welcome and help her catch up with the class. Rarely have I been so wrong. Shortly after Araceli's arrival, the students in her class read a short story and then wrote an essay about prejudice. Araceli's essay not only made me realize my mistake, it also made me question many other assumptions that had been, until then, unchallenged. Here's what she wrote:

My Experiance with Prejudice
by A. Andrade

My experiance happened today right now in this class. There was a lot of empty desks where I could of sitted, but just because I speak Spanish, my English teacher putted me with a bunch of other girls who speak Spanish, like just because we speak the same language we have to be best friends or something. But we do not even speak the same languages. I am from Argentina and we have our own kind of spanish and it is way

*different of the way that gordita girl talks. She sounds like she
came from Tiajuana or somwhere in mexico where the fruit
pickers and cholos live. And that other one, the sad, skinny girl,
she is from nicaragua. In case you are not knowing your geography, it is in central america which is a hole nother continent
from south america where my country is.*

*People always doing that, especial teachers, sticking all of
the spanish speakings in one place like we have to like each
other because we all frijoles and tortillas. But los americanos all
eat hamburguesas and french fries and the teachers do not
think they will always liking each other. And the teachers put
los negros together, too, when they do not know each other. Why
the teachers do that? Do they are thinking we are the same peo-
pls because we all have black hair? Or they cannot tell us apart
one from each other, so they putting us together so when they
call our name they do not have to look at nobody, just look at
our group and we are in it. Maybe you do not even know our
names.*

Quien soy yo?

*You want us to write about a time we saw somebody be prej-
udice and how does that made us feel and what we think about it,
well I cannot tell you all that because I do not know. But it is making me think. Would you do this thing to a white girl?*

After reading Araceli's essay, I talked to her and her classmates, and learned that often there is bitter rivalry among
students from Mexico and South America, for example, or
from El Salvador and Nicaragua. "Everybody always calls me
a Mexican," one boy said, "and it makes me mad. I don't hate
Mexicans, but I'm from El Salvador and I'm proud of my
country. Americans need to learn some more geography."
Several black students said they knew teachers were trying
to be kind, but that grouping them together was a form of
well-intentioned discrimination, because teachers assumed
black students would automatically like each other, which
meant the teachers weren't paying attention to the students'
individual personalities and attitudes.

At the end of our discussion, I asked the students for suggestions about seating assignments. Their suggestions were equitable as well as motivational. Students should be allowed to sit where they wanted, they said, except for people with bad grades. Anybody who was failing class should have to sit in the first two rows, and the last row of the seats should be reserved for students who maintained A's or B's in class. Since many students head for the back of the class when they enter the room, the grade requirement for sitting in the back would motivate them to keep their grades up.

Rules, Grades, Cheating

Your school district will probably have guidelines, perhaps stringent rules, about grading standards and classroom procedures, but I think it's a good idea for you to develop your own basic philosophy before you start teaching. Questions may arise about restroom visits or absences on your first day as a teacher, and if you aren't prepared, you may find yourself making up rules that you'll regret later on.

1. Those ubiquitous rules.

Administrators demand rules. Kids expect them. Teachers have to have them. But I've learned from sad experience that here is one case where less is definitely more. There are students who perceive every rule as a challenge. And even those who don't will be tempted to chew gum just to see if they can get away with it, if you make "no gum" a rule, or snack on a Snickers if you ban candy bars from your room. I'm not suggesting that you let them chomp and chew their way through your exciting lessons. I'm suggesting that you be sneaky, devious, and underhanded—ah-hem, I mean you should use some basic child psychology.

My first year, I made the required rule list and passed it out on the first day of class. I think I had ten rules. I spent a lot of time pursuing and punishing culprits. Then I read some teacher manuals that advised three to five rules as maximum. I also read a brilliant and compelling observation by French author Alexis de Tocqueville: "To render a people obedient and keep them so, savage laws inefficiently enforced are less effective than mild laws enforced by an efficient administration regularly, automatically, as it were, every day and on all alike." In the second semester of that year, I cut down the list and waited until the second day of classes to distribute the list. Things improved, but I still spent too much time on discipline and not enough on lessons.

The following year, I waited until the third day of class, when I was relatively certain that the students I had were the ones I was going to keep. Then I presented only one rule: *Respect yourself and the other people in this room.* Instead of making copies and handing them out, I wrote it on a large poster board and hung it on the front of my desk. The one-rule approach worked much better for a couple of reasons. First, it's positive, not negative. It doesn't tell people what they can't or shouldn't do. It tells them what they are supposed to do. Second, it covers everything else. For example: chewing gum isn't respectful to you or anybody else if you snap it, pop it, and stick on the dictionary when you're finished with it. Those actions are both ill-mannered and disrespectful. But if you chew it gently and quietly, and dispose of it properly when you are finished, you demonstrate self-respect and respect for other people. And that's one of the most important things we can teach our children.

When I explain my one rule to my students, I always use this example, because I think it's important in our society: *I will not tolerate any put-downs of other people based on their ethnic background, skin color, gender, sexual orientation, or religion. Such insults are the most disrespectful of acts because they erase the other person's face, and nobody deserves that.* I give students the opportunity to object if they believe my rule is unreasonable, but nobody has ever challenged it.

There are hundreds of textbooks and research reports that recommend specific rules and methods for assignment consequences. You may find suggestions that work for you. But you may find, as I did, that you will develop a much better rapport with your students if you come into the class with an attitude that you expect them to behave themselves, you expect them to be polite, and you expect them to succeed in your class. When somebody does something disrespectful to me or to themselves, I call that student aside and explain why I dislike a specific behavior. I don't like assigning kids to detention because I don't want to sit there and baby-sit them, and I don't like calling parents and causing more distress. Instead, the student and I discuss the misbehavior privately and we come to an agreement about it. This has saved me and my students a lot of time and trouble.

2. May I be excused?

It seems clear to me that when somebody has to use the restroom, a restroom should be made accessible. Perhaps that is because I have a weak bladder and once wet my pants in school when a teacher refused to excuse me from class. I have never been so humiliated in my life. My face still gets red, thirty-six years later, when I think of it.

What will your restroom procedure be? Will you have a time limit? One person out of the room at a time? A special pass? (I use a stuffed teddy, the Bathroom Bear, which can't be duplicated or rolled up and stuffed into a pocket.) Will there be times when restroom visits won't be permitted? (I declare restroom visit time before whole-group reading sessions because nobody leaves the room when we're reading something important.)

Some schools have a standard policy that nobody is permitted to leave the classroom between bells, in order to prevent problems—cutting, graffiti, fights, and romantic trysts. But it seems to indicate serious problems and a lack of rapport between students and staff if the adults have to resort to an inhumane rule system in order to maintain control. I try to put myself in my students' shoes. If I had a job where my employer refused to allow me to go to the restroom when I needed to, I would find another job quickly. I did have such a job once, and I didn't stay with that company in spite of its excellent salaries and benefits.

If you believe that children should be denied permission to use the restroom simply because they are children, I must ask you—why? Would you make the same rule for adults under your charge? If not, then I ask you to reconsider. Perhaps your attitude was shaped by your own experience; but just because something didn't hurt you doesn't mean it is right. Some people believe denying restroom privileges teaches self-control.

I think denying such basic privileges teaches anger, humiliation, mistrust of adults, and a desire for revenge. (By the way, my doctor warned me that "holding it too long" is not only painful, but can cause medical problems.)

What should you do if you're a pro-potty teacher working for an administration with an anti-restroom agenda? First, ask other teachers whether the rule is strictly enforced and, if so, who is punished, the student or the teacher—or both? If the rule isn't enforced, and ridiculous ones seldom are, then make sure you explain to your students that using the restroom is a privilege. If you let it slip, accidentally on purpose, that you aren't *supposed* to let them go, but that you think they deserve the respect of being permitted to use the restroom when necessary, they will be delighted at your daring on their behalf. (Be sure to add a warning that the first person who abuses that privilege or discusses it outside of class will ruin it for everybody.)

At one school, where a strict no–restroom visit policy was enforced, the principal permitted me to escort my students to the facility when they needed to go. My students knew I had made a special effort on their behalf, by negotiating the arrangement with the principal, and they repaid the favor by working harder in my classroom.

3. Percentage? Curve? Coin Toss?

Grades can be used as incentives, record of progress, punishment—or all three. I opt to use the first two only, because when teachers use grades as punishment, they contribute to the cycle of misbehavior, punitive discipline, and failure that undermines our efforts to teach.

Every teacher must create a grading policy that reflects his or her own ethics and teaching philosophy, but the most effective teachers maintain high standards, a flexible attitude, and a focus on fairness. They keep students informed of their progress at frequent intervals, to avoid surprises and complaints. They also understand that student grades reflect, at least to some degree, their effectiveness as teachers. A gradebook filled with D's and F's is a warning flag.

Your school may use a Pass/Fail option, straight percentages, or a letter-grade system. Your department may add their own criteria—95% required for an A, for example. But it will be up to you to assign the grades. Even a subject such as math, which is more objective than most, leaves room for subjectivity in grading. Will you give credit only for correct answers on homework, for example, or will be you give partial credit for papers that have incorrect answers but indicate considerable effort and understanding of basic concepts? If a student has perfect attendance, does her homework faithfully, cooperates during class, but gets so nervous that she fails every major exam, what grade will she receive? Will you go strictly by percentage? Or will you assign less weight to her exam scores? Perhaps you'll arrange an alternative testing program for her, allowing her to take her exams after school or with a trusted counselor.

The question is not so much *What grade does a student deserve?* as it is *What do you want your students to learn?* Grading strictly by percentage teaches them that they must achieve whatever standards are set for them in a particular situation, but it also may teach them that academic ability is more important than social skills, respect for other people, enthusiasm, or a willingness to learn.

My best advice is to begin by making check marks for completed assignments, without assigning grades, until you have a sense of what your students can do, what their personalities are, and what special needs they have (such as dyslexia or limited English-language skills or test anxiety). Then design a fair and equitable system that suits your students, your subject, and your objectives. Be creative. If your school requires letter or percentage grades, you can still use a Pass/Fail option to encourage risk-taking and creativity from your students. Make each Pass an A or B, and a Fail a D or F. Using this method, students who make a true effort receive a good grade, and you don't break the rules.

At the end of the year, you may wonder whether your grades accurately reflect and reward your students' efforts. You won't be the only wondering teacher. That's why so many teachers ask students to grade themselves, or to write a paragraph or an essay arguing for their grades. I've used a variation of that assignment, with great success. My students enjoy it and I learn as much about my teaching as I do about their learning. My self-grading assignment is called "A Different Perspective."

First, I read aloud to my students the book *The True Story of the 3 Little Pigs* by A. Wolf (as told to Jon Scieszka). The book takes about five minutes to read, and tells the story from the wolf's point of view: suffering from a bad cold, he accidentally sneezed down the pigs' houses while trying to borrow a cup of sugar so he could bake a birthday cake for his grandmother. Next, I assign the students the task of writing letters to themselves, from me. In their letters, they must imagine that they're seeing themselves from my perspective, as they describe their behavior and evaluate their performance in my classroom, as well as giving themselves grades.

Sometimes students become confused by the assignment and need help getting started. I write a few examples on the board: *Dear Joey: Wake up before it's too late! bla bla bla . . . Dear Patrice: It's been such a pleasure having you as a student. You are too wonderful for words . . .*

One or two jokers usually write silly letters, but most students take the assignment to heart. They are brutally honest and more critical than I ever would be. Sometimes a student who has an A in my book assigns himself a lower grade because he really didn't try his hardest. Other times, I realize that a student spent an extraordinary amount of time and effort in my classroom. I rarely lower a grade after reading the letters, but I sometimes raise one. In addition to letting me see whether my grades are on target, the letters also give me insight into my own performance in the classroom. They let me know that I spend too much time on one area and not enough on another, or that I divided my attention unfairly between boys and girls. Those student letters remind me that I must work to earn my own A.

4. What will your exams measure?

Exams are supposed to measure learning. If that is true, then I believe they should be viewed primarily as measurements of teaching. If I teach well, my students won't need to cheat on exams, and their daily work will be a much better record of their achievement and progress. Exams are checkpoints for me, to see whether we are ready to move on or whether we need to back up and recover some ground.

While sometimes a major exam can serve as a strong motivator, I prefer to use other forms of motivation. I tell my students, repeatedly, that I am more concerned with helping them learn to be effective students than in punishing them with bad grades on exams. I frequently ask if they need additional practice before exams, volunteer to refer them to a tutor for extra help, and remind them that tests are for me— as a measure of how well I have taught. Imagine how you would feel and behave if your supervisor informed you that your salary would either be increased on reduced, based on one review of your job performance during one or two hours of one work day. Most likely, you would object, claiming that such a policy would be an unfair and unrealistic method of assessing your knowledge and abilities.

5. Avoid trick questions.

I hate trick questions on exams. Students hate trick questions on exams. They aren't fair, they don't test student knowledge, and they make students feel foolish. Trick questions can be useful to entertain or provoke thought or to stimulate interest in your lessons, but they don't belong on exams that are intended to assess student knowledge for the purpose of assigning a grade.

6. *Reduce anxiety; increase test scores.*

Tests are traumatic experiences for many students, but you can do much to reduce their anxiety by making sure your students understand why they are taking a particular test. Are you checking to see whether they understand certain concepts before you move on to more complicated work? Do you want to know how well you have communicated the information in your lessons? Do you simply want to know who has been paying attention? Whatever your objective, remind students that their daily work and achievement are more important than a single test score. (If that isn't true, and you place more importance on a single exam score than on weeks or months of work, then your exam had better be comprehensive, objective, error free, and tailored to the learning preferences of all the students in your classroom, from dyslexic to kinesthetic—difficult standards to meet in a one- or two-hour period.)

You don't have to make your exams easier in order to improve grades and student motivation in your classroom; you do need to reduce the stress and anxiety your students feel about taking exams. The following techniques and methods reduce stress and, in some cases, actually make the experience enjoyable.

Personalized exams. Laughter reduces tension. You can inspire smiles by personalizing your exams. Replace city names with local neighborhoods, and business names with local stores and restaurants. If a school is mentioned, change its name to that of your school. If you create your own exams, include your students' names in the questions. If you use prepared exams, you can make a master copy and replace names with those of your students. To avoid hurt feelings, keep track of student names you've used and either use all names from a given class on one exam, or include ten names on each exam, rotating them to make sure every student is mentioned. At the end of the exam, thank your students for their time, effort, and cooperation. Thanking them might seem silly or trivial to you, but it won't seem insignificant to them. Trust me.

Group reviews. I use group reviews before all my exams for two reasons. Students love playing games, and I know that as they consider the questions, all of the students in the class are thinking about the information from their lessons. You'll need to tailor your game to fit your students' personalities and abilities, but here is the basic game plan. Place students in teams and ask questions based on the test material. Assign one team point for each correct answer. You may want to stop and give the correct answer when students answer incorrectly, or move on to the next team, and the next, until somebody gives the correct answer. Ask for a volunteer to track scores on the board in front of the room. Don't embarrass students by focusing on mistakes. Allow students to come to the board, when appropriate, to work out math problems, spell words, draw simple diagrams, write brief definitions, and so on. If your students are extremely competitive, you might want to assign one or two monitors to deter cheating (this is a frequent student suggestion in my classes). When the team review is finished, award prizes to the winning team. I usually give bonus points on the exam grade, which really isn't a bonus, because students on the winning team usually earn the highest exam scores—but they think they're getting free points. I also award prizes to the losers—pens or pencils, candy kisses or some other inexpensive treat. I try to limit the competition to half the class period, and use the second half to go over the questions, giving correct answers, so students can take notes on the areas they need to study before the exam.

Group exams. By placing students in groups of three or four, you can reduce anxiety, increase the amount of information covered and the number of questions asked, encourage teamwork, and reduce the number of exams you must grade, which will allow faster feedback to your students. When I use group exams, I try to make sure that each group includes students with varying degrees of academic ability, and different talents (an ace speller may be a poor writer, and vice versa). I also make sure that the exam is too long for any one or two students to complete alone, so that everybody must contribute. Rules for group exams in my classes include: (1) all students in a group may review all portions of the exam and make corrections as needed, (2) all students in one group earn the same grade, and (3) students may either divide the exam into sections and assign one person per section or take turns working on all the sections. In my English classes, a group exam might include four sections: spelling, vocabulary, composition, and literature. In most cases, I announce group members and describe the exam sections a few days prior to the exam date, so they can decide how to divvy up the sections and focus their studies on particular areas.

Practice exams. I often give "practice" exams. I tell the students that I want them to treat the practice exam as they would a "real" exam—do their *best* work and do their *own* work. If the grades are 75% or higher for everybody in the class, I sometimes announce that we won't be needing a "real" exam since everybody knows the material well enough to earn at least a C. Some students will insist that they want to earn a higher grade. In that case, I make the "real" exam an option for those who want to take another exam after reviewing their practice exams. In addition to allowing them to work to raise their grades, this approach also teaches them that it is okay not to be perfect, that mistakes can be corrected, and that they shouldn't give up when they stumble or fall.

I first used practice exams to motivate a class of remedial students in a freshman high school class. They were bright students, but they hated school, earned poor grades, and failed miserably on their exams. Even when I knew they understood the material, they still earned low test scores. The more I encouraged them, the more they insisted that they were the "dumb kids" and that they never did well on tests, never had and never would. Desperate to motivate them, I announced one afternoon that I was no longer going to use my grade book to record exam grades in their class. Instead of one "real exam," we'd have two "practice exams," and any passing grade would do. If they earned a C+ (75%

or above) on either "practice exam," they would be excused from taking the "real exam." If they passed the first practice, however, they could record their passing grade as a safety net, and still take the second practice and real exams, just to see if their grades improved. If not, they could keep the first "practice" score. At first, they were suspicious.

"You think we're too dumb to get A's, don't you?" one boy asked.

"On the contrary," I replied. "I think you are smart enough to earn A's if you want to, but you don't think you're smart enough."

"Don't you want us to get A's," a girl asked.

"That would be nice," I said, "but I will be happy if you earn B's and C's. If you earn a D or an F, I will still like you just as much, but I will also try harder to help you learn and study. It's important for you to do your best work all the time, at home and at school, and to be proud of every job you do, but nobody is perfect. I am happy when you succeed, and sad when you fail, because I've failed myself many times and I know that it hurts. But I also know that I have learned so much from my mistakes, and I know you will learn from yours. The important thing is to try, and to learn. So, I want you to stop worrying about your grades, and just focus on learning."

The three exams were all different. They covered the same lesson material, but contained different questions. After the first practice exam, a few students chose to keep their C and skip the other tests. They worked on journal writing assignments while the other students took the second practice and real tests. Everybody passed the second practice exam, but 90 percent of the students opted to take the "real" exam.

As I watched those students during the "real" exam, it was obvious that they were more relaxed and confident, because they knew they couldn't fail. They weren't worried about failing, because they had already passed the practice exams. The worst that could happen was that they would pass with a C. The grades on those exams were the highest those student had earned all year.

The less emphasis I put on grades, the harder those students worked. They took chances, challenged themselves, pushed a little harder, because they knew if they failed, they could try again. They taught me that children will strive for success and perfection, if they are certain we will still love them when they aren't perfect and when they fail.

Oral exams. If you've recently completed a lesson on a difficult skill or abstract concept, you can check for understanding quickly and efficiently by requiring each student to explain the material to you individually. Assign full credit, or check marks, for those students who grasp the material; repeat the oral exam for those who need to review the material or complete additional exercises to increase understanding. Don't announce the exam, but call students aside, one at a time, while the class is completing another assignment, to avoid having them parrot each other's words. Choose an assignment that requires concentration and time, so that students won't finish early and eavesdrop on your conferences.

Combo exams. Combination exams require different skills— a written report, an oral presentation, and an art or creative project. Combo exams have several advantages. They help you assess more fairly those students in your class who are visual or kinesthetic learners. They can be assigned as portfolios to be completed during class time, at home, or some combination of classwork and homework, which requires students to develop self-discipline, use time management skills, and learn to set priorities. They allow for more in-depth student research, response, and understanding of lesson material. They focus on student exploration of ideas instead of teacher lectures and discussions.

Individual exams. Individual exams are an abbreviated version of combo exams. Instead of requiring each student to complete three or more different components of a single exam, students have the choice of completing one component. This approach increases student motivation and confidence by allowing them to focus on their strengths.

SAT/ACT prep. Sadly, average or remedial students, who most need the skills, often are excluded from exercises designed to improve their scores on SAT, ACT, or other college entrance exams. College-bound students usually have good critical thinking skills, and know how to solve analytical problems, such as multiple-choice analogies. At one school, a notice was placed in all the teacher mailboxes, announcing that study materials for the SAT exams were available from the guidance office. My "regular" sophomores and juniors were very excited about having a chance to complete the practice exams, but when I requested the study materials, I was informed that they were available only for "accelerated" or "honors" classes. Saddened but undaunted, I bought a couple of study guides at the local used bookstores and made my own exams for my students—many of whom went on to college, by the way. Those who didn't go to college left my classroom with improved critical thinking skills and more self-confidence. If college preparation exams aren't appropriate for your subject (auto mechanics or typing, for example), or you don't have time to spend one or more class periods on test preparation, you can still include questions on your quizzes and exams that require critical thinking skills. Analogies, for example, require analytical, logical thought, and can be adapted for any subject or student ability level. A sample analogy worksheet is included at the end of this chapter.

7. *Keep your eyes on your own paper.*

A hot topic in many staff rooms: *How to prevent the little stinkers from cheating during exams.* I've heard a thousand suggestions, some of them remarkably inventive:

- Make five different versions of the same exam by rearranging questions.
- Move the students' desks so that everyone sits back to back.
- Give cheaters a choice of failing or eating the test paper.
- Remove your shoes and tiptoe around the room, patrolling the grounds.

My own philosophy, as you may have guessed, doesn't emphasize deterrence or punishment. I tell my students from the outset that I trust them to be honest in my classes. If they copy homework assignments, I give all students involved in the incident a grade of 50% on the assignment and explain that I've given that grade because I can't be sure who did the work. If I suspect which student did the original work, I call that student in for a conference and try to provide some good excuses he or she can use when other students ask to copy.

"Bring it to me as soon as you come to school in the morning so you won't have it if somebody asks," I might suggest. What if the student who copies demands to see the student's work during the bus ride to school? "Tell him or her that Miss Johnson thinks you're copying and has threatened to tell your parents if it happens again," I say. "If that doesn't work, you come back to see me and we'll think of something else." Children need our help to resist peer pressure. We are much better at making excuses than they are. We've had more practice.

Cheating on exams may seem more important than copying homework, but I'm not so sure. It seems to me that anybody, even an intelligent, hardworking student, could panic or be caught unprepared and be tempted to cheat on an exam. In spite of the breach of honesty, that student is likely to learn most of the material you assign during class. But somebody who routinely copies homework and depends on other people to do the thinking is probably somebody who isn't learning much in your class. Which person would you be more likely to hire if you were the employer—the one who works hard and occasionally makes an error in judgment, or the one who collects a paycheck for other people's work?

"How come you never try to catch us cheating?" one student asked me in front of the class. "It would be real easy to cheat in your class sometimes when you aren't watching us." Everybody paid attention, waiting for my answer.

"I realize you could cheat," I said. "But I trust you not

to. I believe you are honest people, with a sense of honor, and I respect you too much to suspect you of being dishonest just because you are younger than I am." Some of the students applauded my response, but the boy who asked the question wasn't completely convinced.

"So, what happens if I cheat?" he said. "Not that I would, but I just want to know what would happen."

"You would feel like a worthless piece of dirt because I trusted you and you took advantage of me, that's what would happen," I said.

I don't believe that boy ever cheated. But I'm not naive enough to believe that nobody ever did. Occasionally, I even catch somebody in the act. My first response when I do suspect cheating is: *Why did this student feel he or she needed to cheat to pass this exam?* Did I teach the material poorly? Was this student absent frequently during the unit? Is there a lot of parental pressure on this student to earn good grades? Was my exam a legitimate measurement of student learning?

Consequences for cheating in my class depend on the student and his or her attitude upon being caught; I do whatever I think will be most effective. I might assign a two-page essay (to be graded on grammar and composition) on the topic: Why I Felt Compelled to Cheat on the Exam. I might require a series of worksheets that cover the same material to be completed under my supervision during lunch hour or after school. I might simply scare the student with a fierce warning. For first offenses, I think dealing directly and solely with the student is much more effective than a visit to the principal or a parent conference. For repeat offenders, I don't hesitate to call for reinforcements.

Visual, Auditory, or Kinesthetic?

Most teacher education programs include at least a basic overview of learning styles and a recommendation that we should keep them in mind and vary our teaching styles so we don't overlook one group. Some subjects lend themselves to different approaches, but how does a math teacher communicate a complicated mathematical concept to a child who learns by movement? How does an English teacher convey the concept of symbolism in literature—an abstract idea—to a child who needs to see things in order to learn? How can one lonely teacher assess the preferences of thirty or forty children in one classroom? Ask the experts—your students. They will be interested in this lesson because it will concern the most interesting topic in the world—themselves.

1. Teach your students to identify their preferences.

During a freshman English class, when we were reviewing literary techniques for a semester exam, one of my best students sighed loudly and rolled her eyes. "I just know I'm going to flunk this test, even though I never miss class and I do all my homework and study." I asked her why she thought she was going to flunk. "Because I can never think of a symbol in a story when you ask me to," she said. "I can remember the examples you gave us in class, but you always ask us to make up our own examples, and I can't. I know what it means and I can write the definition, but I can't make up an example. It makes me feel so stupid." Several other kids nodded vigorously as Shanna explained her predicament; a few added "Yeah, me, too."

I was at a loss. We had discussed symbols in stories, completed worksheets in class, written about them in our journals—and still some of my best and brightest students insisted that they "just didn't get it." As I stood looking at Shanna's pink cheeks, I recalled a conversation we'd had a few days before. She was failing pre-algebra, although she had been working with a tutor after school twice a week.

"Did you get good grades in math last year?" I asked Shanna. She nodded. "I always get A's," she said. "At least I used to until this year."

"How many of you kids who are having trouble with symbols are also having trouble with algebra?" I asked the class. Several hands waved vigorously. "And how many of you learn the best when you have pictures or drawings or graphs or videos to help you?" The hands stayed in the air. Clearly, it was the teacher and not the student who was the problem. I had designed test questions that visual learners couldn't answer, especially if their brains hadn't yet reached the stage where they could move from concrete to abstract thinking.

We stopped our literature review at that point and spent the rest of the class period talking about the three basic learning styles. The kids were enthusiastic and excited about comparing their experiences and preferences. To help them recognize their individual preferences, I used the example of traveling to my house from the school. First, I gave quick, detailed verbal instructions. A handful of kids, the auditory learners, were confident that they could get to my house without any problems. Next, I drew a map on the board and asked how many kids thought they could make the trip—almost half the class, the visual learners, raised their hands. The third group—the kinesthetic learners—believed that they would be able to retrace the route if they traveled it once, but would have problems with either verbal or written directions.

2. Help students learn to help themselves.

After Shanna made me reconsider my lessons and exams, I realized that my students needed to know how to use the information they now had about their learning styles. Once they understood why they were having trouble with a particular task or concept, they needed to know how to ask for help from both me and their other teachers. Auditory learners are the easiest to help—usually rephrasing or repeating information is enough. Repetition of verbal instruction doesn't do much for visual and kinesthetic learners. Complaining that they "don't get it," doesn't give the teacher enough information. When somebody says that to me, I don't know whether they need me to repeat what I just said, or talk more slowly, or raise my voice so they can hear better. Since I believe it's important for students to take responsibility for their own learning, I assigned my students the task of coming up with suggestions that visual and kinesthetic learners can use to ask for help from their teachers. Working in small groups, they developed these cues:

Visual Learners may say:

"I learn best when I can see some kind of picture of what I'm learning. Could you help me figure out how to present this concept in a drawing or graph or something I can see?"

"I like to see things so I can learn better. Can you recommend a videotape about this particular topic? I'd like to watch it at home because I think it will help me."

"I understand what you're saying, but I just can't 'see it' in my mind. Could you draw a picture on the board to illustrate this concept for me?"

Kinesthetic Learners may say:

"I learn the best when I can do things for myself. Could you help me go through a couple of these problems, step by step, while I do the work, so I can get the hang of it?"

"I have a hard time learning things unless I can move around while I'm thinking. Would it be all right with you if I stand in the back of the class and walk around a little bit if I'm careful not to distract the other students?"

"I'm one of those people who learn by moving and doing. I'm having a problem remembering this new information. Can you help me think of a way I can move things or do some activity to help me learn?"

Encourage your students to choose activities that take advantage of their learning styles. A kinesthetic learner who is struggling with history, for example, might concentrate on activities that will help him improve his listening skills. He also might design study aids, such as taping your classroom lectures and discussions, to use as a study aid for exams. Remind students that having a particular learning style is not an excuse for earning a poor grade if that learning style conflicts with a teacher's teaching style. If there is a conflict, the student needs to seek solutions.

Just as students need to take responsibility for their own learning, we need to take responsibility for our teaching and review our lessons to make sure that we have included projects and assignments that address the needs of all our students. We could allow a kinesthetic learner, for example, to give a demonstration instead of writing a paper when given a choice of projects for a grade. Or we could allow a visual learner to design collages, posters, or computer graphics—projects that will emphasize her talents.

3. Ask the experts.

If you aren't confident in your ability to teach students about learning preferences, find somebody else to present the material. First, contact the guidance or counseling office at your school and ask whether anybody on staff is trained to evaluate learning styles or preferences. If your school counselors are not trained, ask them to refer you to another agency. Contact your district, county, or state office of education and ask for a referral. Call the education department of the nearest university. If you still can't find help, ask the reference library at your public library to help you locate books or academic journals, so you can teach yourself first. The following publications are a good place to start: *Vocational Educational Journal, English Journal, Schools in the Middle, Educational Leadership, Principal.* The research and writing of Rita and Kenneth Dunn have been particularly interesting and helpful to me.

"Problem" Children

Sometimes, I say, as a joke, that BD stands for Bored to Death because so many of my BD (Behavior Disordered) students respond so well when I give them more challenging assignments or ones that are tailored more to their interests than the ones I had planned for my classes. I also sometimes say, and I'm not joking then, that we might just as well lump all of the children who have troubles in school because they don't or can't or won't fit the mold into one group and label them DDWWWWWWTT—Don't Do What We Want When We Want Them To.

1. Other possibilities.

There are plenty of reasons why students misbehave or have trouble concentrating in school. Here are just a few possibilities:

Student chairs are uncomfortable. Try sitting at a typical student desk for forty-five minutes without getting out of your seat. Then imagine doing that for six or seven hours per day, and you'll see why so many kids are willing to risk being punished for a chance to get out of those seats and stretch their aching bodies. One group of researchers reported that the typical school chair forces 75 percent of the student's body weight to be supported by only 4 square inches of bone. Ouch.

Kids are flying high on caffeine and sugar. Check out the vending machines at your school, and try to find some milk or water or unsweetened fruit juice, perhaps a piece of fruit or a whole-wheat cracker. Good luck. You're more likely to find coffee, hot chocolate, and soft drinks filled with caffeine, and every kind of sugary sweet you can imagine. Ask veteran teachers if they notice a change in student behavior after lunch, when students have free access to those vending machines. Then ask yourself if those kids who can't sit still have an attention disorder or whether they're bouncing off the walls because of the sugar and caffeine flooding their young bodies and playing games with their brains.

Pain is distracting. Imagine that your father whipped you last night, as he often does when he can't handle the frustrations of his difficult life, and your back and legs feel like they're on fire. Now imagine that you have to sit on a hard plastic chair and complete one hundred difficult mathematical computations before you can be excused to get out of your seat and stretch.

Life is more compelling than literature. Take any good, well-written, moderately difficult literary book—*Tender Is the Night* by F. Scott Fitzgerald, or *War and Peace* by Leo Tolstoy would be appropriate examples—that requires some mental concentration in order for you to comprehend it well enough to answer questions about the characterization, plot, or symbolism involved. Now, imagine that your mother is gravely ill in the hospital on the other side of town. Or imagine that you were recently informed that soon you would have to leave your home and go to live with one or another relative, although which one has not yet been decided. Or imagine that you didn't have time to eat breakfast or lunch; your stomach is achingly empty, you haven't a penny on you to buy something to eat, and even if you had a penny you wouldn't be permitted to buy anything because you have to sit in that chair right now and read that book and answer five essay questions on the second chapter and they had better be thoughtful, articulate, grammatical answers, too, or else.

I don't mean to imply that there are no children who need and benefit from special programs designed to help them cope with genuine disabilities and perceptual problems. But I do mean that I believe we should refuse to accept any of the many diagnostic labels—Behavior Disordered, Attention Deficit Disorder, Developmentally Delayed, Learning Impaired—that have been placed on our students until we have eliminated the possibility that the child is hungry, bored, worried, ill, frightened, in pain, exhausted, or unable to cope with some other stress.

2. Scotopic sensitivity.

At a high school in California, one of my tenth-grade students, Nick, behaved well in class, except during silent reading periods. During periods when students took turns reading aloud, Nick paid close attention and participated in discussions about the reading, but whenever he had to read by himself, he became so disruptive that I eventually threatened to have the counselors remove him from my class if he didn't sit his posterior down in his chair and read his book. He sat and he read, for ten minutes. Then he stood up and walked to my desk. "Look," he said. "This happens every time I read." His eyes, which had looked perfectly normal a few minutes earlier, were bright red and watery. Tears streamed down his cheeks. "Whenever I read," Nick said, "I get a really bad headache and my eyes hurt and then they start crying all by themselves."

Nick's mother wasn't able to take him to an ophthalmologist, although her insurance would cover the visit, so I took him one day after school because I wanted to make sure the doctor believed Nick. After the eye exam, the doctor reported that Nick had a slight astigmatism, or irregularity in the shape of the eye, but that his vision was fine. There was no medical explanation for his red, watery eyes.

I happened to mention Nick's situation to one of my friends who teaches college students who have learning disabilities. Diane visited my classroom, discussed light sensitivity with my students, and gave Nick a blue transparency to place over the page of his book as he was reading. I was skeptical, but Nick sat down and read nonstop for thirty minutes, with no eye irritation. He used the transparency regularly, and his grades improved enough that he made plans to attend college—an idea he had rejected previously because he didn't think he could handle the reading required. (At present, Nick has successfully completed three years of college.)

A similar experience occurred at a high school in New Mexico, this time with a freshman girl. Regina was one of my top students and a talented athlete, with an outgoing, friendly personality—except during independent reading periods when she became a terror. I knew Regina was an excellent reader. She had read aloud briefly a few times, but she insisted that she hated reading, because it gave her a bad headache and made her eyes "dizzy." Several other students in Regina's class also became problem children during reading periods. They reminded me of Nick, so I called the counseling office to ask if anybody there had been trained to test students for scotopic sensitivity. Yes, there was a counselor, but students had to have a vision exam first, and parental permission to be tested. In the meantime, a counselor agreed to visit my room and discuss scotopic sensitivity with Regina and her classmates.

When the counselor arrived, she handed Regina a white sheet of paper with a series of X's printed on it in the shape of a pumpkin. Regina was to count the number of X's in a given line, using only her eyes, without pointing her finger. All of the students crowded around Regina's desk as she tried to count the X's. She couldn't; neither could half of the other students. (I couldn't, either, so I suspected that it might be impossible, until several students correctly counted the X's in different rows.) The following week, Regina's parents agreed to allow her to be tested, and I excused her from class for thirty minutes. When she returned, she brought three purple transparencies that she placed over her literature textbook and started to read. I couldn't even see the print through the transparencies, but Regina read smoothly and correctly for the remainder of that period and became a regular reading volunteer.

Later in that school year, a team of trained counselors talked to the staff about scotopic sensitivity, which is a relatively recent development and, therefore, still a controversial subject. They explained that scotopic (light) sensitivity is not a vision problem, such as nearsightedness. Rather, it concerns the eye's ability to filter different colors from the spectrum of light. Some people have trouble reading under fluorescent lighting or from glossy pages, for example. Bright, direct light helps some people read better, while others need soft, indirect light. People who suffer from scotopic sensitivity often display one or more of the following characteristics:

- preference for reading in dim, blue or pink light
- difficulty reading words printed on glossy paper
- inability to focus under fluorescent lighting
- black print seems to "float up" off a white page
- eyes focus on "rivers of white" on the page instead of on printed words

During the meeting, several teachers and students shared their own experiences. One young man told about his struggles to maintain a high enough grade-point average to be accepted into college. During his senior year, he had been tested and had purchased a pair of glasses with blue lenses. "Now I'm an A student and going to college," the boy explained. "I just wish I had known about this four years ago when school was so much harder for me."

"I used to think I was romantic," a math teacher said, "because I always turn off half the lights in my classroom and at home I have very subdued lighting. Now I realize that I need dim lighting in order to read well." Another math teacher told about his daughter, who had argued for years that she really could read better by the dim blue light of the aquarium in their living room than under the bright light on her study desk. "She earns excellent grades," the teacher admitted, "but I always thought she was just trying to be unique."

For more information about light sensitivity, check the reference section of your local public or university library for a copy of *Reading by the Colors* by Helen Irlen (Avery Publishing Group, 1991). Or write to request a brochure from the Dyslexia Treatment and Counseling Center, 940 Saratoga Avenue, Suite #205, San Jose, CA 95129, phone (408) 241-3330.

3. BD or bored?

Don't be surprised if nobody tells you that you have BD students in your classroom. From my experience, and from stories other teachers have shared with me, it is common for BD students to be placed in classrooms without notifying the teachers of the students' problem. Don't be dismayed if you find out you have one or more BD students in your classroom. All of the BD kids I've taught earned a good grade in my class—not because I gave them grades or lowered my standards, but because I did not allow them to use their BD status as a crutch or an excuse for misbehaving.

Two years ago, one of my freshman boys grabbed a handful of my hair and yanked it hard. At the time, I was sitting in a student desk, writing an essay with my class, hoping my example would inspire them to write. When Lino pulled my hair, I whirled around and shouted, "What's wrong with you?"

"I'm BD," he said with a grin.

"I don't care what you are or what somebody labeled you," I told him. "You know how to behave because I've seen you do it for a week in this room. So don't tell me you can't control yourself. You can if you want to, and you will if you want to remain in this class. If you can't behave, then you can go back to the special classroom and act however you please. I hope you decide to behave yourself and stay here because I like you and I think you're pretty sharp, but it's your decision."

Lino decided to stay, and earned an A in my class. Once in a while, he seemed to have trouble controlling himself. When that happened, we would move his desk into the hallway for ten or fifteen minutes where he could work quietly without any distractions, then he'd move back into the classroom when he was ready.

Lino's experience was typical of my other BD students. Every one of them chose to accept responsibility for his behavior (interestingly, all of my BD kids were boys) and remain in my classroom. I don't know whether they had emotional or mental or psychological problems that prevented them from having the same control other students have over their behavior. Perhaps they did, but I still don't think that means we should excuse their behavior. If we do, we are giving them license to act however they want, without taking any responsibility for their behavior. Many people have bad tempers or aggressive personalities that are difficult to control, but I think it is our duty as teachers and parents to try to help those people develop as much self-control as possible when they are young.

4. Dyslexic doesn't mean dumb.

Undoubtedly, you will have students in your classroom who have learning disabilities, some who have been diagnosed, others who have not, and it is very unlikely that the administration will alert you to your students' special needs. Occasionally, a student will let you know that he is dyslexic or requires extra time to complete written tasks, but more often, students try to hide their difficulties or are unaware that they suffer from a processing disorder or disability. So you need to be alert, especially during the first few weeks of classes, for signs that indicate potential problems. Students who frequently misspell common words, who can't seem to follow verbal instructions, or who ask you to repeat instructions again and again, for example, may have difficulty processing information.

The most important thing for you, as a teacher, is to understand that learning disabilities do not indicate lack of intelligence. A learning disability or processing disorder is simply that—a "short circuit" that causes information to be misrouted, misinterpreted or misunderstood. Recently, one of the directors of the Dyslexia Treatment and Counseling Center in San Jose, California, told me about a teenage boy who had appeared at the center with his father and asked to be tested. The boy wanted to prove to his father that the school counselors and teachers were wrong, that his failing scores on test after test were not an accurate representation of his intelligence. He believed he was smart, in spite of the evidence. During testing, the staff at the treatment center discovered that the boy was right. When he was limited to the standard time to complete the test, the boy failed, as he had done in school, but when he was allowed to work at his own pace (four times the maximum allotted time for completion), he scored in the 98th percentile. All he needed was enough time for his brain to process information.

In my own classroom, I had a boy who was severely dyslexic. Kyle's manners were impeccable and his attendance was perfect. His attention never wavered during class, he never missed an assignment, and he often volunteered to distribute or collect worksheets. He had difficulty spelling the simplest words, on paper, and struggled to write a simple paragraph, yet when I assigned independent reading projects, he read *The Hobbit* and the trilogy by J.R.R. Tolkien in the same amount of time that his "normal" classmates each read one novel. Kyle created a striking poster and gave a brilliant oral presentation at the end of the unit. During that semester, I excused Kyle from taking spelling exams and allowed him to read his own compositions to me. He met with me after school and gave verbal answers for the questions on the exams that covered literature, grammar, and vocabulary. He earned an A on his report card. Shortly after report cards were mailed, Kyle's mother stopped by my classroom to discuss his grade. She couldn't believe that her son had earned an A in my class. She thought I had given him the grade because I felt sorry for him. Before our meeting, I overheard Kyle and his mother, in the hallway outside my room, arguing in whispers. "Mom, I earned that grade," Kyle said. "You're embarrassing me." He stayed outside when his mother came in to talk to me.

I showed Kyle's mother my grade book, with its rows of A's and B's beside Kyle's name, but she was still unconvinced. She wanted to know how he could earn an A in English class if he couldn't spell.

"I don't give Kyle spelling exams," I explained. "That would be like making a child with one leg run a foot race. It would set him up to fail."

"I see," Kyle's mother said. "But you do know that my son is ADD, don't you?"

"ADD?" I echoed.

"He has Attention Deficit Disorder," she explained. "He can't focus on any one activity for more than a short period of time."

"Well, that isn't true in my class," I said. "Kyle works all period on whatever assignment is due, and he doesn't waste time or distract other students." Kyle's mother looked surprised.

"He stopped taking his medication this year," she said, "and I was worried, but I guess he's doing all right."

Kyle's experience made me even more determined to give my students every opportunity to disprove the labels that other people placed on them, no matter how well-intentioned those people may be.

5. Cowboy philosophy.

Last summer, as I watched renowned horse trainer Craig Cameron, the "cowboy professor," in action at the Southwestern New Mexico State Fair, I was struck by the similarity between breaking wild horses and taming wild students. Cameron worked with two wild horses that afternoon—one that had never been ridden and one that had resisted being forcibly saddle broken. In both instances, Cameron was able to mount and ride the horses within an hour, without raising his voice or using any force whatsoever. As I watched Cameron tame those horses and listened to him explain his actions, I realized that I was in the presence of a master teacher. I took notes.

"Many people set out to break the spirit of a horse," Cameron told the crowd who had gathered outside the round pen where he worked the horses. "The last thing I want to do is break down the spirit of any horse; I'm out to build it up so that I can utilize it. I want to relate to the horse on his own level and on his time schedule. If you want a horse to have a good attitude, you can't force things on him. You have to give him time to decipher what it is you want him to do."

As he spoke, Cameron picked up a saddle blanket and took a step towards the horse he was breaking. The horse took one look at the blanket and started running in the opposite direction (just as our students try to escape from difficult lessons). Instead of chasing the horse, or trying to corner it so he could place the blanket on its back, Cameron stood still and waited until the horse stopped running and, overcome by curiosity, approached the unfamiliar blanket to investigate. Cameron allowed the horse to sniff and nibble the blanket, then brushed it gently over the horse's legs and belly before placing it on the horse's back. Immediately, the horse bucked the blanket off and ran away. Cameron picked up the blanket and waited until the horse returned to inspect it again. Satisfied that it posed no danger, the horse finally stood still and accepted the blanket. Cameron could have saved time by hobbling the horse and tying the blanket to its back, as many people do, but he would have faced the same struggle every time he wanted to saddle the horse.

"People bring me all sorts of 'problem' horses," Cameron said, as he placed a saddle on top of the blanket and let the horse run until he realized the saddle wasn't going to hurt him. "Usually, the problem is the way the horse was taught in the beginning. Somebody tried to force a lesson on him, or he was punished harshly for not doing right. If he doesn't do the right thing, he knows you're going to jerk harder or spur harder or get a bigger bit. So, now he's nervous, scared, and defensive. He is just flat-out turned off to learning." Again, the horse circled the pen several times, then slowed down and walked to Cameron and allowed him to tighten the cinch on the saddle.

Students, like horses, resist having their spirits broken, or being forced into performing uncomfortable or unfamiliar actions. If we give them time to get used to us, and time to understand what we want from them, they are much more apt to cooperate. Horses and children may cooperate temporarily, out of fear or pain or exhaustion, but unless we gain their trust, we're going to have to fight the same battles again and again.

One comment that Cameron made during his training session struck me as particularly applicable to classroom teachers who must deal with students who resist accepting authority. "Horses naturally understand a pecking order," Cameron explained. "Your horse can accept the fact that you are the leader and he is the follower. That doesn't mean that a horse won't test you from time to time. He's going to test you. But you can establish that you are the leader, number one in the pecking order, without causing your horse pain or fear. The way you do that is to control your horse's mind instead of his body."

If you back a student against the wall and demand respect or obedience, you are not apt to receive either one. Like horses, children's natural instinct is to escape when they feel frightened or threatened, or fight if escape is impossible. If you make it clear from the start that you are the leader in your classroom, and that your leadership is necessary in order for you to teach and for your students to learn, you allow students to accept your authority without feeling any loss of dignity. Instead of demanding cooperation, effective teachers make it a choice.

After seeing him work, I bought Cameron's videos, *Gentle Horse-Breaking & Training* and *Dark into Light*, to watch at home, and the longer I watched, the more I became convinced that teacher training programs should assign his videos as required curriculum. If you'd like to read about Craig Cameron, you can find articles about him in many equestrian magazines, such as *Western Horseman* or *The Quarter Horse Journal.* (See the January 1997 issue.) For information about seminars and videos, contact Craig Cameron Horsemanship, P.O. Box 50, Bluff Dale, TX 76433-0050, phone (817) 728-3082 or (800) 274-0077.

Don't Be Afraid of Your Students

Surely, at some time in your life, you have been accused of lying or cheating or some other wrongdoing that you did not do. You also must remember the overwhelming indignation that you felt upon being falsely accused, and the rage that resulted when nobody would listen to your truth. That outrage is magnified in children when they are accused without reason, even if the accusation is left unspoken— *especially* if it is left unspoken. When you are afraid of a child, the child perceives your fear as dislike, mistrust, and a silent accusation of his or her character. To accuse children of being stupid or untrustworthy or criminal because of their native language, their skin color, or their poverty, is the worst kind of psychological abuse because you are telling them that there is something inherently wrong with them—and they believe you.

I wish I could show you the picture of Dante Williams that is indelibly sketched in my memory. An intelligent and sweet-natured young man, Dante was unusually tall for his age and very dark-skinned. He was a student in my English classes during his sophomore and junior years, and during that time, he was unfailingly polite and genial. I never saw him mistreat another person, in or outside of my classroom. Although he was sometimes slow to complete his assignments, he was quick to help other students.

At the end of his sophomore year, Dante stopped by my desk to chat on the last day of school. After we'd talked about his plans for the summer and his excitement at having been notified that a college football scout wanted to watch him play ball, Dante drew a deep breath and said, "I just wanted to thank you, Miss J, because you were the only teacher I've had in this whole school who made me do my homework. All my other teachers are afraid of me. Just because I'm big and black, they act like I'm gonna kill them or something if they talk to me or make me mad." His eyes glistened with unshed tears and he swallowed hard. I wish I had a photograph of Dante's face so I could show it to the people who so foolishly and wrongly believe that all black males are prone to violence. I wish they could see how much it hurts an innocent boy to be accused of criminal tendencies that he doesn't possess.

Fortunately, I had a book on my bookshelf that contained a brilliant essay by Brent Staples, an editor at *The New York Times*, about his own experiences with people who were afraid of him because he is a tall black man. "I learned to smother the rage I felt at so often being taken for a criminal," Staples explains. "Not to do so would surely have led to madness." Instead of going mad, when Staples suspects that people are threatened by his size and color, he whistles popular classical music tunes to let them know he is harmless. "Virtually every-body seems to sense that a mugger wouldn't be warbling bright, sunny selections from Vivaldi's Four Seasons," Staples concludes. "It is my equivalent of the cowbell that hikers wear when they know they are in bear country."

Dante and I sat down and read "Black Men and Public Space" together in my classroom. Reading it didn't erase Dante's pain, but it did help him realize that he was not alone, and that there are intelligent responses to other people's stupidity. Unfortunately, few youngsters have the maturity or self-confidence that Brent Staples possesses. They have no outlet for their rage, but rage demands an out-let, so they vent it, sometimes on themselves, sometimes on other people, and teachers make a tempting target.

Whenever I address student teachers, I ask this question: *Are you afraid of your black and Hispanic students, particularly the males?* If so, ask yourself why. If you have a history of being attacked repeatedly by black and Hispanic people, then your fears are justified. If not, then those fears are unfounded and I urge you to conquer them before you try to teach. You can-not teach children if you are afraid of them.

(P.S.: Given the history of this country and the inequities in our criminal justice system, don't you think it would make more sense for a black or Hispanic teacher to fear being phys-ically attacked by white students than it would for a white teacher to fear being attacked by nonwhite students?)

Sometimes teachers explain that they are afraid of minority males because so many of them are involved in gangs. My argument is that not all youth gangs are violent. Some of them are organized as defense, not offense. Many of my own students have confessed that they joined gangs for protection, not from other gangs, but from police and other authority figures in a society where they feel unwel-come and threatened. Further, I don't believe that I, as a teacher, am the enemy of young gangsters. Of course, we have to use caution and protect ourselves from attack, and not take chances or intentionally expose ourselves to dan-ger, but we also must realize that classroom teachers are not a primary enemy or target of organized gangs.

Yes, I realize that there are exceptions to any generalization, and that there is a very real danger of gang violence erupting in any school, but that danger is a result of our society's failure to address the problems of unemployment, inequality, and injustice—not because young gangsters want to eliminate teachers. Further, I refuse to accept the excuse that it is impossible to make our schools safe from invasion by drug dealers, pornographers, and gangsters. That is an indefensible lie. If we valued the children of this nation even half as much as we value our money, our public schools would be as safe and secure from uninvited guests as our banks and major corporations are. (Okay. Off my soapbox and back to the subject of gangsters in school.)

When I have known gang members in my classroom, I try to reduce the risk of any friction between us by making sure that they are present when I explain my teaching philosophy and my grading policy to my students. My philosophy is that nobody in my classroom is bad or stupid. Sometimes they make stupid choices, but that's part of growing up. I believe that all students can learn, and I am not concerned with their past records. I am concerned with the way they conduct themselves in my classroom. As for my grading policy, I tell them exactly what they have to do in order to pass my class. I offer to help anybody who wants extra help. I keep them posted about their progress, and I give them a reasonable opportunity to bring up low grades—but they are responsible for doing the work and they will receive the grades they choose to earn. They know that if they fail my class, it is because they choose to fail, not because I flunked them. I don't flunk students because that is not my job or my purpose in teaching. My job and my purpose are to help them succeed in school and in their lives.

You Don't Need to Justify Yourself

I'd like to suggest one last issue for you to consider before you begin teaching. Unless you are the lucky one in a million, somebody is going to give you a hard time. More likely, several somebodies are going to give you a lot of hard times, especially if they find out that you are a new teacher. They may settle for a little good-natured teasing or a few "gotcha" tricks. But sooner or later, when you are least prepared to deal with them, the challenge will be posed. Your students are going to ask the same questions you did when you were in their seats:

Why should I do this stupid assignment?
How come we gotta read this boring junk?
When are we ever gonna use this stuff in real life?

Your first reaction, most likely, will be to handle them the way your teachers handled you: attempt to explain although they aren't really interested in your explanation, ignore them, order them to do the work, threaten to flunk them, banish them from the room, call their parents, whisper nasty things when nobody else can hear you. Or you could decide *before* the challenge is made how you will handle the students who resist you. My suggestion is to point out that the students are responsible for their behavior and the choices they make. If they choose to come into your classroom, then they must accept the responsibility that goes with taking a seat—letting you do your job. I'll spend quite a bit of time on the issue of choice and power in the next chapter, but right now I'd like to share some experiences, and some suggestions for dealing, with the new teacher's nightmare—the serious power player.

1. Who do you think you are?

During my first semester of teaching, I was given one class as an intern—no supervisor, no master teacher. I was on my own. The students in that class were supposed to be difficult and unruly, but we quickly came to an agreement about who was in charge. My other assignment, as student teacher for an accelerated (honors) class, was a different story. I observed for a couple of weeks and then my master teacher turned the class over to me. I was ready. I knew the names of all the students. I had read *Julius Caesar* several times. And I was filled with energy and enthusiasm for teaching. I introduced myself to the class and asked if there were any questions. A slim, blond boy raised his hand and smiled sweetly at me. I acknowledged his raised hand with a nod and returned his smile. Immediately, he dropped his hand and his smile and sneered, "Where do you get off coming in here and trying to act like a real teacher?" Nobody laughed. He was serious, and his question was mirrored in the eyes of the other students. Suddenly, they wanted to know, too, what made me think I could be a teacher.

In quick succession, I thought of running out of the room, crying, smacking the kid in the teeth, calling my master teacher on the telephone, sending the student to the office. I ended up tripping over my tongue, trying to answer the boy's question. The harder I tried to convince them that I was qualified to teach them, the more convinced the students became that I was not qualified. I could see the doubt in their eyes. And they, undoubtedly, saw the panic in mine. They took advantage of the situation, as children will do, and made my life as difficult as possible. The harder I tried to control them, the more they resisted. They did the minimum amount of work required to pass every assignment and refused to participate in class discussions. If a student tried to answer one of my questions, the other students would cough loudly until the student gave up. When I turned my back to write on the chalkboard, they would all drop their books flat on the floor. Although I suppose I could have sent the entire class to the office, I didn't think it would impress the principal so much that he'd rush to hire me when I had my full teaching credential.

Finally, the tension reached an intolerable point and I called my master teacher for help. Al Black observed the class from the back of the room for one day, then explained his view of the problem.

"You don't like them," Al said, after the bell rang and the students left the room.

"They didn't like me first," I argued.

"So what?" he said. "You're the teacher. You're older,

more educated, more experienced, and more powerful—
you have the grade book. These are smart kids, and they
need the grades, so you can threaten to flunk them. But that
isn't really fair and it isn't good teaching."

The following day, instead of trying to present my
lesson plan, I talked to those students. I told them how I
had felt that first day, and how their behavior had put me
on the defensive, made me feel that they didn't like me. So
I had retaliated by making them sit in assigned seats and
giving them overly difficult and time-consuming assignments.

"I'm tired of being mean," I said. "Let's call a truce. I'll
be nice to you if you're nice to me. Do we have a deal?" I
like to think they agreed because they were won over by my
natural charm, but I think it's more likely that they were
simply exhausted. It's hard work hating somebody who is
trying to help you.

2. When a student demands your attention, let him have it.

Another student posed the same question (*What makes you
think you're a teacher?*) during my second year as a teacher,
but that time I was ready. "This is not an appropriate time to
discuss such an important matter," I explained to the student who challenged me. "But I am very interested in hearing your thoughts, so I would like you to come and see me
after school."

"I can't come after school," the boy responded. "I'll
come after class."

"Oh, no," I said. "This is far too important to try to discuss during a five-minute break when there will be other
students asking questions. I want to give you my full attention, so let's wait until you can arrange to meet with me
after school. Right now, there are thirty other people who
are waiting politely for us to get on with today's lesson. So
let's not be rude to them." I immediately launched into the
day's first activity.

Both the student and I knew that he wasn't interested

in discussing my qualifications or teaching methods. He was making a power play, but I refused to cooperate. By refusing to play, I let him back down without losing face, but I made it clear that I wasn't going to let him stop me from teaching. I didn't think he would bother to come to see me after school, but he surprised me. I shook his hand and asked him to sit down and share his thoughts with me. He offered a few weak criticisms of my lessons.

"Thank you for taking the time to discuss this with me," I said. "I will take your comments into consideration, but you need to understand that it is my personal responsibility to make the final decisions about what goes on in my classroom. I am the one with five years of education, a professional license granted by the state of California, and the responsibility for making sure that my lessons meet the district curriculum guidelines."

After our private meeting, the student stopped challenging me. I might have breathed a sigh of relief and believed I was prepared to handle such problems if my neighbor, an experienced and effective teacher, hadn't been brought to the brink of resignation by a group of honors students a few weeks later.

3. The issue isn't teaching; the issue is power.

Miss Wilson was a popular and respected English teacher with a pleasant personality and a sincere desire to teach. For seven years, students from her classes had gone on to successfully engage in college studies. Unfortunately, during that particular term, one of Miss Wilson's students was more interested in proving his power than in learning to analyze literature. One day in the midst of a lesson, he jumped to his feet and interrupted Miss Wilson. He announced that her class was stupid, that he wasn't learning anything, and that he wanted her to change her teaching methods immediately. Miss Wilson, caught completely offguard, tried to explain the lesson in question. The boy shouted her down, insisting that she was a terrible teacher. His friends joined the attack and Miss Wilson, her confidence severely shaken, ended up walking out of the classroom in tears. The students, delighted with their victory, rushed to the principal's office to demand a different teacher. Miss Wilson sought solace from her fellow teachers in the staff room, and returned to teach the rest of her classes before taking time to visit the principal after school. By that time, the students had gone home and convinced their parents that there was some merit to their criticism of Miss Wilson. They asked: *If she wasn't a bad teacher, why did she run out of the room?* A parent-teacher-student conference took place, with the students again joining forces against Miss Wilson, who was still in shock from the initial incident. Once again, the students drove her to tears, and she left the meeting shaken and ashamed at her inability to control her emotions.

Fortunately, the principal recognized what was truly happening. He had the integrity to assure the parents that he had complete faith in Miss Wilson's teaching ability and methods, and that the students would not be permitted to change to another class. The parents agreed to reserve judgment until they had seen the lessons assigned to their children. The students were directed to apologize to Miss Wilson and mind their manners in the future. They apologized, Miss Wilson accepted their apology, and life went on. The students eventually found another outlet for their aggression and stopped resisting Miss Wilson's efforts to educate them. They seemed to have forgotten the incident, and left with passing marks on their report cards at the end of the year. But Miss Wilson still questioned herself. Were the students right? Were her lessons stupid? Was she a failure? Of course, she wasn't. It never had been a question of her teaching. It was simply a question of power. It took an entire year of school before Miss Wilson regained her confidence.

After observing Miss Wilson's experience, I kept making mental plans, designing strategies for handling my next challenger. I repeatedly replayed conversations in my mind that I had had during confrontations with students. I realized that my instincts had been correct—I had not let my challengers stop me from teaching. But what if I hadn't been lucky? What if the next kid wouldn't shut up and sit down when I said that it was not an appropriate time for discussion?

I decided that if anybody ever stood up and challenged me and refused to sit down and let me teach, I would walk out of the room—and go directly next door to another teacher's room to call the principal. I would explain that I had a student in my room who had lost control and needed to be escorted to the office to wait until I had time to come for a conference. I would explain to the principal that I needed his or her support in order to maintain an orderly classroom. By removing the student from the room, my message would be clear: I am the teacher. I have a job to do and nobody is going to stop me from doing that job.

A Pound of Prevention: Student Evaluations

My plan for handling the serious power players seemed like a good one, and I filed it away. But still, I found myself watching for warning signs while I was teaching, and I resented wasting so much time and energy on something so stupid and pointless. Then, one day it occurred to me that I wouldn't have to worry so much about dealing with that problem again if I could prevent it from occurring in the first place. I thought that perhaps if I gave students frequent opportunities to evaluate our classroom assignments and make suggestions for improving them, they would be less likely to feel the need to challenge me. So, I began asking students for written analysis and evaluations of lessons and activities—frequently during the first weeks of class—and at least once per quarter during the year. Evaluations are optional and anonymous, and beneficial for both me and my students: I find out when I'm way off track, and they enjoy having their opinions taken seriously.

It has been over five years since anybody has challenged my right to call myself a teacher. (Except maybe me. And I'm too busy to stay after school.)

If you like the idea of using evaluations, you'll probably

want to create your own, but I have included a sample in case you're fresh out of creativity. *Please note*: this sample form is compressed. If you adapt it for your own students, be sure to allow more space for answers to the questions. It's been my experience that the length and sincerity of student responses directly corresponds to the amount of space allotted for those responses.

Informal Course Evaluation

GIVE IT TO ME STRAIGHT; I CAN TAKE IT

(Do NOT write your name on this paper
unless you really really really really want to.)

1. Do you honestly feel prepared to do library research
and write a research paper? If not, what could we have
done in this class to better prepare you?

2. What are your thoughts on journal writing?

3. How did the peer critique groups affect your writing?

4. What did you like best about this class during this
quarter? Why?

5. What did you like least about this class during this
quarter? Why?

6. Which would you prefer (check as many as you like):

_____ *grammar instruction in class*
_____ *self-paced assignments and tests*
_____ *regular homework and quizzes on grammar*

7. In reference to group activities, please check all
those that apply:

_____ I liked changing groups for each activity so I meet new people.

_____ I would like to keep the same groups so we can work together better.

_____ I would like the teacher to choose the groups.

_____ I would like the students to choose their own groups.

_____ I think group activities should count for grades because they are a lot of work.

_____ I don't think group assignments should count heavily for grades because some people mess it up for the rest of us.

8. Please check the box that most closely states your feelings about each subject:

	forget it! yuck!	cut back a little	just right for me	add a little	give me more
grammar instruction					
peer critiques					
Les Brown video					
journal writing					
class discussions					
1-minute speeches					

Thank you ever so much for completing this evaluation form. I truly appreciate your comments and will be sure to ignore them. No! Wait! I'll read them and feel really bad about all your criticisms. No! Wait! Honest, I'll read them and see where I can make changes to the lessons. That's what I'm going to do. Yep. You betcha. Thanks.

The Big D

Discipline Is Not a Dirty Word

If you mention the word "discipline" to most children, they will immediately think of punishment, because they have only been taught one facet of this multidimensional word. In the military services, discipline has a more positive connotation, because military personnel understand that it is discipline that allows them to function as an efficient team, and they know that the self-control and strength of character they develop from good discipline increases their freedom within the rigid military framework.

Classroom teachers can use the same principles of discipline that military leaders use to teach their students how to develop self-control and respect for others. Of course, I'm not suggesting that you conduct your classes like a military boot camp, and order kids to hit the deck and give you fifty push-ups when they step out of line, but I do believe that children need and want strong adult guidance. In spite of their loud protests and complaints, students don't want to be allowed to do whatever they want. The world is a scary place for children, and they want adults to establish boundaries for behavior and set limits for them, so they can relax and learn without having to be responsible for more than they can handle.

Would you like to live in a world that had no laws, no courts, no police, no control at all? Of course not. We want to live in a world where reasonable laws allow us to have the maximum amount of freedom and the minimum amount of danger. Children are no different from us. In spite of all the books and newspaper articles and television programs that tell us today's children are apathetic, learning impaired, developmentally delayed, unwilling or unable to pay attention, impossible to discipline or teach, I don't believe those things for a minute because I've taught so many of those "unteachable" children. Children are naturally curious and eager to learn, but when they are sent to school, unfortunately, their natural curiosity and enthusiasm are replaced by fears—that they can't learn, that they will be attacked by other students, that their parents will get divorced, that they won't be able to get good jobs even if they go to college, that they will die from AIDS or a random drive-by shooting or a drug-crazed mugger on the streets outside their school, that nobody really cares about them. We can't address all of those fears, but if we can create an oasis of calm and order in our classrooms, where students feel safe and protected, where they know what is expected and what will happen, their curiosity and enthusiasm for learning will resurface, and they will apply themselves to the lessons we offer. Discipline is the key to creating that classroom oasis.

Control the Classroom, Not the Student

The first mistake I made as a teacher—and the worst—was trying to control my students when I should have focused my energy on controlling my classroom, instead. After nine years of military service, I was well versed in both giving and taking orders, and I thought I had a handle on discipline. When my master teacher turned over his chalk and left me in charge of his sophomore accelerated (honors) English class, I was determined not to "take any lip" from anybody. Unfortunately, my students didn't care about my determination—they gave me all the lip they wanted to, then went out and found some more. The harder I tried to control them, the harder they resisted, until they finally taught me the lesson I needed to learn: *In order to maintain control in my classroom, I must concentrate on controlling the environment (which is possible), and not concentrate on controlling the students (which is not possible unless they agree to permit it).*

The first time two boys started socking each other on the arms during my lesson, I did the most natural thing—I ordered them to stop and directed them to move to different seats. They stopped hitting each other, but refused to move. Now I had a more serious problem. Instead of a distraction, I faced an outright challenge to my authority. There was no graceful solution. Everybody in the room was focused on the standoff. One of us had to win, which meant one of us had to lose. I felt I couldn't afford to lose, so I quickly reviewed my options: send the boys to the office, call security to come and escort them if they refused to go, threaten to lower their grades or assign after-school detention unless they moved immediately. I threatened them with detention. It worked. I won. At least, that's what I thought at the time.

Later, I realized that everybody in my classroom had lost. I lost my temper, the boys suffered a loss of pride, and the rest of the students lost valuable learning time. But worst of all, we all lost the feelings of comfort and pleasure that come from participating in a class wherein everybody enjoys equal respect. I had to work hard to reestablish the rapport we had lost.

Perhaps you're thinking: Big deal, the kids got out of line and they had to move. They got over it, no real harm done. You have to show them who's boss or they'll take over and ruin your class. To a point, I agree. The kids got out of line. But I think there was real harm done. Instead of teaching them how to deal with conflict calmly and reasonably, I resorted to muscle. We keep asking ourselves why our children are so violent today, why they don't know how to solve problems through discussion. I believe one of the reasons is that we don't demonstrate many alternatives. Although we may not use physical violence, when we control them by threats and punishment, we teach them that power rules. What I taught my students when I threatened them was that I had the authority and the power and if they didn't cooperate, they would be punished. I took full responsibility for the situation and treated them as though they were irresponsible little children. What I should have done, I realized later, was make them responsible for their own behavior. It would have taken a little more time, but it would have been worth it, and it would have prevented other discipline problems in the future.

Not long after that incident, a similar situation arose, and it was a student who taught me a better way to handle the problem. Two boys, Adam and Jaime, who were both well-known gang members, staged a showdown in my remedial English class. Midstory, they both closed their literature books and began arguing loudly about a party they had attended recently. When I asked them to be quiet, they ignored me. Infuriated, I strode across the room and demanded that they stop talking and move to different seats. They not only failed to obey—they didn't even acknowledge my presence! They simply continued talking to each other, as though I weren't there.

I repeated my order in a very loud, stern voice, but still they ignored me. I walked to the phone and picked up the receiver. Before I dialed, I asked, "Would you like me to call somebody who will make you move?" Neither of the boys looked at me, but Jaime said, "No, we would like you to let us sit where we are." Sarcastically, I asked, "Why should I let you sit there when you're disrupting my class?"

"Because maybe we won't disrupt your class if you let us sit here," Jaime said, his voice a perfect imitation of mine. I didn't like the sound of it. Because I recently had made a small amount of headway towards connecting with him, and because I knew his family life was difficult, I relented. "Okay," I told Jaime, "I'm not trying to boss you around, you know. If I wanted to boss people around, I'd have stayed in the

Marines. I asked you to move because I didn't think you could be effective students where you are sitting right now. But if you think you can be good students right there, then I'll trust your judgment. But if you disrupt the lesson again, and interfere with my job, then I will insist that you move and we won't argue about it. Is that reasonable?"

Jaime nudged Adam. "Okay with you?" he asked. Adam nodded. Jaime turned to me. "That sounds reasonable." Jaime looked surprised when I walked over and held out my hand to confirm the deal, but he shook my hand and indicated that Adam also should shake. They both opened their books and behaved for the rest of the class period. Their behavior continued to improve during the following weeks, although they were never at risk of becoming scholarly.

What I learned from that encounter was that a classroom confrontation doesn't have to have a winner and a loser. It can and should have two winners. I won't even pretend that I never succumb to the temptation to try to win, but I do try to remember what my students teach me because they keep giving me tests until I learn the lessons.

There Is a Reason for Every Single Thing a Child Does

Sometimes children's motivations are obvious: they're bored, or tired, or feeling especially feisty. Sometimes they simply need attention. Sometimes they're hoping to be sent to the office because they are afraid they can't complete the current assignment. But sometimes their actions seem completely senseless. How would you explain the following scenarios?

- A usually well-behaved boy shoves several of his classmates and refuses to respond when the teacher speaks to him.
- A straight-A student stops doing her homework and angrily rejects her teacher's attempt to discuss the situation.

- A boy sits quietly in the back of the class, never absent, never causing trouble, never doing a single assignment.
- A student known for his pleasant personality interrupts the lesson and, when the teacher objects, he threatens to hit her.
- An outgoing, friendly girl stands up and curses when the teacher touches her hand in passing.
- An intelligent boy rips his vocabulary test into tiny shreds and throws them on the floor; when the teacher asks him to pick up the pieces, he stomps out of the room.

All of those incidents occurred in my own classroom and, at the time, I was at a loss to explain them. I knew those kids all had reasons for their actions, but I certainly couldn't guess what they were, and when I asked them, I got a shrug and an "I don't know" from each of them. In most cases, I believe they really didn't know, but had felt compelled to act as they had. I refused to give up until I had the answers. I called them at home, kept them after class, tracked them down during lunch hour, and hounded them until they talked to me. When they finally did talk, here's what they said:

Kimboley struck several of his classmates because he wanted to be suspended from school. His grandmother was seriously ill and he wanted to visit her in the hospital. He was so afraid that she would die while he was in school and that he would be left all alone in the world because she was his guardian and sole supporter.

Araceli's father, unable to work because of an injury on the job, was upset that his wife had started attending evening classes to earn her GED so she could get a job and support the family. Although he objected, his wife refused to stop attending classes. So he vented his frustrations on his daughter, who dreamed of attending college. He forbade her to read books or study at home—she had to spend her time cooking and cleaning the house. When her grades suffered, she was ashamed to tell anybody the reason.

Eric had been a good student, earning A's and B's on his report cards, until he overheard his mother and aunt talking one day. His mother remarked that she wished he were more like his cousin, a straight-A student. Eric concluded that since he had been doing his best and it wasn't good enough, there was no point in trying at all.

José was a proud, pugnacious boy who maintained a safe distance from teachers. During a moment of panic, he had written a very personal journal entry about his girlfriend's unplanned pregnancy and his fears about becoming a teenage father. After reading my response in his journal, he became embarrassed that he had made himself so vulnerable. He withdrew from me and when I questioned him, in a desperate attempt to resume his protective privacy, he threatened to hit me.

Letty was an outspoken, friendly girl, but was subject to sudden uncontrollable outbursts of temper. The first time I witnessed an outburst was when I gently touched her hand to get her attention. She refused to talk about her behavior, but I noticed that her worst tantrums came after another student bumped her or touched her without warning. After talking to the school counselors and psychologist, I called Letty's father. When I asked whether Letty often lost her temper at home, he cursed and shouted that he wished he lived out in the country where nobody could hear him because he knew how to make his kids behave, but that every time he tried to control them, somebody called the police.

Danny tore up his test because his father had made him sleep in the garage the night before, even though it was midwinter and the nighttime temperature was below freezing. Why did he have to sleep in the garage? Because his family had visitors and needed Danny's bed for the guests.

I didn't tell you these stories to depress you, but rather to impress upon you that *there is a reason for every single thing a child does.* Finding the reason may be difficult, but punishing children without knowing why they act as they do isn't always effective, or logical, or fair. Of course, we have to maintain order and discipline in our classrooms, but there is a huge difference between discipline that stems from a desire to help students learn how to behave properly and discipline that stems from a desire to punish them for misbehaving. If you operate from a desire to help, and make that clear to your students, not only will you have fewer discipline problems, but you will find that your students will accept the consequences for their misbehavior much more readily.

Nobody Wants to Be a Failure

Who wants to fail this class? Who wants to be disliked?

Ask any room full of students those two questions. Unless there is a psychotic or a smart aleck in the room, you won't see any hands shoot into the air. But if nobody wants to fail or be disliked, then why do so many kids insist on flunking classes and acting so obnoxious that even their mothers are hard-pressed to love them? Because they're kids. They don't spend hours plotting the flight paths of their paper airplanes or considering the consequences of copying somebody else's homework. They simply do whatever they think they need to do to get what they want or need at the time. Adults do the same, but we have many more alternatives, and the experience to make better choices. Children, who have much less experience and far less control, tend to do the first thing that comes to mind— even if it's ridiculous, pointless, obnoxious, or self-destructive. Then, after they have embarrassed themselves, or backed themselves into a corner, the last thing they want to do is take responsibility for what they have done. So, they look for an escape. In school, escape could mean being sent to the office, being suspended, or being put in detention—it doesn't really matter where they go, as long as they get away from all those eyes that are watching with such interest (and sometimes, sadly, with such malice). So, when one of my students acts obnoxious or disruptive, my first thoughts are: *What is this student trying to accomplish right now? What does he think he needs? Why does she want to escape at this particular moment?*

There is no easy answer to the question of why children do what they do, but I have found that by asking questions first, and then responding, I can eliminate most of the potential discipline problems in my classroom. When I assign a grammar worksheet, for example, and one of the boys begins socking his buddy on the arm, I suspect that the one who is doing the punching might not know the difference between a preposition and a pronoun. Either that, or he just doesn't want to work. So, I interrupt the class and say, "Do you know that I studied psychology in college, and one of the things I learned was that when a student is afraid he can't do a particular task, he will often act out, hoping to be sent to the office so he won't have to do the assignment. But I think that's silly. If you can't do the assignment, the last thing you need to do is be absent from class. So . . . let's save some time and trouble. Would all of you who are afraid you can't do this work please raise your hands now, and I will come and help you because that's my job." Eager to show that they are fearless and capable, those problem children usually become intensely interested in the assignment at hand and I make my rounds of the room, offering assistance where needed.

The Principal Difference

A hundred years ago, when I was young, being sent to the principal's office was a very big deal. The principal would paddle you, your parents would paddle you, and your siblings would shun you for embarrassing the family. Today, if you send a student to the principal's office, there is a good chance that the student will simply refuse to leave your room, or that he will leave campus, or spend an amusing hour trading jokes with other students in the waiting area, or sit in a detention room reading comic books.

Even if your wayward student makes it into the principal's office, the result may be very different from what you intended. Principals don't always support their teachers. Students don't always care whether they pass your class or graduate. Parents don't always accept reality or the responsibility for raising their children. And in the worst-case scenario, students or their families may raise legal issues, valid or not, to avoid the real issue of personal responsibility.

1. Avoid the office.

Sending students to the office may not be the best solution to behavior problems in your classroom. In my case, it's a last resort. In seven years of teaching, six of those working with at-risk teens, I sent only two students to the office—and I sent those two only because they made me so angry I was afraid that I might throttle them. Neither of those two argued with me when I suggested that they pay the principal a visit, because I had warned them, as I warn all of my classes, "The only reason I will send you to the principal's office from this classroom is if I am so angry that I'm afraid I will try to kill you with my bare hands." Sometimes students laugh when I say that, but they stop laughing when I assure them that I am absolutely serious. They are never quite sure whether I am serious or not, and I let them wonder. A little mystery is good for children.

2. Break the behavior cycle.

In addition to the other reasons I mentioned, my primary reason for not sending students to the office is that I don't like the cycle of behavior that usually results from it. What we hope will happen rarely does: the student accepts responsibility for his or her actions, learns from this mistake, and resolves to cooperate with the teacher. What usually happens is more like this: the student misbehaves, you send the student to the office, the student becomes angry or embarrassed and blames you for causing those feelings, the student also blames you for whatever punishment is meted out, the student returns to your class still angry or ashamed and eager for revenge, and you're back to the beginning of the cycle, ready for another round. A humane approach can do much to break that cycle.

Imagine how you would feel if your supervisor at work objected to your behavior and, instead of explaining the objection and discussing the situation, marched you past your coworkers to the company president's office for a reprimand? That may sound silly, but an office isn't so different from a classroom. Your students are "employees" whose job is to learn their lessons and complete their assignments in exchange for credits towards a diploma. When they make mistakes or become ineffective workers, they need to be corrected, quickly and without damaging their dignity any more than is necessary.

3. Detention can be a losing proposition.

Detention is another tactic that may backfire on you. If you assign students to detention in your classroom, then you have to waste your valuable time baby-sitting. If you send them to an in-school detention, they will miss your lessons and classroom assignments, which probably will result in lower exam scores and even less motivation to behave well. By sending your students to detention, you may be setting them up to fail your class, which is the opposite of what you were hired to do.

In many schools, the detention room is a joke, a party zone or a place to "chill out." I've seen some detention rooms where kids sat on the desks, listening to the radio and discussing their weekend activities while the attendant either read the newspaper or encouraged the kids to share their stories. I taught at one high school where students in detention were required to complete word-search puzzles from a crossword puzzle magazine. I tried to drop off some assignments for a student who had been absent and was told by the attendant that students were "not allowed to work on classwork in detention because they are being punished."

Once again, let's use the metaphor of student and teacher as employee and employer. Would you be inspired to work harder or learn difficult tasks if your boss sent you to the lunch room to sit for an hour or two whenever you failed to complete your day's work or wasted time talking to your coworkers instead of focusing on your job? Probably not, because that punishment wouldn't address the problem behavior. The same holds true for students. Many children, faced with a difficult academic lesson, are thrilled to have an opportunity to escape to the detention room because then they don't have to deal with the present difficulty. If we want them to learn to focus on difficult lessons and admit that they need help sometimes, we need to insist that they focus and ask for help when they need it, instead of trying to escape temporarily. At the beginning of the year, I warn my students: "Don't act like a turkey, thinking I'll send you to detention. I know you'd rather escape than stay here and learn to read and write effectively. If I have a problem with your behavior, you and I will handle it right here in this room. If we can't handle it, we'll ask your parents or guardians to help us, but we aren't going to waste your time sitting in detention. My time is too valuable to waste, and so is yours." That gets their attention, and I do my best to keep it.

4. Put your ducks in a row.

As early in the school year as possible, it's a good idea to request a conference with the person who is responsible for handling disciplinary problems at your school. In some cases, there will be a different dean or principal for each grade level. In other cases, the principal or a counselor will handle every referral. At your conference, explain how you plan to handle behavior problems in your classroom. Ask if there is a standard school policy that requires specific consequences for specific offenses, or whether the principal has flexibility in assigning consequences. If there is a strict policy, you may be out of the loop after you refer a student to the office. But if there is a flexible policy, ask whether you might make recommendations, based on the particular circumstances of an incident. If a normally well-behaved student becomes very disruptive, for example, you might want to request a more lenient punishment than you would for a student who repeatedly causes serious problems.

When I meet with the principal, I explain that my goal is to keep students in class and help them be successful, not to punish them. I let the principal know that if one of my students shows up in the office during class time, that student is there because I am too angry to be objective or fair.

Unless I specifically request it, however, I ask that the principal not suspend or otherwise punish a student I have sent to the office, until after I have had an opportunity to meet with the principal so that I might suggest appropriate consequences for that particular student—a stern lecture from the principal; a three-way conference with the principal, the student, and me; a parent conference; in-school detention; a behavior contract to be signed before the student returns to class; and so on.

The more familiar your administration is with your teaching philosophy, the easier it will be for them to work with you instead of against you. Quite often, principals are just as overworked as teachers. They resent having to spend their time on trivial complaints. If you send students to the office only after you've exhausted other options, you will find that you will be much more popular with the principal (and her staff) than teachers who send students to the office for minor offenses such as forgetting to bring a book to class, or throwing a paper airplane, or making a smart remark. Your referrals will be taken seriously if you send students only when a serious situation occurs.

Rules of Order

When I meet with parents, we often discuss the question of how to establish and enforce rules that will help children succeed in school. I tell parents that I like to think of rules as a kind of scaffolding for children. They provide support and keep children from falling and seriously injuring themselves. As children grow older, the rules can be relaxed or removed, one at a time, until the children stand alone, making their own decisions, taking as much risk as their confidence and abilities will allow. If we make reasonable rules, enforce them fairly, and adjust them to meet children's changing needs, we will teach children that, instead of rigid restrictions designed to spoil all their fun, rules actually can create more freedom for them.

1. *Rules are not made to be broken.*

Rules and procedures are two very different things. Rules are rigid; procedures are more flexible and can be adapted if necessary. If you make a clear distinction between rules and procedures, you will make life easier for both you and your students.

As I explained in Chapter 1, I suggest keeping your list of rules to a minimum—one or two should be enough. Rules, like laws, make no allowance for individual differences or circumstances. If you establish rigid rules, you may regret it later. Many teachers, in an effort to teach responsibility, make it a rule that they will not accept late work, or that one missing homework assignment will preclude a student from earning an A in the class. What if a student cannot complete an assignment because of a true emergency, such as a serious illness, accident, or death? You have two choices—stick to your rule or ignore it. Either option has disadvantages.

If you adamantly refuse to bend your rules, innocent students will suffer and you may earn a reputation as a harsh and unfeeling person. If you bend your rules for one student, other students will quickly line up and ask for special consideration because they, too, have emergencies (which may seem trivial to you, but very important to someone young). No matter where you draw the line, some students will feel that they have been wronged, that you dislike them, that you play favorites. That's why I suggest making rules only about things that you will *never* tolerate, things that don't happen by accident—swearing, hitting, making racial insults, for example.

Procedures, on the other hand, don't legislate behavior; they provide guidelines for completing specific activities, such as using the restroom, completing makeup work, requesting permission to miss class, how students who arrive at school late should go about requesting admittance to your class. Establishing procedures for your classroom provides clear guidelines for student behavior while leaving you more options. If special circumstances arise, you will be able to make changes without causing a lot of complaints or confusion.

2. Hold students responsible.

When you first establish your classroom rules and procedures, explain to your students that you expect them to take responsibility for their behavior, and you expect them to cooperate with you because you have an important job to do. Make sure students understand the consequences for breaking rules, assign consequences that help students correct behavior problems, and then put the responsibility for everything they say and do squarely on their young shoulders. When a student misbehaves, find out why. If one student instigates trouble, that doesn't excuse another student's misbehavior. If a student has a problem at home or is angry about something that happened at school, offer to help him come up with solutions. Whatever the student's reason, don't allow him to blame somebody else for his own actions.

3. Explain and explain again.

Just as we assume that students know that, as teachers we want to help them, we also assume that they understand why we correct them. But they don't always understand. Ask a student why he or she was punished and you'll hear surprising explanations. Here are some explanations from students who came to me for counseling:

> I don't know why, but that teacher hates me.
> The teacher is prejudiced; I can tell by the way he looks at me.
> That teacher only likes boys/girls/football players/nerds.
> She's on a power trip and likes to make people feel small.
> He's just trying to look bad, like he's tough and all that.
> She gets mad if you ask questions because she's afraid we'll
>   find out she doesn't know everything.

The sad thing is that sometimes those students were right. There are teachers who are prejudiced, power hungry, or afraid to admit they don't know all the answers. But those are the exceptions. Most of us sincerely want to help our students. We need to tell them, repeatedly, that when we correct them, it is to help them be more effective students and successful people. It takes much less time to say, "Sally, please be quiet or else" than it does to say, "Sally, I'd like you to stop talking now because you're distracting me and making it hard for me to do my job, but there's a more important reason I'd like you to pay attention—I want you to pass this class. I want to help you be a successful person." The extra time and effort you spend explaining your requests will pay off and eventually you'll be able to drop the explanation. It shouldn't take more than two or three million reminders before your students get the message.

4. Separate the student from the behavior.

When a student misbehaves, make it abundantly clear that it is the student's present *behavior* you dislike—*not* the student. Hate the behavior; love the child. Don't worry about stating the obvious. What is obvious to you may not be obvious to a child. Remind him that your job is to help, not punish, but that you do have a job to do, and part of that job is to teach children how to behave so that they can go on to become successful adults.

After you correct a student, mention something good about him or her. Don't make up anything; if you try, you will be able to find something good, although it may not be something academic. Perhaps he has leadership ability, quick wit, a talent for solving problems, especially good grooming, or beautiful handwriting. Perhaps she is always on time, prepares neat assignments, has perfect attendance, or a kind heart. Tell the student you appreciate whatever is good about him or her. Then explain why the student's present behavior is inappropriate and what you expect him to do to correct the situation. Don't worry about sounding phony, because you won't sound phony if you tell the truth. No child would object to being told: "You know I like you very much. Your sense of humor adds a lot to this classroom and I enjoy your jokes. But although I like you, I do not like your behavior right now.

I want you to stop throwing staples at Phyllis and settle down and use your good brain to finish this assignment. If you need help, ask me and I will be happy to help you because I like you." (If you don't like the student, don't say you do. If you don't like a lot of your students, then perhaps you should look at yourself to see whether your attitude may be the source of some of your discipline problems. Kids are like puppies. They know instinctively who likes them and who doesn't. When they sense that they are disliked, it hurts their feelings and makes them angry, and heaven help you then.)

5. Be specific.

I felt certain that my one rule—*respect yourself and the other people in this room*—would prohibit just about any inappropriate behavior my students could come up with (putting gum in the dictionary is disrespectful to others who need to use the books, passing notes during class is disrespectful to the teacher, etc.). But I hadn't allowed for differences in interpretation of the word "respect." I assumed that my students would share my definition, and most of them did.

One young man, however, repeatedly interrupted me while I was speaking by loudly clearing his sinus cavities. Then he'd stand up, walk across the front of the room to the trash can near the door, and spit loudly into the metal can.

The first time Rick snorted and spat, I was shocked into silence. I stared, along with the other students, as he made his journey to the trash can and back to his seat. After class, I reminded Rick of the rule and asked him to be more polite the following day. He nodded agreeably and left. The next day, he repeated his performance. After three days of spitting, and three reminders to be polite, I stopped Rick after class and asked him to sit down.

"Why do you persist in being so rude during my lessons?" I asked.

"I'm not being rude," Rick responded.

"How can you say that?"

"What am I doing?" he asked, raising his hands, palms

up. I remember thinking what a good actor he was—he looked genuinely surprised.

"Do you think it's polite to snort while I'm talking, then walk in between me and the rest of the class to spit in the trash?" I asked. "Don't you think that's rude?"

"No," Rick said, "because I'm not spitting on the floor."

That conversation with Rick made me realize that when I think students are ignoring my instructions or requests, that may not be the case at all. They may be interpreting my instructions differently than I had expected them to. When they don't respond as I want them to, I rephrase my request, making sure that my instructions are clear and explicit.

"Settle down" means one thing to me and sometime entirely different to children. So does "be polite." For weeks, I kept urging my sophomores to be polite while we were watching videotapes in class. I warned them repeatedly, but they continued to whisper and giggle. Finally, out of patience, I stopped the tape and flipped on the lights. When the students complained and demanded to know why I had turned off the tape, I told them I was tired of asking them to be polite. They insisted that they had been "being really good." I said I didn't think they were being "good" by continuing to talk when I had asked them repeatedly to be quiet.

"You never asked us to be quiet," one boy insisted. "You just kept telling us to be polite."

"Well, what did you think I meant?" I asked, sarcastically. I hadn't expected an answer, but I got several.

> *"Don't throw candy wrappers on the floor."*
>
> *"Move your desk so the people behind you can see."*
>
> *"Don't open your backpack during the movie because the zipper is too loud."*
>
> *"Don't get up and walk around because you might step on somebody's toes."*

The longer I teach, the more I learn.

6. Big Brother may not notice.

Sometimes, rules will come from your administration or government. In that case, it's much easier to justify an unreasonable rule. All you have to do is tell the students that you are legally bound to comply with district, state, or federal regulations. But occasionally a rule may strike you as being so completely unreasonable that you cannot follow it, although there is no possibility of changing it. Let me give you an example.

One year, during the last week of summer school (a four-week session), the grandfather of one of my students died and the student asked me if I would excuse him so he could attend the funeral. He would be absent for three days because he had to travel across country. I thought the boy's request was reasonable, but the summer school principal disagreed. There was a strict rule, established by the state, that required any student who missed more than twelve hours (three days) of summer school to be expelled with no credit. This rule was established in accordance with state guidelines stating the minimum number of hours a student must attend a class in order to receive credit.

But surely this student had learned the material; had perfect attendance to that date, and had earned excellent grades on all his class assignments. I suggested that he be permitted to attend the funeral, then return and take the final exam with his classmates. If he passed, he would earn credit. The principal said he was sorry, that there was absolutely no way he could make an exception. The boy had to choose whether to attend his grandfather's funeral or pass English.

I hope that principal isn't reading this book, because I lied. The boy went to his grandfather's funeral, I marked him present during those three days, and he earned an A in my class. I'm not proud of myself for breaking the law, but I would have been ashamed of myself if I hadn't.

A Little Less Talk, a Lot More Action

If you take the time to establish that you are in control of your classroom and that the students are in control of themselves, you will eliminate many of the discipline problems that plague teachers. Problems will still occur, however, and when they do, you must be prepared to deal with them. Just as you have your own teacher persona, you will need your model of discipline. What works for somebody else may not work for you. My own disciplinary model is a seven-step plan, with each step requiring more time and energy. When a student misbehaves, I try the first step first, then the second, and so on, until I find the one that works.

1. *Ignore the instigator.*
2. *Send a nonverbal message.*
3. *Speak softly, but carry a big vocabulary.*
4. *Drop a card.*
5. *Just you and me, babe.*
6. *Time out.*
7. *We're off to see the principal.*

1. Ignore the instigator.

Sometimes even the best students will act out, in a moment of temporary insanity, or just to see what your reaction will be. If you ignore the misbehavior, quite often it will go away. I once heard a comedian discussing the difference between people who perceive themselves as "high class" and those who actually possess some social graces. He said something to the effect that if somebody farted in the presence of the Queen of England, she wouldn't acknowledge that she'd noticed the intestinal disturbance. In my classroom, I try to conduct myself with the social grace of a queen by ignoring those little brain farts that so frequently occur in teenage minds.

2. Send a nonverbal message.

When I ignore disruptive behavior and it doesn't go away, which happens about 50 percent of the time, I continue talking but move immediately in the direction of the disruptive students. As I near them I smile at them but still keep addressing the class. My message is clear. They know that I am offering them a chance to gracefully back down. Usually, they will stop talking and behave themselves. I honestly believe that sometimes they just need to be noticed but don't know how to ask for attention in an acceptable way.

When a quick glance and a pleasant smile aren't enough, a deadly stare sometimes does the trick. In fact, a bone-chilling stare is one of the most effective tools a teacher can have. Many times, one such look is enough to stop students in their tracks, but you'd be surprised how many people think they are looking stern when they are actually smiling. Practice glaring in the mirror at yourself. Curl your lip into a sneer. Tilt your chin down so that your eyeballs seem to be staring from the middle of your forehead. Narrow your eyes until they become tiny, mean slits that throw off death rays.

Sometimes even your deadliest warning look won't be enough. In that case, combine it with another nonverbal warning—clear your throat, tap a ruler against your palm, adjust your glasses, heave a long loud sigh, or slap a book down sharply on your desk.

Whatever you do, don't hide behind your desk. Movement can be one of your most effective deterrents. If you stand behind a desk or a podium, you place a barrier between you and your students. They feel distanced from you and are much more likely to misbehave. If you walk among your students as you address them, between the aisles and across the back of the room, you will change the dynamics of your classroom. You will be more accessible to all your students. By removing physical barriers, you take a psychological step closer to them, which helps them to bond to you, and by moving about the room, you are sending the message that you are teaching all of them and not just the few in the front rows of the room.

Make your movements smooth and casual. When misbehavior erupts, continue speaking or reading as you move towards your problem child. If you're writing on the board, stop and look thoughtful, as though a new idea had just nudged you, and ponder this new idea as you stroll about the room. If you're reading from the text, pick up the book and take it with you. Don't speak to the student, and don't reward her by focusing everyone's attention on her, but stand guard near her desk until your message is received and understood. If the misbehavior is corrected immediately, do pause and smile at the student. Just as puppies need a pat on the head to reinforce their good behavior when they perform on the newspaper instead of the floor, we need to let our students know when they have responded to our cues.

If the student is slow to respond, lean against the edge of her desk or place your hand on the back of her chair. Until you capture a student's attention, it's very possible that she wasn't aware that she was acting inappropriately. To a child, showing photos to a friend, humming the latest tune softly to herself, doodling on the desktop, or staring out the window might seem like perfectly logical behaviors.

3. Speak softly, but carry a big vocabulary.

Sometimes you will encounter a student who is determined to test you and will escalate the disruption. In that case, I recommend that you stop suddenly (midsentence is good) and simply look at the student for several long seconds. When you stop talking, everybody will look to see why, and they'll notice you staring at your disruptive student. Now he or she has the attention of the entire classroom.

"He's really gonna get it," the students will be thinking. They'll prepare themselves for the usual skull crunching lecture. This will present a perfect opportunity for you to teach them that they aren't as smart as they think they are, if instead of shouting or clenching your teeth, you say, in a most pleasant and sincere tone, "I would appreciate it immensely if you would not talk/throw paper/pound on your desk/whistle when I am addressing the class, because it is distracting and frustrating to me because I am trying to be an effective teacher for you."

Don't wait for a response, and don't stand there staring at

the student because that could be taken as a challenge to escalate the confrontation. Instead, smile sweetly and say, "Thank you very much. I truly appreciate your cooperation." Then walk away quickly and continue your discussion. In most cases, this method will work. If not, you will have lost nothing but a few seconds of time and a little dignity, and, as author Garrison Keillor once pointed out, "Who needs dignity when you can be in show business?"

4. Drop a card.

By accident, I discovered that a behavior card can be quite effective in controlling student behavior. A boy I liked very much began spitting paper wads into a girl's hair. Since most of the students were engrossed in a writing assignment, I didn't want to interrupt their work by reprimanding Jerome. I grabbed a scrap of paper from my desk and scribbled: "Your present behavior is unacceptable. I know you can be more polite. Please do so. Return this note to me after class."

I tossed the card on Jerome's desk and quickly walked away, to avoid any discussion that might distract the other student. Jerome read the paper, blushed, and turned the paper facedown on his desk. He was quiet for the rest of the class period and disappeared as soon as the bell rang, leaving the note behind on my desk. The following day I called Jerome aside and asked him why he hadn't returned the note to me personally, as I had expected, so that I could talk to him. "It didn't say I had to hand it to you," he protested. "It just said to return it to you, so I put it on your desk." That evening I cut some index cards into thirds, so that my message wouldn't be large enough for a nearby student to read. I wanted the behavior cards to be a personal, silent, communication between me and one student. I revised my instructions so that my final cards read:

> *Your present behavior is unacceptable. I know you can be more polite. Please do so. Return this card to me in person after class. Thank you.*

When a warning look or other nonverbal cues don't work, I pick up a card and drop it on the desk of the student who is talking, reading a comic book, passing notes, or some other minor disruptive activity. I don't make a production out of dropping the card, and I don't say anything. I place the card on the student's desk, smile at him or her, and get on with the lesson. Those cards work wonderfully. When I drop one on a student's desk, he or she always reads it, glances to see if anybody else noticed, then turns it facedown and gets busy with the classroom assignment. Only once did a student ignore the warning. Danny Roberts, a senior with a serious attitude problem, kept trying to draw another boy into a loud conversation during a vocabulary exam. When I dropped a card on Danny's desk, he glanced at it, snorted, and sneered, "Oh, wow. I'm really scared." Then he tore the card in half and stared directly at me, which I interpreted as an invitation to conduct a private discussion on the finer points of academic etiquette, so I invited him outside my classroom for a chat.

5. Just you and me, babe.

We all know that a private conversation is much more likely to be effective that a public reprimand, but more than one teacher has whispered to me, "After I call the kid outside to talk, I'm never sure what am I supposed to say." That makes sense, especially if the student is one you don't know well. My advice is to put yourself in the student's place. If you had done something bad enough that your supervisor felt compelled to call you in for a private discussion, what would make you receptive to what she has to say? Would a list of your shortcomings, followed by a list of your character flaws inspire you to change your ways and work harder? More likely, you would become embarrassed, angry, defensive, and inspired to look for another job. But if your boss made it clear that she was aware of your good points and appreciated your contribution to the company, wouldn't you be more inclined to listen and consider changing your ways?

On the rare occasion, I have had a student who seemed

determined to resist my charm from the first moment he or she stepped into the classroom. (In my case, it's usually a he, perhaps because I'm a woman.) When I am rudely unappreciated, I call the student into the hall for a private conference. We *don't* have a conversation—*I* do all the talking. If it's a girl, of course, I revise my monologue to include feminine references, but the gist of my message is this:

> *I know that you are in a difficult period of your life right now, you're tired of being treated like a little boy, and people expect you to act like a man but they don't always treat you like one. In my classroom, you will be treated like a young man, and I expect you to act like one. You have some serious decisions to make in the next few years, things that will affect your life forever. Right now, you have one decision to make—and that is whether you want to be in my class or not. I like you, and I hope you will choose to stay. I try to be a good teacher, and I will never embarrass you. If you can't read very well, or have some other problems in English, I will help you. But if you choose to stay in my class, then you must cooperate with me. I have many students to teach, and I take my job very seriously. I will not let you stop me from doing my job. So, you will have to decide right now whether you want to stay in this class and cooperate with me, or whether you want me to escort you to the office right now to get your class changed. Which will it be?*

Nobody has ever asked to go to the office. (They don't know that I don't have the authority to change their classes.) But it isn't as easy to get back into my room as it is to get out of it. When the student indicates that he wants to stay, I continue my speech:

> *All right. I'm very happy that you want to stay. I like you already and I don't even know you very well. But you seem to be a bright, intelligent young man. Now, before we go back into that room, I want you to look me in the eye and give me your word of honor as a man that you will cooperate with me. I'm not asking you to be a brown-nose or a perfect little angel. But I*

want your word that you are going to conduct yourself with dignity and self-respect and to respect other people—because those are the behaviors of a real man.

I extend my hand and wait. Sometimes I have to wait quite a while, but I believe it's worth my time. And when a young man gives his word of honor, I treat it as the precious gift that it is. After we shake hands, I open the door and let the student walk back into the room ahead of me. I enter smiling, as though nothing had happened, and continue where I left off. If other students giggle or start to tease the boy or girl, I ask if they would like to step outside. They wouldn't. After that day, if the student who shook my hand slips, all I have to do is stop by his or her desk, put my hand lightly on his arm or shoulder, and whisper, "Remember what you promised." It works. And I have stopped being surprised when those tough-acting kids turn out to be some of the best students I have ever had.

6. *Time out.*

If you don't have the time, or patience, to hold a private discussion with a disruptive student, ask him or her to step outside your classroom and wait for you. Sometimes, that's all it takes and the student apologizes after class. I simply let the student stand out there until the bell rings, hoping he or she will spend the time worrying about what I'm going to do. If I have time, and think it will be worth the effort, I give my speech and shake hands. If not, I hope that the time out gave the student a chance to consider his or her behavior. At the very least, it allows me to focus on the students who are behaving themselves, instead of letting one disruptive student use up all our valuable class time.

7. *We're off to see the principal.*

As I mentioned earlier, this is a last resort, and one I rarely use, because when I send a student to the principal's office, I lose control of the situation and can no longer decide what consequences the student should face. I have seen students suspended or expelled for what I considered to be trivial infractions of the rules.

When I have to use number 5, 6, or 7, I make a personal phone call that evening to remind the student that I like him (or her, of course) and that I hope he chooses to return to my class the following day. I reassure the student that I am not angry and will not carry a grudge, but that I simply cannot accept some behavior because it interferes with my ability to do my job well. I ask the student if he has any concerns he'd like to discuss with me, although I know his primary concern at that moment is getting me off the phone. Before we hang up, I remind him that I look forward to seeing him in class the following day.

You may have guessed that my undergraduate degree is in psychology. But even without that as a foundation, I think I would still be more interested in finding out why a student behaves a certain way than in trying to force the student to change his or her behavior. And I would still believe, as I always have, that every person is entitled to the same respect and basic human dignity.

The Element of Surprise

After just one or two years of school, students know what to expect from teachers. They know what behaviors will earn them a lecture, a demerit, a bad grade, a trip to the office, a phone call to Mom and Dad. They think they have us figured out. They take for granted that they know how the teacher will react, and they are confident they can outmaneuver us. They let down their guard, and that's when we teachers have the best opportunity to capture their attention and earn their cooperation.

1. Reach out and scare someone.

We have all heard a teacher ask, "Do you want me to call your parents?" in order to catch a student's attention. But how many of us have heard a teacher ask, "Do you want me to call you tonight?" Students expect us to call their parents and complain about them. They aren't a bit surprised that all the "old people" are ganging up on them in an attempt to spoil what little fun they have. They are surprised, however, when one of those old folks calls to chat with them.

There are advantages to calling students directly, instead of parents or guardians. First, you will avoid the resentment that often comes with punishments, such as grounding or losing telephone or television privileges. Even though the student was at fault, she will blame you for her punishment, and any change in behavior will be out of desire to avoid further punishment, not a desire to cooperate with you. Second, you will save time because you won't have to explain the situation in great detail. You won't be talking to a third party—you'll be talking to the star of the show. The greatest advantage of direct phone calls to students is the element of surprise. They aren't prepared for battle.

The first time I called a student, I was simply at a loss for alternatives. Derek was a likable boy with a great sense of humor and a surplus of energy. He had good attendance and did well on his assignments, but he drove me crazy during class sometimes. Six out of seven days he'd behave, but the seventh day would be a winner. If he wasn't spitting staples at the girls, he was throwing Gummie Bears at the overhead lights. Nothing he did was bad enough, by itself, to merit suspension or detention, or even a call to his father. He had been sent to the principal's office so many times the previous year that he was on a first-name basis with the principal, so that wasn't a viable solution.

One day, Derek had whistled nonstop under his breath, just loudly enough to irritate me, for thirty minutes. I hadn't been able to identify the whistler, and every time I stopped talking, the whistling had stopped. I'm sure to prepubescent people, it was hilarious to see me wincing and gritting my teeth, so nobody snitched on the whistler. When Derek admitted, on his way out the door, that he was the whistler, I was tempted to throttle him. Instead, I let him escape, but I kept thinking about it, and by the end of the day I was raving. After all the effort I had made to help him, and the special attention I had given him, look how the little twerp repaid me. That evening, after dinner, I grabbed the phone and dialed Derek's number. I hadn't planned what to say, I just wanted to let him know how angry I was.

When Derek's father answered, I asked to speak to Derek. After a brief pause, he covered the receiver and called Derek. From the sound of his voice as he said, "It's your teacher," I knew he was puzzled. Good, I thought. I hope you grill him after he hangs up. Make him sweat. When Derek took the phone and said a timid, "Hello," I said, "Hi, Derek, this is Miss Johnson, your English teacher, the one you tormented all class period today. Remember me?"

"Yeah," he whispered.

"I just wanted you to know that I like you, but I don't like the way you act sometimes and I think you should seriously consider how your behavior affects other people. I try very hard to be a good teacher and plan lessons that you guys will like. So, I don't understand why you want to be so mean to me. Could you explain that to me so I can understand?" Derek didn't have an answer, so I told him to think of one before he walked into my room the next day.

"And don't even think about cutting, Sweetpea," I warned him. "If you do that, we'll both be sorry." Then I hung up.

Derek paid more attention to that phone call than he had to all my other efforts to get him to listen. It worked so well that I started calling kids at home whenever they didn't respond in school. Sometimes parents or guardians would ask why I wanted to speak to the student. I'd say that I wanted to make sure she didn't forget to bring an important assignment or that I wanted to remind him to study for an exam. Then, when the student came to the phone, I'd say, "I'm not going to tell your mommy (or daddy or aunt or grandma) on you, because you're old enough to make your own decisions. I like you, but I didn't like your behavior in my class today. So I want you to decide right now that you're going to behave better tomorrow. Can I count on you?"

When they say yes, as they always do, I thank them and

tell them I can't wait to see them the following day because I truly like them.

After accidentally interrupting dinner a few times, I intentionally began making my calls at dinnertime. Students become very uncomfortable when the whole family is in the same room or the next room, straining to eavesdrop. Often I can hear a parent or guardian, sometimes a curious sibling, in the background whispering, "Are you in trouble? What does she want?"

When that happens, I ask the student, "Do you know why your mom is standing there watching you? Because she cares about you. And so do I. See you tomorrow." Then I quickly hang up and leave the student to explain to his family why I called.

2. Lunch is on me.

Sometimes I buy a student a burger or a soda, and take advantage of the informal situation to connect with students who don't respond to me in the classroom. Lunch in the cafeteria or outdoors at a picnic table is much less threatening than a conference in the classroom, and the student may relax and talk. If the student seems nervous, I keep it short. Five minutes of conversation goes a long way towards breaking down resistance. Please note that I'm not talking about being a student's pal. Just as a boss at work can treat an employee to lunch or dinner in order to have a personal chat without crossing the line between employer and employee, you can buy a student a burger or a soda—or take her to a play or a movie—without becoming bosom buddies. As long as you maintain a professional attitude and maintain an appropriate distance (don't let students call you by your first name, for example), students will appreciate your concern without losing respect for your position as their teacher.

People occasionally criticize me for spending money on my students (although I don't know a single public school teacher who doesn't spend his or her own money on students and supplies). I explain that I consider money spent

on my students as my own direct charitable contribution to
their educations.

Ironically, the most successful strategies I've used to
connect with my students were unplanned—taking students
to lunch, for example. One day, on my way out the door at
lunch, I spied a student who often sat in the back of my class
and kept up a running commentary on my teaching, under
his breath, just loud enough for me to hear. Sometimes
Russell would mimic my voice as I lectured the class. Since
he didn't cause any serious problems, I let it slide. He had
written in his private journal that he didn't like white people. Although I hoped to change his mind, I knew it would
take time for him to learn to trust me. That day, on a whim,
I beckoned to Russell and asked him if he'd like to walk to
the deli with me so I could buy him lunch.

"Why?" he asked.

"I don't know," I said. "Why not?"

Russell shrugged and fell into step beside me. During
the trip to the deli, I knew he expected me to complain
about his sarcastic comments during class, so I talked about
everything except that. I asked him what movies he had
seen lately, how many brothers and sisters he had, whether
he thought rap lyrics should be censored or not. I told him
about my own family, how I missed my sisters and brothers,
and that I was trying to teach myself to play the piano.

When we returned to campus after lunch, Russell
thanked me for the sandwich and soda and took off for his
fifth-period class. A few days later, he asked me why I had
taken him to lunch. I said that I sometimes took students
out to lunch (which was true, although he was the first)
because I wanted to get to know my students better so that I
could be a better teacher—and that I wanted them to realize
that I was also a regular person, just like them. He gave me a
strange look, as though it had never occurred to him that I
might be a person.

Russell didn't become a model student after that, and he
never did join in the friendly banter that most of my students
shared with me, but he did stop making fun of me. And on
the last day of school, when I asked the students to write in

their journals about the most important thing they had learned during the year, he wrote, "I learned that not all white people are bad." From Russell, that was high praise.

3. Hire the "problem" child.

It's tempting to assign extracurricular chores to the most responsible, mature students in your classroom. But those students already know how to handle responsibility. It's the immature, flaky kids who need to learn how to manage their time, set priorities, and learn to focus on one task at a time. If you have a "problem child" who responds to individual attention, but flounders when left on her own, why not enlist her as your student clerk or aide? In most schools, students may earn credits for working as teacher's helpers, but even if no credits are earned, the experience can be invaluable—for both you and the student. She will have the opportunity to watch you at work, to learn new skills, and to enjoy the feeling of satisfaction that comes from being depended on. You will learn new teaching methods and techniques for teaching responsibility that you will be able to use with other students.

The best student clerk I ever had was the last student I'd have chosen at the beginning of the year. José was an intelligent but tough boy who lifted weights every night in preparation for his recreational fistfights during lunch hour every day. José spent more time in the office then he did in his fifth-period math class, which immediately followed lunch. When José's math teacher, who worked closely with me, told me that José was failing because of missing so much work, I jokingly suggested that we should switch José to an earlier math class and sign him up to be my student clerk fifth period.

"Great idea," Mr. Attwood said. "José likes you, and he respects you. If he knows he has to report to you after lunch, maybe he'll stay out of trouble."

I agreed to try it for a month. At the end of that time, I wouldn't have traded José for ten student clerks. He not only stopped getting into fights during lunchtime, but he was the most hardworking, conscientious clerk I've ever had. One day, I was late getting back to my room, and worried that José would find my room empty and assume that he didn't need to check in. I envisioned him wandering the halls, looking for trouble. When I reached my classroom, José was not only there, but he had collared two other boys who were cutting class and had put them to work grading the spelling tests I had left in his work basket. I was thoroughly ashamed of myself for having so little faith.

We've all read the research that proves children live up— or down—to their teachers' expectations. After working with José and so many students like him, I believe that completely. I'm not afraid to trust a student, even if his record shows I shouldn't. When students enter my classroom, I tell them that I don't care what they did the year before or the day before. But I do care what they do from that moment on. And I trust each one of them, regardless of their past records, until I have personal proof that somebody can't be trusted. The knowledge that you expect a child to be honest and dependable may inspire those traits. Sometimes all it takes is one person to believe in him to make a child believe in himself. Of course, that doesn't always happen. But I would rather place my trust in a child, take my chances, and risk being disappointed than to distrust an innocent child, insult his dignity, and risk being responsible for provoking him into an act of dishonesty or revenge.

4. Offer unattractive alternatives.

I once had a class of seniors who balked at the assignment of memorizing and reciting a sonnet by Shakespeare or Elizabeth Barrett Browning (or an original poem of comparative length and depth) in front of the class. These students had been together for three years, they got along well, and they weren't shy about speaking in front of each other. They just didn't want to work that hard. After listening to ten minutes of moans, groans, and complaints, I said, "Fine. I'll give you an alternative assignment." Thinking they had won the war, they started cheering and giving each other high fives. The alternative? Do the entire Hokey Pokey, from right hand to head, in front of the class. For those who weren't familiar with that old favorite, I demonstrated the first verse, complete with mandatory hand gestures, dancing in place, and clapping on the last line:

> *You put your right hand in, you put your right hand out*
> *You put your right hand in, and you shake it all about*
> *You do the Hokey Pokey, and you turn yourself around*
> *That's what it's all about.*

Some kids complained that the Hokey Pokey was stupid. I argued that it would require the same skills as learning a sonnet—memorizing, reciting, public speaking—but that it would be a little easier for those who weren't up to the challenge. One sharp student threatened to go tell the principal about the Hokey Pokey assignment. I told him to go ahead, the principal probably learned it in kindergarten and might like to come and watch those who chose to perform it for the class. Every single student in that class chose to recite a sonnet, and they did a good job of it.

On other occasions, I have made the unattractive alternative more serious, such as writing a research paper instead of a two-page essay, or completing several grammar worksheets instead of reading a story from our literature textbook.

5. Hit them in the funny bone.

My favorite discipline tool is my sense of humor. It works better than anything else I've tried. It can dispel tension, ease anxiety, and prevent minor disruptions from becoming major distractions. Even if you are a serious person, you may find that humor works where other tactics fail.

Here's an example: You pass out a worksheet and one of your students moans and groans and whines that she "doesn't want to do this." She expects you to ignore her or insist that she do it. She doesn't expect you to say, "Oh, well. Doing things you don't want to do is good practice for when you grow up and get married. If you don't believe me, go home and ask your mama." She won't expect you fall on your knees in front of your desk, clasp your hands, and plead, "Oh, please, do this assignment. I'm an old woman, and this is hurting my knees. How can you be so cruel? Would it hurt you so much to do this assignment and bring joy into the life of an elderly woman?" Chances are very good that your student will chuckle, sigh, and do the assignment.

Another example: Two Hispanic wannabe gangsters sit in the back of your room, arms crossed, sunglasses perched on their noses, clearly begging for your attention. They expect you to order them to take off the sunglasses. They don't expect you to stroll behind their desks and softly sing the lyrics to "Lo Mucho Que Te Quiero": *"Nunca hablo a ti con la mentira. Siempre hablo a ti con la verdad. Quisiera que olvides el pasado, que vuelvas a mi lado, que tengas compacion,"* which translates as: I will never lie to you. I will always tell you the truth. I wish you would forget the past, return to my side, and have some compassion.

I did that very thing once, and it worked wonders. Both boys tried to continue scowling but couldn't keep the smiles from their faces, especially when the rest of the students started laughing and pointing at me. It's hard to be a tough guy when you're holding your breath to stifle your giggles.

Here are some other techniques that use humor to make a point, develop rapport with your students, or convince them to cooperate with you.

Be terribly bilingual and sing off-key. It isn't necessary for you to have a perfect accent or be impressively bilingual. Students enjoy learning that a teacher isn't perfect and will be delighted to correct you if you mispronounce a word in their native language. My Spanish-speaking students shriek with laughter when I deliberately fracture the sentences, *"Yo hablo espanol muy bien. Estoy practicando todos los dias"* and they come out sounding like, "Joe HABlow ESSpanYOLE mooEE BEAN. EsTOY prac-tee-CAN-do TOADoss LOS DEEass."

Likewise, nobody cares if you can't carry a tune. In fact,

a terrible singing voice can be a very effective disciplinary tool. When I want my students to settle down, I threaten to sing "Egg-Sucking Dog." The first time, they laugh and dare me to sing. The second time, they beg me to be quiet and let them work. In case you haven't had the pleasure of hearing that great old song, it goes something like this:

> Well, he's not very pretty to look at
> He's dirty and eats like a hog
> And he won't stay out of my hen house
> That dirty old egg-sucking dog.
> Egg-sucking dog,
> I'm gonna stomp your head in the ground
> If you don't quit killing my chickens
> You dirty old egg-sucking hound.

Sing along with teacher. Make up your own lyrics to well-known tunes, or write your own rap songs, and use them as bribes. Tell your students that if everybody gets an A on a particular assignment, you'll sing them a song. If they don't want to hear you sing, then threaten to sing if they don't all earn a C or better. Even if they protest, they'll still get a kick out of laughing at you. And kids are a tough audience, especially teenagers. If you can make them laugh, you can make them do anything.

Here's one of my own fractured songs, "Hush Little Babies," that I wrote to the tune of "Mockingbird." I was inspired to write it when I had a rambunctious class of freshmen who needed frequent reminders to be quiet during spelling exams.

> Hush little babies, don't you cry.
> Teacher's gonna poke you in the eye.
> If that makes you scream and shout
> Teacher's gonna rip your toenails out.
> And if that don't silence you
> She'll hold her breath till she turns blue.
> Then she'll die and you'll be sad
> 'Cause she's the sweetest teacher you ever had.
> So hush, hush, hush little babies.

I may not win a Grammy, but it worked. Those children hushed—and they all passed their spelling final.

Be, like, totally cool. Sometimes a good "shh!" will quiet a class right down and you can forge ahead with your exciting lesson plans. But every once in a while, kids will ignore you when you ask them to be quiet. And the louder you ask, the louder they ignore. You can always try to outshout them, which doesn't usually work. You can cross yours arms and glare at them, which usually works, but takes a long time. Or you can adopt a painfully loud Valley Girl or Surfer Dude whine, roll your eyes dramatically towards the ceiling, and say, "Gawd, like I'm just asking you kids to, like, be quiet for, like, one little itty bitty second, and, like, do you think you could do that? Nooooo, you, like, just keep on talking and acting like I'm not even here which, like, really bums me out. Gawd!" About halfway through this speech, they will beg you to stop. Some will cover their ears to drown out the obnoxious droning. Be merciless. Keep whining until they are absolutely silent. Then smile at them and say, "Thank you very much. I appreciate your cooperation. It's, like, totally cool."

Desperate measures. I don't know a single teacher who hasn't "lost it" at least once. Some of us cry, some shout, some stalk out of the room, some simply sit at our desks and watch the clock until the bell rings. At those moments, we forget that although our students have youthful exuberance and boundless energy on their side, we have the benefit of years of experience in deceiving and manipulating people. The next time your students drive you dangerously close to the edge, instead of leaping (or sliding) down the precipice, why not try one of these emergency actions. They are more likely to work than shouting or crying, and even if they don't work, they may remind you not to lose your sense of humor.

   1. *Flip the lights off and on until your students complain that they're getting dizzy.*

2. *Lie down on the floor and pretend you are uncon-scious.*

3. *Laugh hysterically until they become concerned and quiet.*

4. *Write in tiny tiny tiny letters on the blackboard, using your body as a shield, so they can't read what you are writing. Curiosity will make them pay attention.*

5. *Whisper at them so they have to be quiet to hear you.*

6. *Start rapping. Make up some snappy lyrics and drum the beat on your desk.*

7. *Dance around the room, humming to yourself. Have a good time. Forget them.*

8. *Sing off-key very loudly, preferably an "oldie" that they've never heard.*

9. *Recite, with feeling, a Shakepearean sonnet, inspira-tional speech, or excerpt from a favorite dramatic role. I like to strike a pose and use dramatic hand gestures to accompany this: "Who steals my purse steals trash. 'Tis something, nothing. 'Twas mine, 'tis his, and has been slave to thousands. But he who filches from me my good name robs me of that which not enriches him, and leaves me poor, indeed."*

10. *Threaten to assign singing "Little Ducky Duddle" as a major grade requirement.*

11. *Tell stupid jokes: Q: Why don't cannibals eat clowns? A: They taste funny.*

12. *Walk out and slam the door, then stay out there until they look for you. If they ask you what's wrong, tell them that you are tired of being unappreciated. You could get a "real job" any time you want to. Remind them that they must return to class, sooner or later. You, however, may choose to leave any time you want. Remind them that if you leave, you'll recom-mend an ogre as your replacement.*

13. *Slap yourself on the forehead and say, "Silly old me. I was just getting ready to shout at you because*

you're acting so immature, like a bunch of children, and then I remembered that you are a bunch of children. Please, the next time I forget, and expect you to act mature and responsible and considerate and appreciate my remarkable, wonderful teaching—please, remind me that you're a bunch of flaky kids."

When you regain their attention, remind them that you are a human being and you hate to be ignored, especially when you have worked so hard to create lessons for them that are as interesting and challenging as possible.

Your Teacher Who Loves You

At every opportunity, I refer to myself as "your teacher who loves you." Just in case there is somebody who isn't listening, I add the following note at the end of every exam paper: *This exam was brought to you by your teacher who loves you and wants you to be successful.* I believe that if I say it enough times, eventually they will believe me. And I have found that it's impossible for even the toughest of tough kids to hate somebody who truly loves them.

Motivation

Meet Your Students in the Middle

W hat makes students lack motivation? The usual suspect list goes something like this: apathy, bad attitudes, crowded classrooms, no parental support, poor academic skills, peer pressure. That's a convenient list of problems, but I don't believe those are the true reasons—and I think we do a disservice to ourselves and our students when we perpetuate those false excuses, because believing in them encourages us to give up. We can't change the world, so why bother? The picture is much less bleak if we take a different view and accept these as the reasons why students lack motivation:

- They believe they're bound to fail or be ridiculed for making mistakes.
- Their good behavior went unnoticed and unrewarded for years so they gave up.
- They are tired of being compared to other people their age and found lacking.

• All of their energy is focused on personal problems that they can't handle.

We can do something about those four reasons. It isn't easy, but it can be done, if we give ourselves and our students the time we both need. They need time to see that we sincerely care about them, have something valuable to teach them, and will not embarrass them when they make mistakes. We need time to get to know their personalities and maturity levels, as well as their intellectual abilities and academic needs. It also takes time to create an environment in our classrooms that is comfortable and secure, so students can relax and concentrate on their lessons. We may be the best teachers in the world, but if our students can't concentrate, they can't learn.

One year, I had an entire high school freshman class of poor readers. Those students were obviously bright, but they were unmotivated and apathetic. They were also a joyless bunch. There was little laughter in that room filled with fourteen-year-olds, which I thought was unnatural and sad. Without warning, one afternoon while I was force-feeding those freshmen *Romeo and Juliet*, a class discussion erupted on the topic of violence against women. Unlike most discussions, in which a few students participate and the rest either observe or ignore them, every student in class became involved in the hot controversy. Instead of interrupting and pulling them back on task, I let them talk. Twenty minutes later, the reason for their lack of motivation was clear—every one of those students had significant problems at home, problems they were not equipped to handle. One of the boys said something about his parents arguing, and another boy interrupted with, "Well, at least your mother didn't hit your father with a shovel like mine did." "At least you know who your father is," another boy added. "My father lives on the other side of town, but he never came to see me, not once. He doesn't even care enough to find out who I am." One of the girls stopped the argument when she stood up and burst into tears. She said, "You guys talk about this stuff like it's a joke, but you never saw your father try to kill your mother right in front of you."

Those teenagers couldn't concentrate on schoolwork because their emotional and mental energy was focused on coping with their difficult young lives. Instead of completing the reading assignment, we discussed divorce, abuse, neglect, anger, violence, and ways to cope with them. I gave them my best advice—write down your feelings in a private journal—and I gave them a list of resources, including the school counselors and psychologists, and community social service agencies. I scheduled regular discussions into the curriculum for that class, and by the end of the semester, those students were reading and writing, and laughing, as well as my other classes.

That remedial freshman class taught me something I wish I had learned in teacher training—that before you can teach anything effectively, you need to identify and remove (or reduce) those obstacles that prevent your students from learning. You may be the best teacher in the world, but if you're students can't relax and concentrate on the lessons, they can't learn. There is no guaranteed method for identifying or addressing the obstacles your students must overcome, but if you approach them from a standpoint of genuine respect and caring, your efforts will carry you halfway down the road to successful teaching. Your students must make their own journey down that same road. With luck, you will meet somewhere in the middle.

Expect Your Students to Succeed

Surely you have made mistakes in your life and learned from some of them. Why not assume that your students might have learned something from their past mistakes, as well? If you expect your students to perform as they have in the past, they probably will, especially if their past performances have been substandard or halfhearted. We've all read the reports and seen the statistics: student performance depends much more on teacher expectation than on

IQ scores, past performance, or natural abilities. Even if your expectations are already high, raise them one more notch.

1. Why not start with an A?

A burned-out, frustrated teacher inspired the most effective motivational technique I've ever used. During my first teaching assignment, as an intern, I inherited a class of sophomore students—unmotivated, disenchanted, rebellious under-achievers whose teacher had suddenly decided to retire halfway through the school year. Those students refused to try at all, despite my promise that if they would only make a sincere effort, I would make sure they passed English.

"It don't matter anyway," one girl informed me, "because Miss Shepard done already flunked us all anyway." The other students assured me that it was true. Miss Shepard had told them they were all failures, and she had shown them her grade book with a solid line of bold red F's down the right-hand column where the final grades were recorded.

"Well!" I huffed. "That's the most ridiculous thing I ever heard of. Nobody gave me that grade book. As far as I'm concerned, you all have A's right now. I don't care what you did before I got here. You're starting over, fresh, and everybody has an A in this class, but you'll have to work to keep them. I'll help you, but it will be up to you to keep those good grades."

I don't know who was more surprised by my announcement—those students or me. For one short moment, I worried that I would get in trouble at the office, but the students' excited discussion at the wonderment of this crazy new teacher convinced me to stand by my words. Their faces, which had previously been dull-eyed blank masks, were flushed and animated. Their eyes sparkled the way children's eyes should.

When I confided my plan to another teacher, she was shocked. "You can't just give them grades," she insisted. "I'm not giving them grades," I explained. "I'm just making them feel like they're winners from the beginning, so they'll want to remain winners. When they thought they were failures, they were prepared to stay that way." My teacher friend wasn't convinced, and I began to doubt the brilliance of my plan, but it was too late. I was not about to break a promise to those students. Fortunately, the strategy worked, and it worked much better than I could have hoped. Only a handful of students kept their A's, but nobody failed that class. Those students, who knew they had been expected to fail, did a complete turnabout when they knew they were expected to succeed. All they needed was a chance to change their self-destructive behavior.

Why not try it in your classes? Tell your students that you don't care about their previous grades, that they start each quarter or semester with an A in your class and must work to keep those A's. You won't be giving them anything except encouragement and hope. They will still have to earn the grades, but your faith in them will be contagious. Perhaps they won't believe you at first, which is all right, because when they find out you are telling the truth, it will give you that much more credibility and authority.

2. *Prepare your students to advance.*

Think of yourself as a gardener and your students as an unplanted garden in fertile ground. Whatever seeds of thought you plant in their minds will blossom. Plant tall thoughts. During the course of your conversations with your students, make references to the more complicated tasks they will be asked to perform later during the year. Voice your confidence that they will handle those new, more difficult tasks with ease. "Whew! You guys are sharp. Shakespeare's going to be a piece of cake for this class," or "If you people continue to ace these exams, I'm going to have to bring in some college textbooks for you." They may laugh and pretend to argue, but they won't mean it. In their secret hearts, they will be thrilled that they have finally found an adult who appreciates them and believes in their ability to grow.

Make Mistakes Okay

In my experience, those "bad kids" who sit in the back of the room and refuse to try a new assignment usually are afraid they can't do the work and they can't risk their "hard-core" reputations by making mistakes in public—they certainly can't ask for help. The kids who claim that they are bored, that the lesson is "too easy," when it clearly is not, are quite often afraid that they can't do the work, either. Perhaps a few of those students truly are self-destructive, but most of them are bluffing. If they honestly didn't care about their grades, why would they bother coming to class?

Students try when they believe they can succeed. On the other hand, if they believe they will fail, they will refuse to try. You can help your students develop self-confidence and faith in their ability to learn by allowing them to make mistakes.

1. Face the fear.

I realize that most teachers do try to encourage children to experiment, to improve their skills, to risk making mistakes. Unfortunately, many teachers forget to allow a margin of error for those mistakes when it comes time for report cards. If we punish children for every mistake they make, they soon learn not to make mistakes. In my English classes, that means they won't try to use new words in their essays, or complex sentence structures, because they don't want to lose points for misspellings, misuse of words, or faulty punctuation.

It's important, I think, to acknowledge students' fear of failure and to discuss this fear with your classes. All of my students, from remedial to honors level, read "To Err Is Wrong," by Roger Von Oech, which is included in the essay collection *Viewpoints* (Lexington, Mass.: D.C. Heath & Co, 1989). Von Oech explains: "Most people consider success and failure as opposites, but they are actually both products of the same process . . . the same energy which generates good creative ideas also produces errors." He goes on to discuss ways to use errors as stepping stones to success and how to use negative feedback in a positive manner. To illustrate his points, Von Oech quotes a number of successful people who aren't afraid to risk failure, including baseball great Carl Yastrzemski and Thomas J. Watson, the founder of IBM, who is credited with this unexpected advice: "The way to succeed is to double your failure rate."

After we read Von Oech's essay, I ask students to share examples of mistakes they've made in school, or failures they have experienced, or times when they were afraid to try. To get them started, I tell my students about the time I blew up my Bunsen burner in chemistry class and earned my first failing grade, and the time I opened my algebra book, leafed through the pages, and started crying right there in class because I knew I could never do all that hard stuff. Students who have been afraid to try often will make an effort when they realize that everybody makes mistakes, including the teacher and the top students in class.

2. Make mistakes mandatory.

Assign a difficult task or project and instruct students to complete the work on their own (individually or with a partner). Give them a specific amount of time in which to complete the task, then ask for volunteers to share what they have accomplished. If you have a group of shy students, you might want to allow them to assemble in small groups and select a speaker for the group. After they have shared their work, including the problems they encountered, share your own method for completing the assignment. Next, have them write in their journals about the mistakes they made and what they learned from those mistakes that might help them with future assignments. Give full credit to all students who made an effort and described those efforts in their journals. By assigning a grade for imperfect work, you will be showing them that you are serious about allowing them to make mistakes without sacrificing good grades, and that the process of learning is as important as the end goal.

3. Provide fix-it time.

Imagine this scenario: Your supervisor at work gives you a task to complete within the next hour. You received some instruction pertaining to that task, but you don't remember it clearly. You leaf through one of the manuals on your desk and locate the pertinent instructions, but they aren't complete, and you recall that your supervisor provided some additional verbal instructions which you can't remember because you had a migraine that day, or you needed a cup of coffee, or you were worried that your checkbook was overdrawn. You go to your supervisor's office and knock softly on the door. You say, "I don't remember exactly how to do this task." She sighs and shakes her head. "I went over this twice already, and it's in your manual. Don't be so lazy." You walk next door to a coworker's office and ask for help, but your supervisor immediately appears, interrupts, and says, "No cheating. Get back to your office. Do your own work." You complete the task to the best of your ability. A week later your boss informs you that you made several mistakes on that task, and reminds you that you'd better shape up and perform that task correctly next time, because performance appraisals are due soon. You can't remember exactly what you did a week ago, because you've worked on so many different tasks since then, but your supervisor doesn't explain your mistakes or give you an opportunity to learn how to do that task correctly. How do you feel now? Cooperative and motivated? Frustrated and confused?

If you apply this analogy to children, then you understand why they cheat, or copy their classmates' work, or give up. For high school students, the frustration and confusion are multiplied. Imagine repeating this same scenario with six or seven different bosses in one day.

You can help avoid frustration and keep your students motivated to learn by giving them the chance to correct their errors on classroom exercises and homework assignments. Let them rewrite essays and reports, and redo assignments that miss the mark. Please note: I'm *not* saying that we should overlook laziness, missing assignments, undone homework, and failure to study for exams. Those are another matter entirely and must be dealt with differently. But I believe you will have more assignments and homework completed (with better results), and higher final exam scores, if you allow students to correct their mistakes without penalizing them.

Whenever possible, correct assignments in class, immediately after they are completed. Don't let papers pile up on your desk until you have time to correct them, because teachers rarely have enough time. Corrections need to be made as soon as mistakes are identified, before the misinformation becomes stored in students' long-term memories, or before they forget the original lessons. If you don't have time to do it yourself, enlist a student aide, ask for volunteers who finish their work early, or exchange papers and let students grade each other's. If you do exchange papers, I'd suggest collecting them and distributing them yourself, to avoid having students correct the papers of their best friends or worst enemies. My favorite method is to have students use ball-point or felt-tip pens to complete the assignment and pencils to correct papers—this eliminates the temptation for students to change answers to make the other person's grade higher or lower. If it's a difficult lesson that might require erasures, I distribute pencils to complete the assignment, then collect the pencils and distribute green or blue pens for student corrections.

4. What about exams?

Some teachers balk at the idea of allowing students to retake exams to raise their grades. Certainly, I don't advocate allowing them to take the same exam twice, because that allows too many opportunities to cheat or to memorize answers without understanding the material. But what is wrong with allowing students a second chance if they are willing to work and study to fill in the gaps in their knowledge? Some people seem to think it is unfair to the students who are extremely bright, or who study very hard, or who were born under a lucky star if those students who aren't bright, who didn't work as hard the first time around, or who are unlucky are allowed to retake an exam and raise their grades. Why is that unfair? The students who earned good grades the first time don't lose anything, except perhaps a sense of superiority. The students who try harder and retake the exam aren't getting something free. In fact, in some cases, they will have done twice as much work for the same grade.

I failed my driver's exam three times before I finally managed to make a three-point turn on a snow-banked street. Maybe I didn't try as hard as the other students in driver's ed. Maybe I was less coordinated, or more nervous during my exam. Does it matter? I earned a 100% on my third try and have had only one accident in nearly thirty years of driving, but I didn't ace the test the first time. Does that mean I shouldn't be allowed to drive as often or as far as those drivers who whipped through their driving exams the first time? More recently, I had to rewrite a book five times before my editor and I were both satisfied with it. Should I have been paid less for that book than for the one following it which required only one rewrite? I think we make too much of our mistakes and too little of the opportunity to learn from them.

Treat Students as Individual Learners

In one of my sophomore English classes, a husky boy with a full beard and mustache sat next to a skinny boy who still had the face of a baby, covered with soft down, not a whisker in sight. The husky boy spoke in a deep baritone, while the skinny boy sounded like a human flute. Another boy in that same class had a few random hairs sprouting from his chin and a voice that cracked and leaped from octave to octave without warning. All three of those boys were fifteen years old, and all were good students. As I observed them throughout the course of that year, I noted differences in their mental development that corresponded to their vastly different physical development—yet they were all expected to be able to learn the same information and skills at the same rate of speed. The skinny, baby-faced boy, Carlin, seemed to be the brightest of the bunch, articulate and quick-witted, yet he had the hardest time trying to grasp abstract concepts such as symbolism or characterization. Apparently, in spite of his intelligence, Carlin's brain hadn't yet made the switch from concrete to abstract thinking. He knew he was capable, and his failure to succeed frustrated him.

"It drives me crazy when I can't learn stuff that isn't even hard," Carlin wrote in his journal. "I know I'm smarter than a lot of guys in this class, but they get better grades on some of the assignments because my brain just won't let me do them. Maybe I'm not as smart as I thought I was or maybe I reached my peak and now I'm getting dumber. What do you think, Miss?"

I think we do our children a great disservice when we lump them together by age, for the convenience of administration, and expect them to be able to learn difficult information and skills at the same rate, in spite of their different rates of development. People learn in different ways, at different rates of speed, and all people are capable of learning. When we throw them all together and demand uniformity, they end up divided into three categories: the "smart" kids who are developmentally advanced for their age, the "slow" kids who are developmentally delayed (often in only one area), and the "average" kids who fall somewhere in the middle. Unfortunately, those labels often stick for the rest of their lives. Although some people have strong enough personalities to shrug off the school experience, most adults still think of themselves in the same terms they did when they were in school. People who think of themselves as "slow" or "average" often accept work that is below their capabilities because they don't believe they are as smart as their coworkers or supervisors. And I know you've met at least one supervisor who believes the word "supervisor" was derived from the word "superior," because he was one of the "smart" kids for so long that he doesn't realize the rest of the class has not only caught up, but some of the "slow" kids have left him in the dust.

I wonder how adults would respond if we were expected to be able to perform as well as everybody else our age at a given task. Imagine being graded, promoted, and paid according to your ability to efficiently handle ten simultaneous incoming telephone calls on a multiline telephone system, or operate a steam shovel, or balance your checkbook, or cook a seven-course dinner. It sounds ridiculous and it is, but that's what we do when we compare children to each other, without making allowances for differences in mental and physical development, individual interests, and varying levels of natural ability.

We can fight the system, but that requires more time and energy than most teachers have left at the end of the school day. Within our classrooms, we can wage the same battle on a smaller scale, with a much better chance of winning, by treating our students as individual learners. One good teacher can overcome the influence of an entire system. I know, because I had one of those teachers when I was a child very much like Carlin, and her perception of me as a talented individual became a lifeline that helped me survive the school system.

1. Don't compare students to each other.

One student's D is another's A. Absolute fairness is difficult to achieve in any classroom, but it is impossible to grade students fairly if you compare them to each other. You'll come much closer to fair if you set a standard for your classroom and encourage each child to meet that standard. For some children, your standard will seem easy; for others, it will be a tremendous challenge. I often remind my students that life isn't fair. "We all have talents, but we all have different talents. Perhaps your talent is for dancing, or playing soccer, or raising children, and not in learning English grammar and composition. You may have to work a hundred times as hard as the person sitting next to you to pass this class, but that doesn't mean you can't earn a good grade. It simply means that in this one area, you will have to work harder. Your success in life is a matter of how hard you are willing to work to achieve whatever goals you set for yourself."

When you encourage students to compete against themselves, to try to improve their own skills and performance, they will work harder than they would if they felt they had to compete against impossible odds. Anybody can learn to read a little bit better than he already does, or learn one new math skill. Those little bits add up.

2. *Allow students to choose their levels of achievement.*

One of the hardest lessons I ever had to learn as a teacher was that students have a right to choose the grade they want to earn in a specific class. When I started teaching, I wanted all of my students to want an A, and I became very upset if an intelligent, capable student set his or her sights on a C and wasted the time and talent that would have earned an A. The first time I encountered a brilliant student who maintained a C- grade-point average and a mediocre attendance record, I spent hours trying to persuade him to change his ways. He listened to my lectures each time without arguing, then quietly went on doing the same spotty work, missing one or two classes each week. Frustrated, I asked my master teacher, Hal Gray, for advice. He surprised me by telling me to leave Bryant alone.

"But he's so smart," I argued, "he could carry a 4.0 GPA and get into any college he wanted to. He could be anything."

"He doesn't want to be anything," Hal told me. "He is already what he wants to be—a darned good trumpet player. Lots of jazz bands hire him to play with them. He could work full-time right now, if he didn't have to go to school. He's that talented."

"Exactly," I said. "He's very talented and he should be earning A's in all of his classes."

"Why?" Hal asked.

"Because he should be, that's all."

"But why?" Hal repeated.

"Because somebody who could earn all A's should want to," I explained, although as I said the words, I realized they didn't sound very convincing.

"Bryant doesn't care about high school," Hal said. "He

only comes to make his parents and his teachers, like you, happy. He does enough work to pass all of his classes. You're the one who's always talking about respecting students and giving them responsibility. Why can't you respect Bryant's right to live his own life? He's far from being a failure. In fact, he's one of the most successful young people I know."

Busted again! I hate it when my own words come back and smack me square in the face. It doesn't happen often enough to make me feel like a total hypocrite, but it does happen often enough to keep me humble.

3. Beware of labels.

Let me preface my remarks by pointing out that I realize there are many children who have been correctly diagnosed as learning disabled or developmentally delayed, and the special programs created for those students serve a real need. But there are many more children who are incorrectly diagnosed and labeled—children who suffer from a temporary condition, or who are allergic to the foods they eat, or who live on a diet of sugar and caffeine, or who are unable to cope with the serious troubles in their personal lives. When we reach the point (as we have in many schools) where one out of four or five students in any given classroom has been diagnosed as having learning disabilities or behavior disorders, it seems obvious to me that we should be asking ourselves whether there is something wrong with the system, and our teaching methods, instead of placing so much fault on the students.

I believe there are a number of reasons why labels have become so popular. First, it takes some of the pressure off parents and teachers who haven't been able to teach children successfully. Second, special programs generate staff positions and programs that receive government grants and other moneys. Third, labeling children is so much faster and easier than changing the philosophy and structure of our school system so that teachers can effectively teach today's children. If teachers were encouraged (and permitted the time) to focus on teaching children how to learn in their own individual styles, instead of focusing solely on curriculum to meet an arbitrary curriculum ladder, we would have better-educated children and more effective teachers. We would spend less time on rote memorization and regurgitation of information and more on the actual process of understanding and long-term retention of information. (And if I were Queen of Education, there would be a federal law limiting class size to twenty students in all schools, public and private, from kindergarten to college.)

If you give your students the benefit of the doubt, and tell them that you aren't interested in what they did yesterday or last year, that you are going to base your opinion of them—and their grades—solely on how well they behave and how hard they work in your classroom, I would bet my giant teacher's salary that most of them will succeed in passing your class. And I'll add another dollar to the pot and wager that they will appreciate you and remember you for the rest of their lives.

4. Vary your teaching style.

Keep in mind that each of your students has an individual learning preference that may not coincide with your natural teaching style. Try to vary your teaching and include visual aids and movement to help those students who are visual or kinesthetic learners. When a student says, "I don't get it," about anything in your classroom, assume that the problem is yours and not his. Find a new way to explain the concept or skill, instead of simply repeating your previous instruction. If you can't think of a new way, ask your students for suggestions. They may surprise you by offering good ideas that never would have occurred to you—after all, you have your own learning style, too.

5. Reassure the concrete thinkers.

If you teach a subject that involves abstract principles or concepts, such as business ethics, algebra, or economics, be aware that some students may have problems because their brains have not yet developed to the point of being able to comprehend abstract ideas. There is a point in every child's development, and that point is different for each child, when the brain makes the switch between concrete and abstract thinking. This switch has nothing to do with intelligence; but depends on the child's individual rates of development. Conscientious, industrious students who are used to succeeding in school often become frustrated when they cannot grasp new concepts. If that occurs in your classroom, you can reassure those students by explaining that although they are intelligent, they may not be ready for abstract thinking. I also would suggest making some allowance on assignments and exams for those students. For example, when we study symbolism in literature, many bright students understand the definition and the examples I give to illustrate the technique, but they cannot create their own examples. Instead of deducting points for their immaturity, I give those students credit if they can define the concept and remember some of the examples that I gave to the class. My hope is that later on, when they are able to understand, they will recall those examples and use them as a model for creating their own.

6. Teach students how to learn.

If you ask students how they learn, you will be surprised at their ignorance. Most children (and many adults) seem to think it's some sort of magical process, or something that happens by osmosis, simply from being surrounded by teachers and textbooks. Even good students often are at a loss to explain how they know what they know, and poor students often believe that they are lacking some essential brain function that makes them unable to learn as well as other people.

Teach your students the difference between short-term and long-term memory. Explain that it takes time and repetition for any information to be stored in the brain's long-term memory. Depending on the difficulty of the material, and a student's effort, the amount of time it will take to learn something will vary. A difficult textbook chapter, for example, might take a week or two of daily reading, discussion, and review before the information is stored. A simple concept, such as adding or subtracting, may take only a brief review on one or two days.

If you have access to a university or library research system, you might look for journal articles or research that show the results of long-term practice for playing a musical instrument. Stated very unscientifically, if a musician plays the same scales and exercises repeatedly over a period of years, the portions of the brain that are involved in performing those scales and exercises get bigger. You might also share with your students this anecdote about Einstein's brain:

Lowell Catlett, a professor and lecturer from New Mexico State University, during a speech to a group of teachers and parents, said that when Albert Einstein died, scientists studied his brain, eager to see if they could find out what made him a genius. They were delighted to discover that Einstein's brain contained more of one particular chemical than most brains do. At first, the scientists believed they had discovered the secret to intelligence. After more research, they learned that when people think, their brains create more of that particular chemical, which suggests that the more we think, the smarter we get. Perhaps we actually can think ourselves smarter.

I can't claim to understand brain chemistry, but I have seen students who supposedly had low IQs and students who had failed miserably in school for years, who finally decided, after weeks of constant encouragement and positive feedback, that they were smart and could learn—and they did. Don't let your students convince you that you can't teach them because they can't learn. They *can* learn if they are willing to work.

Everybody can learn. Students tend to forget that when they face something new and difficult. If your students start to lose faith in their ability to learn, remind them of the many things they have already learned—many without any training at all except trial and error. They can walk, talk, speak, tie their shoes, use a telephone, navigate safely on foot through city traffic, read, write, perform basic mathematics. They also may be able to do other things, such as play a musical instrument, read sheet music, bake a cake, drive a car, dance the *macarena* or the two-step, operate a power lawn mower, swim, water-ski, ice-skate, skateboard, use a computer, ride a horse, raise a healthy pet, speak a second language, operate a camera, list the names of ten sports figures, give the batting stats of their favorite baseball player, reel off the words to a favorite rap song—hundreds of things that demonstrate they can learn if they want to. And if they want to, they can learn the subject matter you teach in your class.

Make Your Classroom a Safe Place

You probably will have at least one student in your classroom who claims not to care one tiny bit about earning passing grades. Balderdash, I say. Students who truly don't care about school don't sit in those uncomfortable desks all day long, especially those big kids who can barely squeeze themselves into the seats. Students claim they don't care precisely because they *do* care and are afraid they will fail. Instead of considering a classroom as a place where they test their skills and improve them, many students spend their school days pretending they aren't afraid that their lack of knowledge or skills or abilities will make them a target for ridicule, embarrassment, or humiliation.

1. Kids hide because they're scared.

Black leather and combat boots, hair that covers half their faces, diamond-studded noses and pierced eyebrows, shaved heads and do-it-yourself tattoos, and belligerent attitudes all do a good job of diverting attention from the real issue—the world is a scary place and children don't want to be hurt. A hundred years ago, when I was a child, the worst that could happen to a girl in school was having her hair pulled or her heart broken by the local heartthrob. The unluckiest girls got pregnant and were shipped off to stay with a distant relative for a few months. Boys had to be prepared for a poke in the nose by the schoolyard bully or ridicule by the reigning beauty queens. If a student dropped out of school but was willing to work hard, he or she could find a job and make a decent living. Today, the stakes are much higher—the bullies carry guns and knives, the heartbreakers often carry herpes or AIDS, and most dropouts can look forward to a life of back-breaking or mind-numbing work, if they are lucky, and poverty, crime, or incarceration if they aren't lucky. It's no wonder that our children are frightened. We can't change the world, but we can provide an oasis of physical and emotional safety in our classrooms.

2. *Teacher, bar the door.*

Many teachers lock the doors to their classrooms, some cover the windows with posters to prevent passersby from looking in, some keep pepper spray canisters in their top desk drawers. Some people (usually those who romanticize childhood and recall their own school days with nostalgia) criticize those teachers.

"We shouldn't lock up our children," the critics say. "We can't turn our schools into prisons."

My response to those critics is, "Yes, we should lock up our children, so we can protect them from harm, so they can relax and stop worrying and start learning. And there is a huge difference between locking a prison and a school. You lock a prison to keep people in; you lock a school to keep people out."

If there are locks on my classroom doors, I use them, and assign one of the students sitting nearest the door to be the monitor. If a student leaves the room to go to the office or restroom, the monitor unlocks the door when the student returns. He or she also unlocks the door to accept messages from the office staff, teachers, or other familiar people. But, if somebody the monitor doesn't recognize knocks, he or she calls me to answer the door. When I first established this procedure, I wondered whether it might make my students nervous, but it has had the opposite effect. They know that nobody is going to burst into their classroom and hurt them unless they can get past me. My students know I'm not Superwoman, and I can't stop a bullet, but they also know that I am going to do my best to protect them from any outside intruders.

3. Protect those fragile feelings.

Just as I try to give my students a sense of physical security, I also try to help them feel emotionally and psychologically secure by creating an atmosphere of mutual respect in my classroom. No putdowns of other people are allowed. If somebody makes a mistake, or voices an illogical idea, we don't laugh at them. We can't learn without making mistakes. In fact, mistakes are often our best teachers—both our own and other people's. I refuse to tolerate racism, sexism, homophobia, or other ignorant prejudices in my classroom. Of course, I can't eradicate prejudice among my students, but I can require them to keep those opinions to themselves.

"Prejudices are like underwear," I tell my classes. "Most of us have them, but it is tacky and ignorant to go around showing them to other people, especially strangers." They always laugh, but they always get the message.

When a student slips and makes a rude comment or laughs at somebody else's efforts to learn, I immediately ask that student to step out of the room and think about what he or she said. I remind the class that I respect their right to think what they want, but that their rights do not extend to hurting other people. After class, I warn the student that disrespecting other people is the one mistake I will not forgive. This method works well. I have had students with every political persuasion from white supremacist to black militant, but I have yet to have a student who couldn't learn to keep his or her mouth shut in my classroom. Of course, I must make my classes interesting, exciting, and challenging, so those students are willing to shut up and sit down.

4. *The puzzle of prejudice.*

I think racism should be included in our school curriculums because it is such a persistent problem in our society. I believe one of the reasons the problem persists is that people don't understand how or why prejudice happens. If we ever hope to achieve a measure of peace in this country, we need to help our students understand the insidious nature of prejudice, and how ignorance can lead to violence when people begin thinking of other people as objects instead of human beings.

There is a movie called *Season of Justice* that tells the story of Jewish attorney Morris Dees and his fight against the Ku Klux Klan. Dees convinces a black woman whose son was brutally murdered by young Klan members to take the Klan to court. Although Dees and the woman win the case, the verdict isn't what my students talk about or write about in their journals. What captures their attention, and changes their thinking, is seeing how the young white supremacists were indoctrinated. White students inspect their own opinions, looking for pointless prejudices, and black students gain a new understanding of the impersonal nature of prejudice. They realize that white supremacists don't hate them personally, because they don't know them, but that their hate is fear turned inside out and aimed at anything that threatens their small world.

If your students are mature enough and interested in learning more about the hidden history of our country, you might consider reading them excerpts from some of Malcomn X's speeches concerning the roots of slavery. Few students are aware of the halfway points where slaves were tortured and convinced to accept their servitude. Often my African-American students are amazed to discover the wealth of information available about their ancestry, and the other students begin to understand the reasons for the tense situation we now face in this country. (Two books are suggested in "A Few of My Favorite Books," which follows the last chapter of this book.)

Give Students Choices

I can't take credit for the decision to give my students choices. My students taught me the importance of including their input in my lesson planning—and it took more than one lesson to convince me to pay attention. After reading *The Taming of the Shrew*, I assigned a two-page essay about the characters and plot of the play to one of my sophomore classes. A few students dutifully took out their pens and pencils, but most of them started moaning and groaning that they were tired of such hard, stupid, boring, dumb assignments. I said, "Fine. What can you do to show me that you understand the characterization and plot of this play?" One girl shouted, "I could write one of the scenes in real English and me and my friends could act it out." Another girl said she could make a comic book that showed the most important scenes in the play. A boy shouted out that he could write a rap in that "goofy Shakespeare talk."

I agreed to let them design their own projects, as long as they agreed to follow these guidelines:

a. Each student must write a description of his or her project.

b. Each student must sign a contract stating that the project would be completed by the deadline or no credit would be given.

c. No more than three students could work together on any project, and they would all receive a failing grade if I saw that one or two people had done all the work.

d. No foul language or dirty pictures.

e. Each student would be required to critique in writing at least three other students' projects, noting specific pluses and minuses of the project.

Those sophomores put more time and effort into those projects than I would ever have dreamed of demanding.

They took more responsibility for their projects and worked harder on them than they did when I supervised and dictated. They learned much more than they would have if I had forced them to write papers—and they reminded me that learning is allowed to be fun. (See the sample project assignment/contract at the end of the chapter.)

A similar situation occurred with my juniors when we were reading *The Merchant of Venice*. One of the boys asked why we couldn't read the modern version of the play, and I told him there was no such version. He countered that he and his classmates could write one and then read it. I'd like to point out that this was not a class filled with scholars, but rather with students who read below grade level, tended towards truancy, and would rather go to the dentist than write a short essay. They were members of a special program for at-risk students who were bright and talented but stubborn and persistent underachievers. I told them I didn't think they really wanted to rewrite Shakespeare, but they insisted that they could do it, that everybody would participate, and that I would be proud. Reluctantly, I agreed, but I made it their project for the entire quarter. They had to read the original version, rewrite the entire play, then perform their play for me—all without my help.

If I hadn't seen it happen, I never would have believed that the boys in that class would settle their differences and work together. There were two leaders of rival neighborhood gangs, one black and one Hispanic, who refused to sit on the same side of the room. But those two boys took over the class and worked the rest of the class to death. The only real trouble occurred when they were assigning names for their characters. I was in my office when I heard loud voices. I went to the doorway to see what was happening, and saw Cornelius and Rico facing each other in the middle of the room, both standing with their arms crossed and their feet firmly planted on their half of the turf.

"What's the problem?" I asked.

"These Mexicans said we are discriminating because we named all the characters," Cornelius explained. He waved his big hand in the air to prevent me from interrupting.

"They got a point. We did take over, so here's what we're going to do. We're going to let the Mexicans pick two names. Go ahead." He nodded at Rico, who jutted his chin into the air and said, "Three." They agreed and went off to finish their play, which they titled *The Lonely Tycoon*.

On the afternoon of their theatrical debut, those students arrived in class with cardboard crowns and performed a play that would have made Shakespeare applaud. After the final curtain, an old bedsheet, fell, Cornelius explained to me that they had changed the courtroom scene where Shylock is forced to renounce his religion because that wasn't right. "Shakespeare messed up a little on that one," Cornelius explained, "because nobody has the right to mess with a man's religion. So we just had them take his money instead, which is okay because he could get some more, but if somebody took your religion and all the stuff you believed in, then you wouldn't have nothing left to live for. You would think a smart guy like Shakespeare would of figured that out."

Those juniors took what would have been a straightforward exercise in composition and turned it into an assignment that required reading comprehension, creative writing, public speaking, and a discussion on moral and ethical values. Not bad for a bunch of underachievers.

I finally learned the lesson. I am now a firm believer in the power of choice and I give that power to my students whenever possible. Instead of deciding that we should begin with grammar and vocabulary, move on to literature, then speech, and finish the year with composition, for example, I write "Grammar," "Literature," "Speech," and "Composition" on the board and ask the students to write down on slips of paper their first, second, and third choices for the area we should study first. Then I collect the papers and let the students tally the answers (they don't trust me not to rig the vote), and we study the units in the order the students select. It doesn't seem like a big deal to me. After all, they don't get to choose the topics, they simply get to choose the order we study them. But they seem to think it's a very big deal, probably because it gives them some sense of control over their lives.

I also try to allow individual choices within assignments, including exams, whenever possible. This sometimes makes my job harder, as far as scheduling units and projects, but it always makes my teaching better because it helps me understand my students' needs and it makes them feel more powerful. Perhaps you can recall what it felt like to be instructed and controlled all day long, without an opportunity to make even small decisions about your own life, such as what to eat for dinner or what brand of toothpaste to use. That's not fun. It's particularly difficult for children over ten years old to accept the multitude of rules they must follow because they're beginning to feel like "big kids" and want so very much to be treated as such.

The students aren't the only ones who benefit when you include them in your lesson planning. By giving students the chance to make choices in your classroom, you can help them feel more powerful, which will make them more inclined to cooperate with you. Let's say you want your students to write a report on a particular topic. Why not give the options of writing a report, giving a speech, creating a visual presentation, or even writing a musical composition on that topic? You may discover talents in your students that you might otherwise have overlooked. I had one student who could write a rap song about anything—and a good rap, too—yet he simply couldn't bring himself to sit down and write a report. I knew he could write, because he wrote good essays often enough to keep a passing grade, but when I gave him the option of writing and performing a rap song every now and then, he worked much harder on the other assignments for which rap wasn't an option.

Another student spent every free minute drawing caricatures of people or creating his own "movie posters." He refused to take art classes in school because he "couldn't draw boxes and designs and all that stuff the art teacher likes." Once, he insisted that he simply couldn't write an essay because he didn't have any words in his head. I told him to write a few words and illustrate his essay with pictures. He wrote his first full-page essay that day, and when he realized that the more he wrote, the more illustrations he could include, he began writing two or three pages for each assignment.

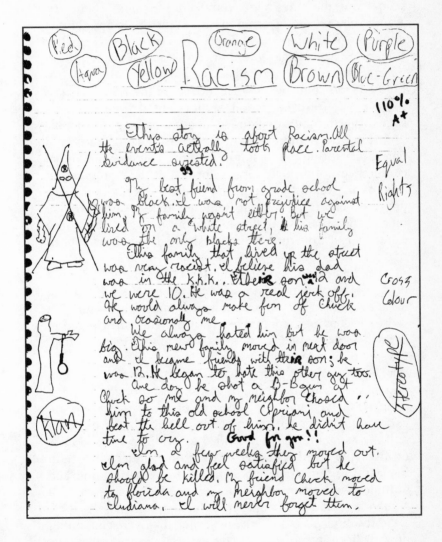

Give Students Frequent Feedback

It's ironic that the students who claim to care the least about school are the ones who complain the most about the grades they receive. During my first year of teaching, I had one class of accelerated and one class of remedial English students. The college-bound students accepted their first-quarter grades with a few sighs and moans, but the self-proclaimed "too-cool-for-school" students in the remedial class spent an entire class period arguing about their grades—some begged, others demanded an audit of my grade book.

After the deluge of post–report card complaints and objections during that first quarter, I tried holding individual conferences to keep students informed of their progress, or lack of it. Next, I tried giving students periodic written progress reports. When the semester report cards arrived, moans and groans were down by about half, but clearly, the other half of my students believed I had somehow robbed them of their due.

The first day of second semester, I offered my students a deal. Anybody who came to every single class, earned at least a C on every classroom and homework assignment (without copying), cooperated with me and participated in every lesson, would earn a passing grade, even if they flunked their exams.

"What are you trying to do, psych us out?" one boy asked. Ryan was one of the brightest, least motivated young people I'd ever had the pleasure of trying to teach. He earned an A on every assignment he did, but he did only half the assignments, so he ended up with a 50% and an F on his report card. Ryan wasn't the only underachiever in his class. Failing grades, missing credits, truancy, and bad attitudes were common in his class, which was part of a "school within a school" program for at-risk teens.

"Absolutely," I said. "I am trying to psych you out. I don't believe it's possible to come to class every single day, and honestly try to learn, and complete all your assignments by yourself with a passing grade, and still fail to learn what I'm teaching. Anybody who does all those things, and who has a functioning brain, will pass. You all have functioning brains, so that's the deal I'm offering you. Why not try it? You don't have anything to lose, and you might find out you're a lot smarter than you think you are."

Ryan took me up on my offer and started doing all the assignments. His grades were at the top of the class, but he couldn't believe he was passing. It seemed too easy. Every day, he'd ask to see his grade in my grade book. It didn't matter that I had told him the day before. He had to see it for himself, in writing, on the page. Soon, other students started joining Ryan, clamoring to check their grades. Although they'd sit down if I threatened them, they couldn't concentrate on the current lesson until they had seen my grade book. And, since I wouldn't allow one student to see other students' grades, I had to show them one at a time, we wasted fifteen valuable minutes of class time every day.

1. Chart their progress.

I'd like to be able to say that making giant wall-mounted progress charts was my brilliant idea designed to motivate my students, but it wasn't. It was a self-defense tactic that turned out to be an excellent motivator, even for my most unmotivated students.

Tired of wasting time talking about grades every day, I decided to make a chart so the students could see for themselves whether they were missing any assignments. On a large sheet of poster board, I printed the names of the students in Ryan's class down the left-hand side of the sheet and divided the rest of the sheet into small squares. Above each square, I wrote the name of an assignment, using abbreviations, such as w/s for worksheet and T for test (i.e., Spell w/s 1, Spell T 1). If a student completed an assignment with a passing grade, he or she earned an X in the square for that assignment. I drew a green box around the square for students who failed or were absent. If the assignment was made up before the deadline (which I wrote under the name of the assignment so there would be no doubt about due dates), then I placed an X in the box to show that the assignment was completed with a passing grade. After the deadline, I put a big red zero in the box for any assignment that was incomplete or failed. (You'll find a sample progress chart at the end of the chapter.)

I have yet to find a student who could stand to sit in a room and ignore a string of red zeros placed beside his or her name. Even my most unmotivated, apathetic students couldn't resist checking the chart to see their own record of progress (or lack of it). They didn't rush into my room and run to check the chart; they'd shuffle in, yawn, and sidle a few steps until they could check the chart while pretending to glance casually over their shoulders at something much more compelling.

The chart didn't contain any grades, because I don't think it's a good idea to try to create competition for grades to motivate kids. Some people simply can't spell, for example, and although spelling doesn't indicate intelligence, it makes poor spellers feel like failures if you constantly compare them to somebody else. I wanted my students to compete with themselves—to make sure there was an X in every box.

"If you have all X's, there is no way you can fail my class," I assured them. "The quality of your work will decide whether you earn an A or a D. But if you do every single assignment, take every test, and make up any work you miss, you will pass my class. If you get bad grades in one specific area, we'll work on that area."

During the first report period that I posted the chart, the students in my lowest-achieving class complained that it wasn't fair, they couldn't make up all those missed assignments. I made a super-duper, incredible, onetime offer: a three-week grace period to make up all missing or failed work; after that, deadlines would be nonnegotiable. It worked. There were still a few red zeros on the chart when the next report cards came out, but every single student passed my class. That's when I realized that students will try when they believe they can succeed, even those students who have failed repeatedly in the past—*especially* those students who have failed repeatedly.

When my other classes saw the progress chart for Ryan's class, they demanded similar charts for their classes. Even the good students, who routinely took home report cards filled with A's and B's, wanted tangible proof of their progress and assurance that there was an end to the daily mental torture. As the line of X's grew on the chart, they could see themselves moving towards the end of the grading period, one step closer to graduation.

Our progress charts worked wonders for me, too. They eliminated those constant, irritating questions, "Am I missing anything? When is my worksheet/essay/report due? What's the deadline for making up my spelling test?" They also eliminated most of the arguments about report card grades.

2. Personal grade reports.

Wall charts are convenient because they keep students informed without requiring a lot of your time, but many students still want to know their letter or percentage grades. Some teachers follow the college-style procedure of posting grades for each class on a bulletin board, using student ID numbers instead of names. I don't like that procedure for a number of reasons. First, it doesn't protect student privacy, because names usually are listed in alphabetical order. Second, even if students can't figure out whose grade is whose, some students feel like losers because they couldn't earn top grades, although they may have worked much harder and made more progress than students who did earn top grades. Third, it's a cold and impersonal method of communicating with students.

In addition to the wall charts for each class, I make brief personal visits to students, at their desks, to let them know where they stand. Instead of diverting valuable lesson time for grade reports, twice each month, I visit students while they are busy working on class assignments. I write down the percentage and letter grade on a slip of paper, 98%-A, for example. I stop by the student's desk, place the paper face-down, and say, "Right now you have this percentage in this class. I'm very proud of you. Thank you. It's a pleasure being your teacher." I shake the student's hand and move on. If a student is struggling to pass, with a 67%-D+, for example, I might say, "This is your grade right now. You're moving up. Keep working and you'll have a C pretty soon. I'm proud of you. Thank you for your cooperation and hard work."

Regardless of the grade, I shake the student's hand. If a student is struggling to pass because the work is difficult, the handshake works as a reward and motivator. If the student is failing on purpose, to get attention or upset parents or irri-tate teachers, my visit and handshake often work as shock therapy. Instead of the expected lecture about "working up to potential," or some other boring old-person idea, I say, "Your grade is not passing right now, but I know you can bring it up. If you want some help, let me know. I appreciate your coming to class and making an effort. You're a bright young man/woman, and I'm glad I got to be your teacher this year." It may sound too simple, but it has worked for me many, many times.

For those cynics in the group, yes, I have encountered students who refuse to shake my hand. I believe that those students are the most frightened, the most angry at the world, and the most in need of reassurance. In that case, I say, "It's all right. You don't have to shake my hand. But don't worry, I still like you." Once in a while, a student still fails my class, but most of the time, they decide to try just this once, and see what happens.

3. Computer printouts can be powerful.

At one high school, my department had the good fortune to have computers and software for electronic grade books. At first, I resisted taking the time to type in all the students' names and lists of assignments and exams, because it re-peated the information in my paper grade book (which had to be completed and turned in at the end of the year). With the help of a student aide, I managed to get all the information into the computer, and our efforts paid off many times over. Not only could I determine any student's average at the touch of a button, I could determine problem areas by separating grades into different categories—literature, spelling, vocabulary, participation, composition, speaking. If a student had poor grades in one or two categories that resulted in a lower grade overall, I could call that student into the English office and pull up his or her record on the computer. By inserting higher grades in place of poor grades, I could show the student how easy it would be to bring up a grade from a C to a B, or from a B to an A. Also, I could print out a grade report for each student, showing all of the grades or just the category percentages. Those grade printouts showed students the results of their work and showed them which areas needed work. They also gave them a written record for comparison when report cards were issued (in the unlikely event that their wonderful, charming, yet humble teacher made a mistake in her grade book).

Challenge Your Students

Instead of "dumbing down" your curriculum when you have students who are unmotivated or performing below par, why not "smarten up" your lessons? If you teach very young children, give them "big kid" tasks. My stepson has proudly informed me at least twelve times that his sixth-grade class is doing "ninth-grader work" in math. If you teach junior or senior high school, give your students college-level assignments. By making your assignments more challenging, you send a clear message that you believe your students are intelligent and capable—and they will believe what you tell them about themselves. (Be prepared to make some allowances in grading for the increased difficulty of the work—but also be prepared for your students to surprise you by not needing those allowances.)

1. Use analogies.

My freshman students used to complain about vocabulary worksheets. "Too boring," they said. "Too bad," I said. "You have to learn vocabulary, and the only way to learn new words is to study their meanings and use them in sentences." Still, they insisted, why did it have to be so boring? I didn't have an answer for that question, so I did my homework. I bought a study guide for the Scholastic Aptitude Test and selected twenty words for the next vocabulary assignment, instead of the easier words from the district-approved word list. My students were appalled. They couldn't learn those hard words, they said. Those were for college students. "You are just as smart as college students," I said. "You may be a few years younger than they are, but that doesn't mean you can't learn to use nice, big, juicy words."

Until then, most of the students recognized half of the words on each new vocabulary list, so they didn't have to work hard to learn the new words. For the first time, nobody in the class recognized the words on the list. They had to work. And when they passed the exam, as they all did, they knew they had accomplished something difficult, and they were so proud of themselves. After a few weeks of college words, I raised the stakes again by adding five analogies, worth 10 bonus points, at the end of the worksheet.

"But we don't know how to do analogies," my students complained. "That's not fair!"

I said, "I'll teach you: Finger is to hand as toe is to— what?" Foot, they said. Very good. A surgeon uses a scalpel and a carpenter uses a—what? Hammer, somebody said. Saw, somebody else said. You know how to do analogies, I told them. Figure out the relationship between the first pair of words. Look at the answers and find the pair of words that has the same relationship—that's the correct answer. It's a piece of cake. (See the Introduction to the Analogy Worksheet at the end of this chapter.)

At the end of the first year that I started using SAT words and analogies on our vocabulary worksheets, I was sitting in the back of the room grading papers one afternoon when one of my at-risk program students, Joey, pulled a friend into the room. "Miss J," Joey said, "can Lance take our vocabulary exam? He says the Academy classes are easier than his classes, and I told him they're just smaller, but they're not easier."

I pointed to the word list that was hanging on the wall in the front of the room. "Why don't you just sit down and write one sentence using each word, Lance? If you still want to take the exam after you've finished, I'll find a copy for you."

Lance grinned at Joey and opened his notebook to a blank page. He pulled out a pen and gazed at the word list. I returned to my work. A few seconds later, Joey called out, "Thanks, Miss J." I glanced up to see that Lance was no longer with us. "He's in an honors class and he thinks he's a hotshot," Joey said, "but he didn't even know one of the words on our list. Guess we're not so dumb after all, huh?"

2. Step aside and let students learn.

It's tempting to want to control everything that happens in your classroom, to avoid messes, mistakes, frustration, fights, noises, and laziness, but students learn much more when teachers step back and let them make noisy, messy mistakes, and figure out how to handle frustration, arguments, and partners who are lazy.

We used to read one story at a time from the literature textbook, discuss the story, complete the questions at the end of the chapter, perhaps add some creative project to liven up the class. I thought my lessons were good, but my students complained that they were boring. "They aren't boring," I insisted. "They require all kinds of critical thinking and evaluation and higher-level thinking skills."

"But you and the book are doing all the thinking," one precocious boy said. "If we don't like a story, and the textbook says it's a good story, then we're automatically wrong, so what's the point of evaluating these stories. They're all in the book, so they must all be good literature." I couldn't argue with him; he was right.

Instead of completing the textbook unit, I assigned my students to groups, three per group, and gave them two weeks to complete the project: What Makes a Good Short Story? (A sample assignment sheet can be found at the end of this chapter.) The first step was to read seven short stories: four from the textbook, one from *The New Yorker*, two from literary journals. The students were to read each story, aloud or silently, and make notes about each one for reference— names of main characters, basic plot summary, things they liked and didn't like about the story. When they finished reading all the stories, they were to discuss them with each other and decide what key elements make a good short story (minimum of four elements). After identifying those key elements, each group had to compare the stories and rate them according to their own criteria. The final step was to design some visual representation that defined those key elements, compared the stories, evaluated the stories according to the group's criteria, and rated the stories from worst to best. A spokesperson for each group would explain why they rated each story as they did and give specific examples to support their choice of the "best" story.

My students came up with a variation of the textbook definition of a good short story: they wanted interesting characters, exciting or thought-provoking action, realistic dialogue, and a satisfying conclusion. In addition to those textbook elements, my students added, "get to the point without too many boring details." They learned the same information they would have learned from studying the text, but they were much more excited because they learned it from their own experiences.

3. Make your assignments/exams meaningful.

If students seem less than inspired by your assignments and exams, check yourself first. Sometimes lessons that we think are fun or interesting are not fun or interesting to young people. Writing your own obituary may sound like an amusing or thought-provoking composition assignment, but some students become so upset at imagining themselves dead that they can't do the assignment. And some of the lessons included in teacher editions of textbooks are insultingly simple. If most of the questions on your worksheets consist of filling in blanks or matching, your students may need to be challenged with questions that require higher-level thinking skills. If you have doubts about your assignments, do them yourself. If they bore you, they will bore your students. It may take you more time to grade complex and sophisticated assignments, but the quality and quantity of student work will improve.

4. Join the class.

One of the most effective ways to generate interest in an assignment is for you to take a seat with your students and complete the assignment along with them. They may think you're sitting with them to keep them from cheating, or to amuse them. Tell them you're doing the work because you think it's important. If you are willing to take your time to do the same work you have assigned to them, they will believe that it is important.

The first time I did a student assignment, I did it because one of my students accused me of giving them work just to keep them busy until the bell rang. I assured him that my intentions were much better, that I hoped they would learn something valuable from the assignment. He refused to believe me, so I grabbed a worksheet and took a seat beside him. He watched me for quite a long time, then finally began writing on his own paper. When we finished, I gave him my worksheet to grade. He gave me an A+. I gave him a B. After that day, I made a practice of doing all assignments that I give students. It keeps me on track and lets me know right away when my lessons are too difficult or too easy for my students.

Rewards

When I announced to my class that I intended to deduct five points from the grade of any student who was late for the exam the following day, one student raised his hand and asked, "Why don't you give five points to the people who are on time, instead?" Not only was his idea good, it reminded me that I was approaching my classes backwards. Instead of rewarding their good behavior, I had fallen into the old familiar habit of punishing bad behavior. I took his advice and gave points to the punctual students. I also made myself a note and hung it over my desk: *If we want students to cooperate and behave, we must reward them when they do.*

For the next journal assignment, I asked all of my students to suggest behaviors they thought deserved rewards, good behavior that usually went unnoticed. Their list of unrewarded good behavior included: not fighting, not swearing, not arguing with the teacher, helping other kids, collecting papers without being asked, picking up trash off the floor and throwing it away even if it wasn't yours, staying in your seat during lessons, participating in class discussions, bringing pencils and notebooks to class, putting back chairs and desks that other students moved out of place. When I read their journals, I realized that I had been ignoring about 90 percent of my students behavior—their good behavior—and focusing my attention on the negative 10 percent.

I turned over a new leaf immediately. From that day, I started rewarding kids for doing the things I wanted them to do. Sometimes my rewards were as simple as a smile or a thank you. Other times, I'd interrupt the class to thank somebody for a particularly positive behavior, such as offering to lend a pencil to another student, or getting up to close the window when noise outside the room began to interfere with the lesson. Every day, I'd announce, just before the bell rang, "Thank you very much for coming to class today and working with me. I appreciate your cooperation. It has been a distinct pleasure being your teacher and I look forward to the next opportunity."

My students responded so well to the positive feedback that I decided to take it one step further by staging random rewards in the form of homework or attendance lotteries. For a homework lottery, I collect the homework papers, write the student's name in one corner of the paper, and tear off the corner. For an attendance lottery, I write the names of all students present in class on slips of paper. All the names go into a paper bag or jar, and a student draws one name. The winner receives a prize. The prize doesn't have to be big—a piece of bubble gum will generate the same excitement as a disposable camera. The prize isn't the point. The point is that attendance improves and students do more homework if there is a chance they'll win a prize just for doing what they're supposed to do in the first place.

When I run out of money for prizes, I ask local merchants to donate gifts. They respond by giving pens, notebooks, videos of hit movies, CDs, audiotapes, certificates for free hamburgers and fries, reduced admission at local movie theaters, candy, and whatever else they have on hand. One woman who operated a security service started bringing in bags of goodies that had been discarded from local conventions. Her contributions included backpacks, three-ring binders, baseball caps, pens, chocolate candy bars, and pads of paper. She supplied us with enough paper for weekly spelling tests for years! The receptionist at a local office complex started collecting magazines from all the lawyers and doctors in her building at the end of each month, and sending the magazines to my students. We received hundreds of magazines, which we used for independent reading assignments and various art and writing projects during the year.

Help Students Learn to Set Goals

Unsuccessful students are rarely good goal setters. They blame their failure on other people, circumstances, or luck. One of the most valuable lessons you can teach your students is how to set realistic goals, make a list of steps to move them forward, evaluate their progress, revise goals when necessary, and to set a new, higher goal, once a goal has been reached. This doesn't have to be a separate lesson. Regardless of your subject, you can incorporate this into your present curriculum by asking students at the start of any grading period to set a goal for their grade in your class. Ask them to write down their goal for the grading period. Ask them to list three things they can do to move closer to that goal. Finally, have them list three things they can do today to get started. Collect the goal sheets and file them where they will be handy. At regular intervals (I'd suggest weekly to keep them on track) take out the goal sheets, have students evaluate their progress, and revise goals if necessary. (See the sample worksheet at the end of the chapter.)

If you have the time and inclination, you might expand this exercise to include personal goals, such as setting a target weight for bench press, losing 15 pounds, finding a job, improving a relationship with a family member, becoming a published writer, performing as a dancer or singer in public.

Don't worry about the handful of students who refuse to play the game. Focus on those students who appreciate learning to use this valuable skill, which will help them succeed in college, their careers, and their personal lives.

Perhaps you've seen an article about John Goddard (there was a feature in *Bay Area Parent*, January 1989). Goddard, author of *Kayaks Down the Nile*, sat down at age fifteen and made a list of 127 goals that he wanted to accomplish in his lifetime. A voracious reader, Goddard listed many exotic locales and unusual adventures, including mountain climbing in Peru and New Zealand and studying primitive cultures in Borneo and Brazil. His list also included less taxing feats such as typing 50 words per minute, owning an ocelot, building a telescope, learning to play polo, and lighting a match with a .22 rifle.

Goddard's story and his list of goals (which was published in *Life* magazine some years ago) make an attention-getting introducton to goal setting. After reading his list, students who couldn't think of a thing they wanted to do often create long lists of goals for themselves. Your own list of life goals might be just as intriguing and inspiring to your students. How you approach the topic isn't as important as providing a model for students to follow. Children who have had no experience in setting goals often throw their hands into the air and give up when faced with this new and challenging concept. These students need the lesson the most.

Teach Problem-Solving Skills

Until your students can deal effectively with their personal problems, they won't be able to concentrate on your lessons, so it is to your benefit to teach them problem-solving skills. The model I use in my classes is a combination of models I was taught during military training and corporate seminars. There are many good books available on the subject, and some contain worksheets and sample exercises.

Basically, problem solving is a cycle, much like goal setting. You begin with a stated problem, brainstorm for solutions, analyze solutions to pick the one most likely to be effective, implement the solution, evaluate your progress, and start over again. Some teachers like to present a real problem that their students face: gang violence in schools, peer pressure to use drugs or alcohol, a schoolyard bully, a personality conflict with a teacher, fighting with parents or siblings. You may want to use something less personal to give your students a chance to practice the model without becoming upset over personal issues. I like to use: *My friends always want to copy my homework,* or *A few students disrupt the class and make it hard to learn.*

Brainstorming is often students' favorite step in the problem-solving process, but often they forget that the key to successful brainstorming is not to make any judgment about suggestions during the brainstorming session, no matter how outlandish or silly the suggestions may sound. A silly suggestion may spark a truly innovative and effective solution to a problem, but the spark will never ignite if people laugh at each other's ideas. Another thing to keep in mind is that brainstorming in a large group tends to disintegrate into a series of smaller conversations, leaving one or two people working with the group leader. Smaller groups, with three to five people, are more effective for brainstormers.

Since children tend to act first and think later, the second step—analyzing the problem—is the most important for them to practice. Students also need frequent reminders that a problem isn't solved simply because they choose a solution. They must evaluate the effectiveness of the solution, and select an alternative if the first choice isn't successful. At first, this process may seem too detailed or time-consuming for students (and teachers), but with practice it becomes a quick and easy habit—and one that will help them effectively handle problems that arise in their future careers and personal lives.

Showcase Students' Individual Talents

Perhaps you've read one of the recent books about intelligence, and the expanded definitions that include spatial, emotional, and musical intelligence, among other abilities. Stand in front of any class filled with children and you will be facing budding singers, dancers, composers, poets, scientists, inventors, philosophers, and athletes. Give those students an opportunity to use those talents that are not normally acknowledged in an academic environment and you will see flowers blossom before your eyes.

A class of especially rambunctious sophomores convinced me to allow them to include music and dance in their class projects one year. The projects were so successful, so much more sophisticated and polished than any previous group's projects, that I expanded the assignment to include whatever talents students chose to display. (An assignment sheet and contract are included at the end of this chapter.) Some students chose to stick with researching and writing reports or composing essays, but more than half of the students designed their own projects. Here are some samples of what students did:

- One young man wrote a poem in Spanish, set it to music, sang it for the class while accompanying himself on guitar, then translated the song for those non-Spanish speakers.
- Two young men wrote and performed a rap song about the real meaning of the word "respect"—that it comes from within the heart, not from holding a gun.

- One young lady wrote and performed a rap song that included (correctly) fifty vocabulary words from lessons in our class.

- Three students staged a "talk show" in class and the guests discussed the issue of interracial dating and marriage—a hot topic at our school.

- Four girls choreographed and presented their own dance routine, then gave a brief lesson in dance to volunteers from the audience.

- One boy played samples of classical and jazz music on his saxophone, then gave a brief biography of the music's composers.

- One young man gave a demonstration of kung fu, complete with displays of physical strength, but the emphasis of his presentation was on the mental discipline and spiritual aspects of the martial arts.

Inspiration via Quotations

You can harness the power of words to motivate and inspire your students by displaying inspirational quotations in your classroom where students will see them every day. Some teachers ask their students to discuss the quotations or write responses to them in their journals. Others let them speak for themselves. Whether you discuss them or not, your students will read them and think about them—although they may never admit that they do. Here is a list of my students' favorite quotations:

> *Nobody can make you feel inferior without your consent.*
> *—Eleanor Roosevelt*

> *Great spirits have always encountered violent opposition from mediocre minds.*   *—Albert Einstein*

The hardest thing about success is finding somebody who is truly happy for you.   —Bette Midler

There are two tragedies in life. One is to lose your heart's desire. The other is to gain it.   —George Bernard Shaw

He who angers you enslaves you.   —Author unknown

If your only tool is a hammer, you tend to see every problem as a nail.   —Author unknown

One often learns more from ten days of agony than from ten years of contentment.   —Merle Shain

Just because you're right doesn't mean I'm wrong.
                    —Shirley Johnson (my smart mom)

If you do not tell the truth about yourself you cannot tell it about other people.   —Virginia Woolf

Light came to me when I realized I did not have to consider any racial group as a whole. God made them duck by duck and that was the only way I could see them.
                    —Zora Neale Hurston

You see what power is—holding someone else's fear in your hand and showing it to them!   —Amy Tan

Do you know the hallmark of the second-rater? It's resentment of another man's achievement.   —Ayn Rand

If you don't decide which way to play with life, it always plays with you.   —Merle Shain

Hold fast to dreams for if dreams die, life is a broken-winged bird that cannot fly.   —Langston Hughes

You cannot make yourself feel something you do not feel, but you can make yourself do right in spite of your feelings.
                    —Pearl Buck

If you can imagine it, you can achieve it.
If you can dream it, you can become it.
                    —William Arthur Ward

INTRODUCTION TO ANALOGIES

(which can help you learn to think better)

An analogy shows the relationship of one thing to another thing, written in a special format using colons. If Tony's favorite food is ice cream and his brother Alex's favorite is pizza, you could compare the two brothers' taste in food by writing this analogy:

Tony : ice cream :: Alex : pizza
(Tony loves ice cream. Alex loves pizza.)

The most important thing about analogies is that they have to be expressed in the same order. In our example, if you changed one of the word pairs around, you would NOT have an analogy.

Tony : ice cream :: pizza : Alex
(Tony loves ice cream. Pizza loves Alex.)

An analogy problem has two key words written in capital letters, followed by three or more word pairs. Figure out the relationship between the key words, and then look for the answer that shows the same relationship. Here's an example:

MECHANIC : WRENCH :: (a) saw : carpenter
(b) scientist : microscope (c) doctor : hospital

The correct answer is b. (A mechanic uses a wrench. A scientist uses a microscope.) If you chose a, check again. (A saw uses a carpenter.)

The best way to solve analogy questions is to make a sentence of the key words and repeat that sentence to find the answer that fits the same pattern. This may seem too simple when you're using basic, obvious comparisons, such as this one:

HAND : FINGERS :: foot: toes
(A hand has fingers. A foot has toes.)

But it won't seem too simple when you start dealing with more complex ideas, like this:

RAIN : FLOOD :: (a) wreck : auto
(b) lightning : fire (c) earthquake : volcano

The answer is b. (Rain can cause a flood. Lightning can cause a fire.)

Here are some samples of common patterns you will find in analogy problems. See if you can figure them out before you read the answers.

1. HOT : COLD :: (a) freezing : icy
(b) steam : water (c) wet : dry

(Hot is the opposite of cold. Wet is the opposite of dry.) *Antonyms (opposites).*

2. HAPPY : GLAD :: (a) silly : smile
(b) sad : ecstatic (c) smart : intelligent

(Happy is the same as glad. Smart is the same as intelligent.) *Synonyms (same).*

3. WARM : BOILING :: (a) cool : frozen
(b) big : little (c) water : ice

(If something gets warmer, it eventually will start boiling. If something gets colder, eventually it will be frozen.) *Degree.*

4. BOXER : DOG :: (a) kitten : puppy
(b) bark : howl (c) Siamese : cat

(A boxer is a kind of dog. A Siamese is a kind of cat.) *One of a type or kind.*

5. PAINTER : BRUSH :: (a) writer : pen
(b) chisel : sculptor (c) janitor : clean

(A painter uses a brush. A writer uses a pen.) *Tool or characteristic related to person.*

6. TURKEY : THANKSGIVING ::
(a) love : heart (b) happy : smile
(c) dove : peace

(A turkey is a symbol for Thanksgiving. A dove is a symbol for peace.) *Symbols.*

7. HAMMER : POUND :: (a) scissors : cut
(b) saw : blade (c) chop : ax

(A hammer is used to pound. Scissors are used to cut.) *Object and logical action.*

8: WOOL : SHEEP :: (a) cotton : plant
(b) leather : suede (c) horse : saddle

(Wool comes from a sheep. Cotton comes from a plant.) *Source or composition.*

9. LIGHTBULB:ELECTRICITY :: (a) hat : head
(b) house : roof (c) car : gas

(Lightbulbs use electricity for power. Cars use gas for power.) *Object and function.*

10. BIRD : FLOCK :: (a) sheep : school
(b) fish : bunch (c) cattle : herd

(Many birds create a flock. Many cattle create a herd.) *Part and whole.*

Here are some examples of analogies that focus on particular school subjects. Analogies are a good way to assess student understanding, because students cannot memorize the answers as they can for matching and they are less obvious than most multiple-choice questions. To increase the difficulty and decrease chances that students can guess answers correctly, add more answer choices to the problems.

Math—PERIMETER : SQUARE ::
  (a) ellipse : oval (b) area : triangle
  (c) circumference : circle

Science—HEART : CIRCULATORY ::
  (a) nervous : kidney (b) lung : respiratory
  (c) skeletal : bone

History—WWII : D-DAY :: (a) Dunkirk : WWII
  (b) Civil War : Gettysburg (c) WWI : Pearl
  Harbor

Geography—MADRID : EUROPE ::
  (a) Cairo : Africa (b) Sydney : Australia
  (c) Rome : Asia

Art—MONET : WATER LILIES ::
  (a) Raphael : roses (b) Matisse : cats
  (c) Van Gogh : sunflowers

You will find a more detailed explanation of analogies, and lots of practice quizzes, in the many handbooks and study guides for college entrance exams. Some vocabulary-building books also contain sections on analogies.

INDIVIDUAL PROJECT ASSIGNMENT SHEET

You may work by yourself or in a group (3 people maximum). Your project design is up to you, but you must have my approval. (No weapons, drugs, or other contraband may be used during demonstrations.) You may select one of the following categories.

• **A research report** of at least 3 pages (typed, double-spaced) on any topic. You must turn in an outline or a rough draft at least two days before the report is due. Your outline or rough draft must be written during class time. Your final report must be typed, double-spaced, with a list of references. You may include illustrations or photos.

• **An art project** such as a painting, drawings, clay model, collage, etc. If you choose to draw, you must submit at least five drawings and at least one must be drawn in class. Other art projects may be approved.

• **An oral presentation** on a topic of your choice. How-to speeches, poetry, researched reports, movie reviews, storytelling, stand-up comedy are all acceptable.

• **A musical presentation.** You may sing, dance, play an instrument, recite a poem to music, present an original rap song, or perform another music project of your choice.

• **A skit** such as a TV show, radio show, scene from a play, etc.

You will have at least two class periods to work on this project.

Your progress report or rough draft will be due on_____

ALL PROJECTS ARE DUE ON_____
NO EXCEPTIONS.

Here are some projects kids have done in the past: Dating Game TV show, lip-synching, guitar solos, how to cut/perm your hair at home, how to change the oil in your car, children's story hour, folk dances, how to play the saxophone, how to drive your parents crazy, keeping fish as a pet. You may bring in small animals—no spiders or snakes.

If you can't think of anything to do, ask your teacher who loves you to help you think of something. She is filled with ideas.

P.S.: What's the point of this assignment? Use your skills and talents. Share your ideas with the class. Work on your communication skills. Have some fun.

PROJECT CONTRACT:
READ, FILL OUT, AND SIGN.

I understand that I am responsible for designing and completing my own project. If I choose to work with other people and they do not complete their part, I will still be responsible for completing my project—*or* I will fill out a new contract and give it to Ms. J so she knows that I have changed my plans.

My project will be (describe in detail):

_____

_____

_____

Check one:

_____ I will do my own individual project.

_____ I will be working with _____

and   _____

           _____

I understand that my rough draft or progress report is due on _____

and the final project is due on _____.

If I do not turn in my project or if I am not prepared to make my presentation on that date, I will receive a zero for this assignment.

_____

(student signature)

WALL PROGRESS CHART

deadline =	9/6 Journal #1	9/15 Spelling #1	9/20 Vocab Worksheet #1	9/25 Vocab Quiz #1	10/3 Literature Worksheet #1	Journal #2	Spelling #2	Speech #1	Vocab w/s #2	Vocab quiz #2	Journal #3						
X = done / □ = missing / ☒ = made up / ⊘ = no credit																	
Aguilar, M.	X	X	☒	⊘	X	X	X	X	X	X	X						
Bailey, T.	X	X	X	X	X	X	⊘	☒	X	X	X						
Chavez, L.	⊘	☒	☒	☒	X	X	X	X	X	X	X						
Cohen, N.	X	X	X	☒	X	X	X	☒	X	X	X						
Dexter, P.	X	X	X	X	X	X	X	X	X	X	X						
Farley, S.	X	X	X	X	X	X	☒	X	X	X	X						
Hong, K.	X	X	X	☒	X	X	X	X	X	X	⊘						
Holly, M.	⊘	X	X	⊘	X	X	☒	X	X	X	X						
Jones, J.	X	X	X	X	X	X	X	X	X	X	X						
Langley, M.	X	X	X	X	X	X	X	X	X	X	X						
Newton, R.	X	X	☒	X	X	X	X	X	X	X	X						
Porter, J.	X	X	X	X	X	⊘	X	X	X	☒	X						
Quintera, A.	X	X	X	X	☒	X	X	☒	X	X	X						
Steiner, R.	X	X	X	X	X	X	☒	X	X	X	X						

2nd Period – English II

SHORT STORY ANALYSIS EXERCISE

Instructions: In your group, you will read the five short stories listed on the board. Three are from our literature textbook, two are stories from literary journals that I have copied for you. (You may read the stories silently or aloud in your group.)

Complete the following four tasks, in order.

1. After you read each story, jot down a few notes about your reaction to the story. What did you like and dislike about the story? Why? **Find a few phrases or sentences that show specifically what you liked or disliked. Copy these down for future reference. (**You will need this information later, so don't skip this step. Each person is to take notes on each story for himself or herself.)

2. Discuss the five stories in your group and decide what makes a good story. What key elements must a story have to be good? List and define them.

3. Create some kind of visual aid (chart, graph, poster) that compares the five stories according to how well they use the key elements you identified. Rate the stories against each other, using some system that you design.

4. Select one or two people from your group to present your visual aid to the class on _____ and give a brief explanation of your comparison.

Note: You may use posterboard, paint, a video camera, computer graphics, collages, the white board in our classroom—whatever you need for your presentation. You also may read selections from the stories if you choose.

Your *next assignment* will be to write an individual critique of one of these stories—including a citation from the story to support your ideas. That's why you will need your notes on each story. Hang on to them.

Let me know if you have any problems or questions. That's my job—to help you be successful.

Thank you for your cooperation on this assignment. It is a distinct pleasure and an honor to be your teacher and I look forward to your presentation.

GOAL-SETTING WORKSHEET

Name: _____

Long-term goal: By _____, I will _____
    (date 6 months from now)

Mid-term goal: By _____, I will _____
    (date 3 months from now)

Short-term goal: This month, I will _____

Three things I can do today to work towards my goal are:

   1. _____

   2. _____

   3. _____

For each Check-up Period, see how much progress you've made. Do you need to revise your plan because it was too easy or to hard? What works for you?

30-day Check-up:

60-day Check-up:

90-day Check-up:

120-day Check-up:

150-day Check-up:

6-Month Evaluation: Did you reach your goal?

_____Yes. Congratulations! Write about this experience in your private journal.

_____No. If not, don't despair. The only failure is the person who doesn't try. How can you use this experience to help you achieve future goals? Write about this experience in your private journal. Set a new goal.

Psychology & Sales

Education Is the Product;
You're the Salesperson

Observe a number of teachers in action and you will see that those who are most effective in connecting with students from a broad spectrum of cultural and economic backgrounds, who demand and receive excellence from students, and who truly enjoy their work, are those teachers who combine scholarship with psychology and sales.

Effective teachers know and love their subjects, and their enthusiasm is contagious. They love learning, and they aren't afraid to admit they don't know all the answers. They encourage students to ask challenging questions, and when they don't have the answers, they do their homework and report back. By their example, they teach students to question constantly, to search for answers, and to learn for the pure joy of learning.

Effective teachers are classroom psychologists—when they want to understand students, they listen more than they talk. They listen to what students are not saying, by paying attention to body language, posture, facial expressions, and other forms of nonverbal communication. And, like psychologists, instead of threatening or ordering people to change their attitudes and behaviors, they try to discover the motivation for self-destructive behavior and help students realize that they have the power to change their own lives.

Effective teachers understand, instinctively, that they are selling education and students are their customers. The primary challenge facing teachers is convincing students to buy what we have to sell. Any good salesperson will tell you that making a sale depends more on establishing rapport with the customer than on the product itself.

During my first year in front of the class, I made the mistake of trying to teach before my students were ready to learn. I assumed that teaching would be as simple as it appeared in my education textbooks: I would present my lessons, and my students would learn them. I didn't understand, at first, that before I could teach, I had to sell myself and my subject to a group of tough customers. I didn't understand that my students needed to trust me before they could accept what I had to offer. Fortunately, those children were relentless. They refused to give up—or to let me give up—until they taught me how to teach. They were excellent teachers. The lessons they taught me have enabled me to successfully teach students ranging from high school freshmen who couldn't speak a word of English, to at-risk adolescents and gangster wannabes, to honors-level college students. This chapter contains those lessons.

Accept, Don't Judge

If you want your students to accept you and cooperate with you, then you must accept them. This sounds simple, but it can be very difficult to do when you have students who have green or purple or no hair, pierced eyebrows and tongues, terrible taste in music, no fashion sense, skewed values, and limited (if any) social graces. Perhaps it will help if you can recall some of the stupid things you said and did and wore when you were a child. I remember having to lie down on my bed so my friend could zip my pedal pushers because they were so tight I couldn't do it myself; today girls wear pants that are big enough to hold themselves and a few of their friends. Kids today like to shave a swatch out of the middle of their skulls; my mother said she and her high school friends all bleached a broad white four-inch streak in the middle of their hair. Why? Because it upset their parents. One of the tasks of adolescents is to create fads and crazes that adults don't understand, as a way of marking their generation.

1. Beware of potential insults.

If you make derogatory comments about teenage mothers, welfare families, gang members, or fanatic religious groups, for example, you may be insulting the friends and relatives of your students, including their parents. I have had many students in my classroom who were second-generation gang members, and many whose parents were married at age twelve and parents by age thirteen. Because I don't share their values or customs doesn't mean that those people aren't responsible, effective, loving parents. If you insult your students' families, you can forget about earning their trust and respect.

Cultural differences create many opportunities to put your foot in your mouth. Once, during a presentation to a group of student teachers, I mentioned that I sometimes touch students to calm them down during class. As I made my point, I touched one of the nearby students gently on the back of his head to demonstrate what I thought was a nonintrusive touch. He didn't respond or move, but after my speech, he stopped me in the hallway to tell me that in his country touching somebody's head was the ultimate sign of disrespect. I was so embarrassed! He assured me that no offense was taken, because he knew I had been acting out of ignorance and not disrespect.

Most students will forgive you, as that student forgave me, if you unknowingly break a cultural taboo, but I prefer to avoid making those errors. After that speech, I made a note to discuss different cultural practices with my classes, so we all know how to show respect for each other. We talk about customs and taboos, particularly behavior that is inter- preted as disrespectful. I still make mistakes, but not nearly as often, and my students appreciate having a chance to be the resident experts.

2. Instead of criticizing, ask questions.

If you remember your childhood at all, you probably remember what happened when an adult criticized your taste in clothes, people, or music or your values, opinions, and choices—you either felt compelled to defend your choices or determined to stop people from "bossing you around." You'll be much more likely to get students to listen if you ask questions instead of offering your own opinions about their terrible tastes and mistaken choices. If a baby outbreak occurs in your school, for example, and girls are actively trying to get pregnant (I've seen this at three differ- ent schools), don't tell them they are stupid and will regret their youthful stupidity later. That won't change their minds and it won't make them trust or respect you. Ask them why they want to have babies, how they plan to care for them, whether they will miss the social activities they will have to sacrifice, how they would feel if their mothers had had them when they were twelve or fourteen or sixteen years old (some of them will be able to speak from experience). Try to help them see past the romance to the practical aspects of motherhood. Some of them will still have babies, but a baby is a baby, not a fatal disease or a death sentence. I've had many teenage mothers who earned excellent grades during high school and went on to college, baby in hand.

When a student makes a comment in favor of gangs, I am tempted to dismiss gang members as stupid, antisocial misfits, but I know that if I do, I will destroy any chance I had of changing that student's mind because he will perceive my comment as criticism of his intelligence and judgment. Instead of thinking about his choices, he will focus on defending them. Again, I ask questions: Why do kids join gangs? What do gangs offer that kids really need? How long will you stay in a gang? Is being in a gang as great as you thought it would be? How will being in a gang affect your life? What if somebody wants out of a gang? What can kids do to avoid gangs without becoming a target of gang violence?

Question your students about ripped and ragged jeans, T-shirts bearing skulls and death masks, music that sounds like cats being strangled, pierced tongues, cults and cliques, glamorizing gangsters and shoplifting for kicks. Ask your students to articulate the reasons for their choices, or at least think about them. Your students will try to resist thinking about your questions, of course, but every now and then, one of your questions will hit its mark, although you may never know it. If you can inspire your students to think about why they do the things they do, and realize that they have a variety of better options, you will have given them a priceless gift and a lesson that will last a lifetime.

Respect Students as Fellow Human Beings

If you want respect, first you must give it. We've all heard that adage, but sometimes it doesn't seem to work. You walk into your classroom, filled with respect for your students, and they refuse to return the courtesy. They don't even acknowledge that you offered it in the first place. What should you do? Keep offering. You may have to give respect for a long while before you get any back, because so many young people have spent their entire lives without ever having been genuinely respected, and they don't know how to respond. Some of them may suspect that you are making fun of them. They have been treated disrespectfully for so long by so many people, particularly adults, that they have no models to shape themselves after, no standards to follow.

1. Set the example.

When I show my students the film version of *To Kill a Mockingbird* (after we've read the book, of course), invariably, they protest loudly when Gregory Peck's character quietly stands his ground without reacting when a filthy drunk man spits in his face. My students shout, "Smack him! Kill him!" At that point, I always stop the videotape and ask if anybody in the room would have that kind of self-control and strength of character, to stand quietly and refuse to be manipulated into fighting. Nobody raises a hand. They can't imagine anybody not wanting to annihilate the guy. I tell them there are people who are strong enough to resist that temptation, and they are impressed. Children have an innate sense of fairness and justice, and a natural respect for strength of character— they just don't have many opportunities to experience those things in action. I ask them to think about their heroes (who are usually movie stars, athletes, and singers, with an occasional author thrown in). I ask if they have any heroes who are admired because of their integrity and sense of honor. They can't think of any. I ask if they would like to know some people like that. Yes, they surely would. Guess what? You're it—the role model they're looking for. Show them honesty and integrity, honor and respect. They'll listen, and eventually, they'll learn.

2. Speak their language.

You will be much more effective in communicating with your students if you learn to speak their language, literally and figuratively. You don't have to be multilingual—learn a few words or phrases in whatever languages your students speak. A Filipino child will be thrilled if you answer a question by shaking your head and saying, "*hinde*" instead of "no." Your Spanish-speaking students will giggle delightedly if you insert a "*no te preocupes*" (don't worry) or "*de prisa*" (hurry) into your lesson. Don't worry about whether your accent is perfect—they'll enjoy correcting you. They love to be the experts for a change, and they know that if you have trouble learning their language, then you will appreciate how difficult it was for them to learn a second language. If you ask students to teach you phrases, you might check them out with an adult or language book before saying them in public. One little imp told me he was teaching me to say, "It's been a pleasure to meet you," when he actually taught me to say, "Your mother is a so-and-so."

Speak the universal language of music. Children love music and you can take advantage of that love to help bridge great ethnic, economic, and social gaps. Ask your students to let you listen to their favorite songs. If you've never listened to rap, you may be in for a pleasant surprise. (I admit it. I sometimes put on a headset, turn down the volume on the heavy metal songs, and pretend I'm listening.) If you don't like the music, lie. Say it's interesting and ask what else they like. Introduce them to different styles of music. I've had students who never heard of jazz and who thought classical music was created for elevators and to serve as background on PBS television programs. Bring in a cassette recorder or a CD player and play a little Bach during an exam. Let students take turns selecting music to play before the bell rings at the start of class. (You'll have fewer tardy students.) Use music as an incentive. If everybody finishes an assignment early and well, let them listen to music for five minutes at the end of the period.

One vocational agriculture teacher brought the chassis of an old car into his classroom and wired a cassette player so students could sit in the front seat and listen to music as a reward for completing assignments ahead of time or for doing excellent work. That car was a more effective motivator than any of his lectures, threats, or promises.

You also can make great strides in connecting with your students if you pay attention to the people they admire. When we're in the midst of a vocabulary lesson, for example, and a wannabe rap star loses his motivation, I can get him back on track by reminding him that Coolio and his cohorts wouldn't have been so successful if they hadn't known a plethora of words from which to create their rhymes. Learn the names of the dancers and singers and athletes your students admire, so you can drop a name at an appropriate point in your lesson and show them that you've been paying attention.

What about street slang? English is a constantly evolving language, even in academic circles; the proper grammar of today would have sounded vulgar and crude to Benjamin Franklin or Jane Austen. Instead of trying to stop students from speaking street slang (which won't happen), I prefer a more pragmatic approach. I tell my students that they must be bilingual in order to succeed in the business world as it exists today. If they choose to speak street slang with their friends, fine, but if they expect to attend college or compete for jobs in major corporations, they must learn to speak the language of commerce—at least until they obtain jobs and achieve a high enough level of authority to challenge the status quo. In private journals, informal discussions, and essays, I let my students use any language they feel will best communicate their ideas and feelings. On formal essays and discussions, however, they must use proper grammar in order to earn good grades.

If you listen to the slang your students speak, I think you'll have to admit that some of it is quite pithy and apt to become acceptable in the future. I wouldn't recommend mimicking student slang in an attempt to be accepted by them, because I don't think it's appropriate for teachers (and because it doesn't work). But, sometimes, for fun, I intentionally misuse one of the popular phrases. Once, I informed my students that the principal had "dissed" me from the staff meeting early. They howled, delighted at my not knowing that to "dis" somebody meant to disrespect or publicly humiliate him.

3. Names are important.

I once had a student named Boerneges (pronouced bo-er-NAY-hez), an intelligent and well-mannered young man, who asked me to talk to the counselors in the office for him. They had changed his name on his official record to José. When I asked why they had made the change, one of the counselors told me that his name was too difficult to pronounce. (This wasn't a case of ethnic discrimination; one of the counselors was Hispanic. They were simply lazy and oblivious to the effect of their behavior on Boerneges.) When I told the counselors that Boerneges told me they had changed his name "like he was a pet rabbit or something," they realized they had made a mistake and quickly corrected their records to reflect his given name.

Names are important. Children are proud of their families, their heritage, and their cultures. Learn to pronounce their names, no matter how difficult they may be. Ask them to correct you until you say them right. If they offer favorite nicknames, use them, but don't create nicknames to make life easier for yourself. If you make the effort to learn to pronounce their names correctly, your students will get the message that you respect and value them as human beings. Their dignity is precious and their egos are fragile, so treat them gently.

4. Reprimand in private.

If you have to reprimand a student, do it in private, even if it means stopping the class for a brief discussion outside in the hallway. Certainly a child's dignity and self-respect is as important as whatever lesson you're teaching. If you simply must reprimand or correct a student in front of the others, use the same tactful approach you would want your boss to use if she felt the need to correct you in front of your peers.

5. Don't damage their kidneys or their dignity.

Imagine that you had to use the restroom at work, but first you had to knock on your boss's door and ask for permission, knowing that it might be denied. Wouldn't you find another job?

This is one area where I advise breaking—or at least challenging—the rule, if your school does not allow students to use the restroom during class time. Not only is it inhumane to refuse to allow children to use the restroom when they need to, forcing them to "hold it in" can cause medical problems.

6. *Tardiness isn't a felony.*

Students may have valid reasons for arriving late to your class or not having homework completed or forgetting to bring a book. I've had students whose relatives were murdered, whose houses burned down, whose families were in automobile accidents. I've had students whose parents couldn't seem to get out of bed to drive them to school on time, students whose parents intentionally interfered with their study time, and students who were forced to baby-sit for six or seven young children every single night. I've also had students who had to work seven days per week, after school, so their families could eat. I think it is a horrible disrespect to young people to establish classroom policies such as: all tardy students must report to detention, or no late assignments ever will be accepted, or one missing homework assignment means a drop in the letter grade, because those policies are, in effect, telling students that they don't have the right to have problems. I realize there are some industries where tardiness means losing your job, but in most cases, supervisors realize that tardiness is a fact of life. They don't encourage it, but they don't overreact to it, either.

If we want students to have self-respect, and to respect other people, then we must teach them by our own examples. When students are late to my class, for example, they know that I expect them to act as college students or business employees would if they were late to class or a meeting: they are to walk quietly to the nearest available seat, or stand in the back of the room, and pay close attention to the current assignment or exercise so they can bring themselves up to speed. After class, they must meet with me to explain what happened and find out what they missed and what work, if any, can be made up. If the excuse is valid, I allow them to make up the missed work with full credit. If it is a matter of simply dawdling or getting caught up in a personal conversation, for example, they can make up the assignments but won't earn full credit. If repeated tardiness becomes an issue, then I try to help the student solve that problem.

7. Tried everything and they still hate you?

Often, teachers tell me that they do respect their students, and have been doing so for a long time, but still can't seem to establish a good rapport with them. Two reasons come to mind. First, it is possible that the students will never respond because the self-appointed leaders of the class are exerting more influence than those teachers. In that case, teachers can try to win over the leaders, try to remove them from class, or accept the fact that we can't always win. Second, it may be that the teacher is going through the motions of respecting students, or overlooking things that students consider important. Some teachers believe that simply addressing students as "Mr." or "Miss" demonstrates respect, but it doesn't. You can't fool kids. If you don't truly respect them, they will sense it. They'll see it in your body language: eye contact, posture, tone of voice, facial expressions, tenseness in your muscles.

It isn't difficult to decide whether an act is respectful or not—just imagine how you would feel if your principal or superintendent treated you the way you treat your students.

Listen and Talk; Talk and Listen

I honestly believe that most children's behavior is a response to one of three emotions—anger, fear, or confusion. If you intend to truly teach, which requires you to know your students, expect to encounter those emotions in the process of getting to know them.

1. Don't take students' anger personally.

Don't ignore it, either. Address the issues that concern them so you can understand why they are angry. Let them talk about the things that upset them—the impersonal school system, abusive or neglectful parents, divorce and death in their families, racism, sexism, poverty, homelessness, the government, unfair police practices, warped justice system, elitism, misused affirmative action programs, and so on.

I know, I know. You can't just walk into a room and launch a deep discussion with teenagers. Perhaps you've tried to initiate a discussion during class, only to have students refuse to participate, ridicule you, make fun of the students who do respond, or make a mockery out of the exercise. Before you can expect your students to risk making themselves vulnerable in public, and to express their ideas sincerely and articulately, you have to do a lot of talking yourself.

2. Talk to them.

Whether your students talk to you or not, talk to them. You may think they aren't listening, because they like to pretend they don't care what adults say, but the reason they pretend is that they care so very much. They want our help, but they hate to admit it. So, help them out. Talk. Spend a few minutes each day delivering a monologue about the problems you faced when you were growing up, or pronouncing your opinions on some current event or social condition or problem in society. Make provocative statements, such as, "I read an article the other day in which the author claimed that girls have life a lot easier than boys do. I wonder about that." Or perhaps, "I read an article about some kids who started their own business and they're making a lot of money. Maybe we should let teenagers quit school and work if they want to, if they have the brains and know-how to succeed." Someday, somebody will respond. A student will interrupt with his own opinions, and another student will argue. Encourage them to exchange ideas and opinions, but don't allow anybody to laugh at somebody else's idea. Make it clear that thinking is permitted, changing your mind is perfectly acceptable, but belittling other people is not acceptable.

3. Give them time.

If a student who has challenged you or been disruptive during your lessons makes an attempt to talk to you, don't remind the student of his or her past sins. Realize that most disruptive behavior is a cry for attention, and that the student may have decided that it's safe to drop his guard and risk talking to you. If a troublesome student makes any attempt to talk to you, consider it an apology and a request for help. Be receptive. This is a child who needs your help but doesn't know how to ask for it. Young people have a difficult time initiating serious conversations. Often, they don't know how to bring up the subjects that concern them, so they stop by your desk after school and say, "How's it going?" Or they come to your classroom early in the morning and just "hang out."

When one of your "difficult" students visits, sit down in one of the student desks, near enough to talk but far enough to allow a comfort zone, and just smile at your young visitor. He or she may not say anything at all, but that doesn't mean he or she didn't have anything to say. It may take two or three quiet visits before the student finally feels comfortable enough to talk. In the meantime, thank your visitor for stopping by to see you. Tell him or her that you appreciate it when somebody remembers that teachers are also human beings.

4. Help them learn to handle conflict.

When your students do open up and begin to talk, don't feel compelled to solve all their problems. You can't—and they don't expect you to. Sometimes, you will be able to offer a solution, but in most cases, young people just need somebody to listen. When your students have vented their anger, and calmed down enough to listen, explain to them that the best way for them to combat those things that enrage them is to educate themselves, to care for their bodies and minds so they are physically and mentally strong, to choose their battles carefully, to think for themselves and make their own choices, to harness their anger to help themselves, to get revenge by succeeding in the face of those who would rather see them fail. Try to find examples from their own lives to illustrate those ideas. Irritating teachers and belligerent classmates are two examples of situations my own students have faced, and here's the advice I give them for coping with those situations:

Example one. Let's say a teacher says or does something that makes you really angry. You mouth off, and you get suspended. Now you become even more angry because it isn't fair to punish you for something the teacher initiated, so you mouth off some more, and you get kicked out of class or school. Who wins this battle? The teacher who taunted you. He got what he wanted—you're out of school, facing an uphill battle to finish your education, and he's still sitting fat and happy in his classroom. There is no revenge. Even if you attacked that teacher, it wouldn't improve your position. You still lose.

Example two. Some other student at school taunts you or challenges you or insults your mother. You hit the student and you are then suspended or expelled. You let that student control your mind and your behavior. Even if that student is also suspended or expelled, he will have achieved his goal—getting you in trouble. Usually the students who set up this kind of situation are poor students, with limited options and not much hope for a bright future. They see you succeeding and achieving and they want to bring you down with them, so they egg you into a fight. You don't have to play that game. It takes a lot more strength to resist a fight than it does to throw a punch. I'm not telling you not to defend yourself if somebody attacks you. I am telling you not to let people sucker you into playing their game. When somebody tries to make me fight with them, I think to myself, "This sorry so-and-so is not important to my life. I refuse to make him important." Out loud, I say, "I really don't want to fight with you. I have something else to do right now." And I get out of Dodge before I give in to the temptation to smack him in the kisser.

If you let somebody make you angry, you give that person control over you, at least for a while. Remember, it takes much more strength to keep your mouth shut and your emotions under control than it does to talk back or strike out. Be selfish. Don't let people control your mind. Control it yourself. Use it for your own benefit. Let the bully find another victim.

Student Input

What started as a self-defense strategy turned out to be an effective teaching tool and a good way for me to judge the quality of my teaching. As I described earlier, one of my fellow teachers had become so despondent that she nearly quit teaching after a group of honors students attacked her, challenging her lessons, her teaching style, and her right to be a teacher at all (she was an excellent teacher, by the way). I wanted to make sure I never faced that situation, so I tried to think of ways to avoid such a confrontation. If I give them a chance to evaluate me, I thought, then they won't be as tempted to belittle me or challenge me because they will believe I value their opinions (which I didn't, at the time).

My first evaluation didn't ask for much, because I didn't really want my students to give me much feedback. I simply wanted to ward off the "monster" students. My students took the evaluations seriously, however, and turned the papers over to add more comments on the back. My plan had been to toss the papers in the trash without reading them, but after I glanced at a few, I took them home and read every word. Some of their comments were plainly silly, but most of them wrote thoughtful critiques of my lessons and my teaching style. One of the students evaluated my evaluation form itself as "not very well designed for thoughtful input." Busted! After I got over feeling insulted because they didn't realize I was a perfect teacher, I looked over my lesson plans and saw that they were right. My worksheet on symbolism was too easy and didn't explain the concept well enough, but some of my writing assignments and exams were too long for the time allotted.

The evaluations were unsigned so that students would feel free to be honest, but I posted them on the bulletin board where they could read them and see the notes I had made in the margins about things I planned to change on future assignments. Even the students who pretended they hated school and didn't care about anything that happened in the classroom spent time standing in front of that bulletin board, reading those evaluations.

1. *Consider students' feelings.*

Many of my classroom policies and strategies have come from the student evaluations. An especially important one was suggested by a sophomore boy, an African-American student who objected to reading *Of Mice and Men* because the word "nigger" upset him and he thought it meant that John Steinbeck was prejudiced. I explained that Steinbeck was trying to paint a realistic portrait of the lives of the people at that time, and that the people who used the word "nigger" were ignorant, poorly educated, and unsuccessful people. I asked him if he would do me a favor—read the rest of the book, since we were on the fourth chapter and the book only contains six—and then tell me whether he thought the book was worth reading, in spite of the way it made him feel. I told him I was seriously interested in his opinion, as well as that of the other students in class. Derek agreed.

When we finished the book, I asked the students in Derek's class to evaluate the book in their journals, paying particular attention to the way it portrayed black people. Most of the students, including Derek, found the prejudice upsetting but felt that the book was so good they should still read it. After reading their journals, I told my students that I was glad the book upset them, that decent, thinking people *should* be upset when anybody is treated unfairly and unjustly. Then I asked them to discuss the book in small groups and decide (1) whether I should assign the book to future classes and (2) if so, how I should present the issue of prejudice.

The final verdict, suggested by Derek's group and voted unanimously by the class as the best course of action: read the book in the sophomore classes, but not at the beginning of the year. As Derek explained, "You shouldn't read a book that has some kind of prejudiced people in it right at the start of the year, because you won't know all the kids in your class and you won't know if they are prejudiced, so you feel funny when you get to those parts. If you read the book later, when you know the kids in the class, and you have the rule about respecting people, then kids won't laugh or make jokes when you're reading and you can relax and get into the story." I couldn't have said it better, but I wouldn't even have thought about it if Derek hadn't evaluated that literature assignment.

2. Encourage independent thinking.

One of the biggest complaints students make about teachers is that they don't let students think for themselves; they insist that students come up with the "right" answers about issues that are subjective and should be open to interpretation. When you allow your students to think for themselves, and reward their mental efforts even when their ideas aren't brilliant or logical, you teach them far more about the process of learning than you do when you require them to tell you what you already think. Encouraging your students to think independently may inspire you to reassess some of your own ideas.

During our class discussion about the merits of *Of Mice and Men*, one of Derek's classmates studied the front cover, then turned the book over and read the blurbs on the back. He leaned towards Derek, held out his book, and pointed. When I asked Nate what he was doing, he said, "It says here that this guy won a Nobel Prize for literature. That's a big deal, isn't it?" I assured him that it was, indeed, a big deal. "Well, then, doesn't that mean this is a good book?" Nate wanted to know.

"What do you think?" I countered.

Nate shrugged. "Well, whoever gives that prize probably knows more about literature than we do."

"Maybe they do," I said, hoping Nate would continue to explore his idea.

"Who picks the winners for that prize?" he asked. I crossed my legs to keep from jumping up and down with glee.

"Who do you think awards that prize?" I asked the class. Most of the kids shrugged, but Derek looked at Nate who nodded and looked at me.

"White guys. Right?" Nate said. "Just like the school board approves the books we're supposed to read, and they're mostly white guys."

"I think that's very likely," I said. "We can research it in the library later, but right now I'd like to pursue this idea. You said, 'white guys,' as though they couldn't be trusted to recognize good books. You're a white guy and you have pretty good taste."

Nate blushed and glanced at Derek who was grinning at him. "You know what I mean," Nate said. "Old white guys don't always like the same stuff that other people like."

"That's very true," I said. "Thanks for reminding me to tell you why I put so much emphasis on reading and writing. I want you people to be good critical thinkers, who trust your own brains and come up with your own ideas. I don't want you to accept everything people tell you without thinking about it. When you read an article in a newspaper or magazine, I want you to analyze the political perspective of the publisher and the writer before you accept the article as factual and objective. When you read a review of a movie you've seen, I don't want you to think that there is something wrong with you if you didn't like a movie that some critic said was wonderful. I don't want you to accept a book as good just because some teacher tells you it's good. If you don't like something that is supposed to be good, or you do like something that is supposed to be bad, I want you to be able to express your arguments in an intelligent and articulate way."

I pointed to a cardboard sign hanging among the quotations I had posted to my walls to inspire thought. This particular sign read: "The surest way to corrupt a man is to teach him to esteem more highly those who think alike than those who think differently. —Nietzsche."

"That's what I'm talking about," I told Nate and his classmates. "Don't be afraid to think for yourself. It's dangerous to let other people think for you."

Nobody said a word for several seconds, and I thought they were busy appreciating my wonderful speech. Nate broke the silence and brought me back to reality when he grinned and said, "So, who says this Nietzsche guy is so smart?"

Acknowledge the Difficulties Students Face

Life is magnified and feelings are intensified for children. When they are sad, their hearts ache; when they are angry, they could just kill you; when they're scared, they think they're going to die. When adults tell them to "cheer up" or "grow up" or "forget about it," they don't become cheerful, mature, or forgetful—they become more of whatever they were in the first place. Perhaps one of your teachers told you that you "weren't working up to your potential." I'll bet you said, "Why, thank you for that insight, Miss Teacher. I see the error of my ways and I am going to apply myself and become a serious scholar from this moment on. How can I ever repay you for making me see the light?" Ha.

Maybe you can't remember feeling that the world revolved around you, that everybody noticed you, and nobody over twenty-five understood you. You couldn't possibly go to the dance because you had a horrid zit right on the end of your nose where everybody would see it. Everybody else had friends to walk with between classes, but you always ended up alone. Your older brother tormented you unmercifully but your parents never believed you. Or your parents were so unreasonable and cruel—refusing to let you buy a motorcycle or borrow their car to go camping with friends in the forest 200 miles from home, or making you come home hours before all the other kids—that you spent hours lying in bed at night, imagining how sorry they'd be if you ran away, or picturing them grief-stricken, howling into their handkerchiefs at your funeral.

It is human nature to see our problems as significant, even though we may realize that our neighbor's problems are much worse. To a child with a bad case of acne, those pimples are every bit as important as another child's broken family. "Maybe his mother left," the child reasons, "but at least he doesn't look ugly and disgusting like I do." Pointing out that another person has more serious problems doesn't help a child forget her own. Even if she recognizes that other children suffer more than she does, she won't quit feeling the way she does, although she may now add feeling guilty for being selfish to her list of worries.

Please do point out that everybody suffers, that pain is part of life, and that every time we pass through a painful period, we emerge stronger and better equipped to face future problems. But don't belittle your student's concerns. Acknowledge their feelings, accept their right to have a bad day or a worry, just as adults do. If they ask for your advice, tell them that you understand how they feel right now, and that you understand their feelings, and try to help them think of solutions for their problems. Just don't tell them that their problems are trivial. Nobody appreciates that.

Show Interest in Your Students as People

Not every child can be an ace student, but that doesn't mean they all aren't lovable and interesting people, and if you notice them, they are much more likely to be lovable. I'm sure I miss a few things, but I try to notice at least something about each student once or twice a week. I don't spend a lot of time on the little things. I might pause and whisper "spiffy haircut" or "nifty shoes" or ask the name of a dance the students were doing in the back of the room before the bell rang. If they wear T-shirts with slogans or logos on them, I ask what they represent and why the student likes a particular brand or person or musical group. (I don't comment on their lack of taste in music or fashion.)

1. Personalize your lessons.

When I hear students talking about hobbies or interests, I make notes so I can incorporate those things into my lessons. If I have a baseball nut or a weight lifter in my class,

I might bring in a sports editorial about the designated hitter rule, or a magazine article about the benefits of weight lifting as a way to develop self-confidence and discipline. Students respond to seeing their own interests reflected in the lessons.

As I mentioned earlier, an easy way to give an ego boost to every student in class is to include their names on your worksheets and exams. Keep a roster handy as you create your lessons, and check off the names as you include them, because if you skip one name, you'll hurt somebody's feelings. Also keep in mind the context of the sentences in which you include student names. For example, I once used a student's name in a vocabulary exercise, and he took offense at being associated with the word "pugnacious. " My student's name was Doug and the sentence read, "Doug is a good boxer because he's _____." I should have said, "Doug's friend Dexter says a good boxer has to be _____ and confident." (There was no Dexter in that class.)

If your subject doesn't lend itself to inserting names on student worksheets, you still can write their names in the margins of the worksheets before you make copies. Again, it's a little thing, but it gets a big reaction.

2. Build your own library.

When the library has sales, look for books that reflect student interests—race cars, athletes, animals, true adventures, nursing, movie stars, outer space, ghost stories, brain teasers and puzzles, science fiction, yucky horror stories. (I admit it: I censor the books I buy. I don't bring in true crime stories or books with graphic violence or pornography because it is my job to protect children from harm, and I believe those things can be harmful to young, immature minds.) Occasionally I give a book to a student; usually I keep them in my classroom to use as an incentive—students who complete their work early are allowed to browse and read until the bell rings.

If you take the time to locate books on topics that appeal to your students and create a library just for them, you will reinforce the message that they are valuable human beings who are worthy of your time and attention. If you tell them that often enough, eventually they will begin to believe it themselves.

3. Remember their birthdays.

Birthday gifts are always a big hit. I used to buy frozen cakes and keep them in the staff lounge so I could give kids a piece of cake on their birthdays, but the teachers keep eating the cakes. I'm serious. The cakes were too expensive, anyway, so it was just as well. I switched to "magic pencils." When the birthday student is seated, I grab a pencil and sneak over to the student's desk. I lay the pencil on the desk and whisper in the student's ear, "Happy birthday. This is a magic pencil. You can only earn good grades with it. It's true. I'm a teacher, and you know teachers never lie." Even the "tough" students can't resist a smile. I can tell it hurts them sometimes, but a little pain is good for them. It builds character.

I buy pencils with psychedelic patterns or cartoon figures on them and keep them in my desk. I have a stack of index cards for each class, which I have the students fill out during the first week of school, and the student birthdays are recorded in the upper-right-hand corners of the cards. I keep the cards in order by date and pass out the pencils when the birthdays arrive. For weekend or holiday birthdays, I either give the pencils the Friday before or the Monday after their real birthdays. During the last month of the school year, I give pencils to all the summer babies. You would be surprised at how excited teenagers get over a little thing like a pencil. Sometimes they smile shyly or blush, but often they jump to their feet and hug me for remembering their birthdays.

If you can't afford pencils, buy those sheets of cartoon stickers and some blank index cards. Slap a sticker in the corner, write "happy birthday" and the student's name, and you'll have a personal card. They won't care that you didn't spend much money; they will care that you took the time to remember them. If you've got the time and personality, you might solicit gifts from local businesses—stationery stores, fast-food franchises, insurance agencies, computer companies. Do be careful to give the same gift to all students in a particular class period to avoid giving the impression that you like some students more than others.

Note: We don't sing Happy Birthday in my classes, unless a student advertises his or her birthday. I leave it up to the individual students whether or not to publicize birthdays. Some kids don't want the attention, and some are afraid of being hit over the head with books, pelted with raw eggs, covered with shaving cream, thrown into the swimming pool, and other disgusting or potentially dangerous customs.

4. Use journals to communicate your care.

Private journals are my favorite way to notice kids. I supply each student with one spiral notebook at the start of the year. I buy them just before school starts when they go on sale for 29 cents at the local department store. During the first days of class, I pass out the notebooks and tell my students that they may write anything they want, whenever they want to, in those journals and they will be kept completely confidential. Unless they show them to somebody else, I am the only person who will read them. To make sure journals remain confidential, I write a letter or number code inside the back cover of each journal, where the code cannot be seen by other students. For one class, I'll use CC, DD, EE, and so on. For another class I'll use 50, 51, 52, and so on. (I don't start with A or 1, because students quickly memorize the alphabetical roster and can then identify journal owners.) I keep a record of the codes in my grade book, so I know whose journal is whose, but the students do not write their names on their journals. Within a few weeks I can identify most of the journals by the students' handwriting.

I give regular journal writing assignments three or four days each week, sometimes composition assignments concerning literature, sometimes free writes when students are free to write anything they want as long as they meet the length requirement (one full page for freshmen, two for sophomores, three for juniors and seniors). The length requirement forces students to develop their ideas more fully.

When I have time to sit down and read journals, I take a few extra seconds to add a personal comment to the student. I may thank somebody for being polite to the new kid in class, or for being punctual or kind or for working so hard in my class, or whatever is special about that child. A Los Angeles man named Fred, who read my book *The Girls in the Back of the Class*, wrote to tell me that he pretended he was one of my students as he read the book. When he finished reading, he wrote to tell me about the experience: ". . . Those journals you had them write really must have made them feel like someone cared. . . . Most people don't get me. They think I'm a weirdo or they don't think anything at all about me. . . . I still feel so invisible . . . thanks again for making me feel like I shouldn't hate myself."

You would be surprised to know how many students believe that nobody cares about them or notices them, that they are invisible. If you use private journals in your classes, please read what your students write. I know it's difficult to find the time to read journals, but if you can't make time, perhaps you shouldn't use them. How can you help your students learn to develop their thoughts and improve their writing skills if you don't read their writing? A check mark at the top of the page may be a quick and easy way to give credit for writing, but students tend to interpret a check as a sign that the teacher doesn't think the assignment—or the student—was important.

When you read your students journals, be prepared to have your heart broken and to be faced with decisions about legal and ethical issues. One young man wrote about having stolen a pistol from his friend's father and hiding it under his bed. Legally, I was bound to report the student, who would have been sent to juvenile detention or placed on probation. Another young man wrote about a time, five years earlier, when his cousin had taken him for a ride in his car. My student, who was eight at the time of the incident, sat in the car and watched his cousin blow a boy's brains out with a handgun. I won't tell you how I handled those incidents, because

I believe every teacher has to wrestle with ethical and legal issues and decide where to draw the boundaries.

Legal and ethical issues don't occur often via student journals. More often, you'll find your funny bone being tickled or your heart being touched by student writing. Each interaction with a child supplies you with important information that may help you understand the next child. When I asked my students to write their autobiographies, one young lady described her life when she was two years old. That she chose to focus on only one year of her life gave me a lot of insight about her self-image and attitude:

My big brother used to take care of me every day except on weekends. He was about eight. His friends used to come over and he didn't want to take me along so he would put a box and sit me in it and close it and stick my bottle in it and put a stick on top so I wouldn't be able to open it. I couldn't hardly breathe. Another thing he used to do is drag me by the hair if I would do something bad. He would change my diaper only once a day and never feed me. He would give me spoiled milk. He would be too lazy to give me fresh milk. That's the end of my life story.

A young man, given the same assignment, wrote about his persistent troubles in school:

Ever since I remember I have been disobeying my parents' authority. The first really disrespectful thing I did that I remember was in preschool at a Catholic private school and in those schools they have permission to spank and slap you. When I acted up, they tried this on me. This old woman was about to slap me and I kicked her in her vital area. After that school I got a bad reputation at various other schools. I'm not saying I was a bad student, I'm just saying I lack discipline.

When I got into junior high I started getting into more serious trouble. My grades started to slip and I got into trouble with the police. I flunked a bunch of classes in 8th grade, but I didn't fail because the principal didn't want to ever see me again at that school.

When I got into high school, I thought I would be able to change, and I did well for the first month, but then I got back to my old habits. I got into a lot of fights and got suspended about five times in one year. . . . The next summer my parents, who were divorced when I was about three, had a talk and decided that I should move to my father's house. They thought I would have more discipline there. So, in Labor Day weekend, I moved to my dad's and stepmother's house. It seemed to work. In the 10th grade I only failed one class, and it was only gym. I totally changed my attitude about school and my teachers, and I hardly ever get into fights with my parents any more.

That one change in my life probably saved my future.

By sharing his experiences with me, I understood that this boy was asking me to be strict with him, because he needed adult guidance and strong discipline. I also knew that he had been very upset about his parents' divorce and had acted out his feelings in school. He wanted me to know that he wasn't a "bad kid," in spite of his school records.

Help Your Students Become Successful People

I think students sometimes forget that our job as teachers is to help them succeed, not to convince them that they are unteachable or unworthy of success. Unfortunately, I think some teachers lose sight of that fact, too. Perhaps you had a teacher yourself, during your school days, who seemed bent on trying to prevent his students from receiving his precious A's. That attitude never made sense to me, and it's unfair to students. We need to remind students (and ourselves) that our job is to help them be successful students because the same skills that enable them to succeed in school—responsibility, respect, self-confidence, cooperation, and hard work—are the same skills that will make them good employers, employees, friends, spouses, and parents. At every opportunity, remind your students that your goal is to see them graduate with good grades and go on to lead successful lives.

1. Correction is not punishment.

Remind your students frequently that you correct them because you're trying to help them be successful people, not because you want to embarrass them or order them around. They are much more likely to cooperate if they perceive your corrections as guidance rather than punishment.

As you know, I advocate making any criticism or correction of students in private, to avoid embarrassing them and playing into the misbehavior cycle where you take turns getting even. Sometimes, we have little choice but to correct students publicly. When you need to have students change seats, for example, to prevent distractions or conflict, you can't very well do that privately. You can, however, remind the students that you are asking them to move because you want them to be successful students and you don't think that will be possible unless they move. In the chapter on discipline, I recalled an incident where two boys and I reached an impasse when I asked them to change seats and they refused to move. Only after I explained that I wanted them to move because I was trying to help them, and not boss them around, did they agree to move.

2. Teach them to read their transcripts.

Another way I let my students know I'm trying to help them succeed is by teaching them to read their transcripts. In spite of all the guidance that counselors try to give, few students understand their transcript or realize they can be corrected if they contain errors. It didn't occur to me that my students knew so little about their own records until one of my seniors arrived on my doorstep in tears one day because she had just been informed by the guidance office that she couldn't graduate with her class. She was missing one-half credit for math. I was as upset as Stacey because the counselors had visited my classes at the start of that semester and distributed transcripts to all of the seniors. I assumed that my students had followed the counselor's instructions to review their records and report any mistakes to the office immediately. Stacey not only couldn't read her transcript—she didn't know the graduation requirements. Since she was a bright young lady, I deduced that there were many other students who had no idea of where they stood in terms of academic achievement.

Stacey's situation stemmed from a course she took as a freshman. She failed one quarter of the first semester and was supposed to make up that quarter during the following three years. She forgot, and nobody in the office noticed the missing half-credit until it was too late to make up the work. Fortunately for Stacey one of the math teachers agreed to create a personal curriculum for her, and spend his own time working with her and administering the necessary exams for her to earn the half-credit. Thanks to that teacher, Stacey was able to wear her cap and gown and graduate with her class.

When the counselors scheduled their presentation at the start of the following school year, I asked them if I might make copies of all my students' transcripts so we could keep them in our classroom. They agreed. I created a form on my word processor that listed the specific graduation requirements for our district (see the sample at the end of the chapter) and made a copy for every student so they could see exactly what they needed. We spent an entire class period learning how to read the transcripts and comparing them to the graduation requirements for our school district. If there was an incorrect grade or a missing credit, I showed my students how to write a memo to the guidance office and keep track of the request until the correction was made. Guidance office personnel are among the most overworked people in the school system, so I don't blame them for making an occasional error. As I explained to my students, "It may be the counselor's job to make sure you have the right classes, but they are people and they can make mistakes. They want you to graduate, but it's your responsibility to make sure that you do. If your transcript isn't accurate or you don't have all the credits you need, they will say they are sorry, and they may be very sorry, but you are the one who won't graduate. Don't expect somebody else to be responsible for your success."

I gave each student a file folder to label, and we filed

their transcripts in a file cabinet near my desk. I explained that their grades were personal and they had the right to share them with others, but I would not allow them to see anybody else's grades. After each reporting period, when report cards were issued, we spent a few minutes recording the new credits on the graduation checklists. Invariably, several students would stop by my desk on their way out of the room on those transcript days and thank me for helping them. I'd smile and say, "You're welcome, but you know it's my job to help you be successful."

3. Teach them how to talk to adults.

Another obstacle to student success that you can help address is the failure of students to communicate effectively with adults. I'm sure you've seen the worst cases—the kids who can't seem to talk to teachers, counselors, principals, or parents without getting into an argument that makes both parties want to scream. In most of those cases, I don't think the kids are trying to be irritating. I think they don't know how to discuss or argue without putting people on the defensive. They don't possess a shred of tact. And, therefore, they think adults are unreasonable and ill-tempered.

Teach your students how to talk to you and other adults. Role-play with them taking the part of the teacher or parents, and you or another student taking the part of the student who wants to argue about a grade or ask for additional help with a difficult lesson.

Bad timing is the primary cause of student-staff communication problems. The worst time to argue about grades or request help is just before or after class. Teachers have a hundred little tasks to perform during those three or four minutes, and they may become exasperated or irritated by student demands. Tell your students that if they want to talk to you or another staff member, it's fine to approach you before or after class, but only to ask when it would be convenient to have a longer talk. When the teacher or counselor names a date and time, the student needs to write that time down to confirm the appointment and as a reminder.

Making the appointment is the first step; the second is gathering information. If a student wants to discuss his grade on an exam or report card, he needs to bring the exam or report card with him to the meeting. If the student wants to request help on a difficult lesson, he needs to bring the textbook or assignment with him and be able to pinpoint the place where he is having trouble.

The third step is the most important. Students need to use tact in their discussions with teachers. Stalking into the teacher's room and announcing that he or she made a mistake and needs to fix it immediately is not likely to inspire the teacher to say, "Why, certainly, Johnny, let me just grab my grade book and change that to an A." The teacher may very well have made a mistake, but that doesn't give students license to be rude. Nobody likes to look foolish, and teachers are in a particularly vulnerable position because they have to safeguard their authority in order to be effective in the classroom. So, when they are accused of making a mistake in grading, they are very likely to say, "That's the grade I gave you because that's the grade you earned." Or they may open the grade book, glance at it, and shut it firmly.

Instead of demanding, students need to discuss. Here are several suggestions:

> *I really want to earn a good grade in your class. Could you tell me what I need to do to bring up my grade?*

> *I've been trying to keep track of all my grades in my classes at home, and I must have made a mistake because I thought I had an A (or B) in your class. Could you go over my grades with me and show me where I went wrong?*

> *I really studied for this test and I don't understand some of these answers. I wondered whether you could go over them and explain where I got confused.*

These approaches give the teacher an opportunity to correct an error without losing face. There may be a mistake in the grade book, or the teacher may realize that a test question was ambiguous or that the student turned in work that was not recorded.

4. Use the power of suggestion.

Words can drive people to tears, make them fall in love, incite them to murder—and inspire them to succeed in your classroom. You've probably read reports of researchers using mental imagery and positive affirmations to help cancer patients. Children have the best success, because their minds are so fertile. You can plant seeds of hope and confidence in your students' minds by teaching them to use positive affirmations. (If that terms strikes you as too New Age metaphysical, or tutti-fruitti as my Grandpa Carl would say, call them something else—positive suggestions, perhaps, or thinking positive.)

I explain to my students that we're going to conduct an experiment, using positive suggestions, to see whether we can develop more self-confidence and be more successful by sending ourselves positive suggestions. For two or three minutes at the start of each class, we write our motivational phrases in our private journals. Quite often, students ask me for suggestions. I write several on the board and ask them to choose as many as they want to write in their journals. These are the most popular:

I am a smart person and a good student.
I am lovable and good.
I like other people and they like me.
I am successful and happy.
I deserve to be successful.
Every day, I am stronger and more confident.
I am a shining star.
I am a brilliant person.
I am healthy and happy.
I am intelligent, lovable, and kind.
I deserve to be happy and successful.

Note: This assignment should be completely voluntary. Don't pressure students to participate or punish them if they choose not to. You can't force children to become more confident any more than you can force an adult to quit smoking or drinking.

You can help your students develop self-confidence and a positive attitude by teaching them to pay attention to what they are saying. In her book *Feel the Fear and Do It Anyway*, Dr. Susan Jeffers explains how we can use words to change our self-destructive thinking. For example, instead of using phrases such as "I can't," "I should," "It's not my fault," Dr. Jeffers suggests using "I won't," "I could," or "I'm totally responsible." When students use strong statements, expressed positively, their perceptions of themselves change from powerless to powerful, from fearful and weak to strong and self-confident. Dr. Jeffers' "Pain-to-Power Vocabulary" chart is a good place to start. Ask your students for more suggestions of power words, add them to the list, and make a chart to hang on the wall of your classroom as a reminder to take advantage of the power of words.

Be Human

1. You and them against the world.

Students hate grammar textbooks, and they love to hate them with me. At some point during the first week of school, I point to the textbooks, which I have stacked on a counter or windowsill or some other obvious location. "How many people like those grammar books?" I ask. When the booing and hissing subside, I hurry to check the hallway to make sure nobody is listening. My students are intrigued as I close the door and place my finger against my lips to warn them that a big secret is about to be revealed.

"I hate those books, too," I tell them. "They are boring. And they're the same books you've had for how many years? Three? Four?" They nod. They've had them forever. "Well, I'm going to leave them right there on that shelf, because if you haven't learned that stuff by now, you're never going to learn it. Is that okay with you—if we don't use those books?" It's all right with them.

During the course of the year, I do teach grammar, but I make up worksheets with my students names on them, using the exercises in those grammar books as a guide, but my students don't recognize the exercises as coming directly from the text because they never paid much attention to them in the first place. Most of them copied the answers when they had to do those textbook exercises, or they got the answers from older siblings, or they already had good grammar sense instilled by their parents' example. And, whenever a grammar question arises, we use those books as a reference, but that's all right because we don't actually have to study them. It makes sense. Honest, it does.

If you have a lesson that must be taught, but you can't think of a way to make it interesting, don't pretend you think it is interesting. Admit that it may be dry and a little boring, but that students will have to use this information later in order to understand future lessons. If you can create a "Teacher and Students vs. Curriculum" attitude, instead of "Teacher vs. Students," your students will be more cooperative during those dry periods when you can't find a way to make your lessons creative and exciting. Tell them that you realize the lessons may be a tad on the boring side, but that you want them to be well-educated, so you are going to get through those grammar lessons, or that tedious classic literature, or that mandatory testing preparation together—and the harder you work, the quicker you'll get on to something more interesting. Also, remind them that if all we did was have fun, it wouldn't be fun anymore because it would become the boring, old norm. Say that with a straight face and they will believe you.

2. If something makes you mad, say so.

I'm not suggesting that you should pitch a temper tantrum every time something annoys you, but if something really makes you angry, tell your students and tell them why. I used to try to maintain a calm and pleasant attitude in my classes, no matter what happened, thinking it would make the students more calm. It didn't. It made them take advantage of me because they thought I would accept anything they did. One day, after trying for thirty minutes to get my

juniors to complete a worksheet on an important skill (giving specific examples to support opinions)—a worksheet I
had spent four hours creating and an hour copying at my
own expense—I lost my temper. I said, "You make me so
mad. I spent a long time working on this because I'm trying
to help you learn, because I want you to be successful people, and it really hurts my feelings that you won't even try. I
feel unappreciated and now I'm angry. I don't even feel like
helping you. If you don't want my help, then get out your
textbooks and learn this skill yourselves. And next year,
when your teacher expects you to know it, tell her you
were too busy goofing around last year to learn it."

Stunned, those juniors sat for a long while, looking at
me, then they did the worksheet. They learned their lesson
and I learned mine. They needed to understand that teachers are human beings, not anonymous, unfeeling authority
figures; I needed to understand that I didn't have to hide my
humanity and try to appear perfect. Several students
expressed their surprise, the following day, that I still liked
them and was happy to see them. They thought, as many
children do, that anger erases love. I realized then that losing my temper had been a positive influence on my students
because it provided the opportunity to demonstrate appropriate and intelligent nonviolent responses to anger, and it
provided a model for my students to use in dealing with
their own angry feelings.

3. Admit your mistakes.

If you didn't get a chance to grade their papers as you
promised you would, tell the truth. Tell them you had a hot
date, or vegged out in front of the TV, or had an apathy
attack. Then promise to get those papers graded tonight, and
get them graded. Don't worry that they'll lose respect for you
if you admit you aren't perfect. Just the opposite will occur.

When I first started teaching, if I designed a worksheet
or assignment that flopped, I'd pitch the papers in the trash
after class and forget about them. If a student asked, I'd say
they were on my desk. I'd stall until they forgot about them.

Then I realized I was being hypocritical. After all my talk about making mistakes and using them as stepping-stones, I was hiding mine, ashamed not to be perfect, afraid to make myself vulnerable to ridicule. The next time that happened, I distributed those same worksheets the following day and said, "I don't know what's wrong with this lesson, but it didn't work. I'll tell you what I wanted you to learn and the purpose of this worksheet. Then, I want you to get into small groups and discuss the worksheet. If you can come up with a way to fix it, we'll make a new worksheet. If you don't think it's fixable, then I'd like you to see if you can come up with a way to learn this concept or skill." I was amazed at what a good job they did of evaluating and redesigning my worksheet. I shouldn't have been amazed. After all, students are the experts at learning. They're also pretty good teachers.

Occasionally I slip into my old bad habits, and when my students discover a mistake on one of my exams, or catch me making an incorrect statement, I tell them that I made the mistake on purpose, just to see if they were paying attention. They never believe me.

Tell Your Students Every Day That You Like Them

(If you don't like your students, please please please find a different job.) You may not be able to like every student personally, but if you look long and hard enough, you will find something good about every child. Focus on the little bits of goodness and try to remember that they are reacting to a crazy world in a way that makes sense to them. Children don't have the resources and options that adults have. If we hate math, we can hire somebody to keep our books and manage our money, but children are stuck doing math for twelve years. If you remember your childhood at all, you must remember that twelve minutes is an eternity. Twelve years is beyond comprehension. So, children try other tactics to avoid having to face the math book, such as acting so obnoxious that the teacher sends them out of the room temporarily. Truly desperate children may opt to be sent out of the room—or out of school—permanently. In that case, it is the teachers and the system who have failed, not the child.

1. *Your teacher who loves you.*

It makes sense for teachers to assume that our students know we care about them and like them, or we wouldn't have become teachers, but what makes sense to us rarely makes sense to students. One unforgettable Friday afternoon just before graduation, one of my cocky seniors made a derogatory remark about teachers being losers and I said, "Excuse me. Do you think I'm a loser?" He quickly said, "No, but I wasn't talking about you. I was talking about the other teachers." I explained that those other teachers also chose to be teachers, most for the same reasons I did. I wrote "Why do you think somebody becomes a teacher?" on the board and asked them to give me their honest responses. Here's what they said:

So you can get the summers off. (*A lovely fantasy few teachers can afford.*)

For the paycheck. (*When I stopped laughing, I explained that it was the best job, worst pay I'd ever had, except when I worked in a plastics factory when I was eighteen.*)

Because you like to boss kids around. (*If only they would let me.*)

Because you can't get a real job. (*As opposed to this pretend one?*)

It's hard to get fired. (*Trust me, it isn't that difficult.*)

You want to get paid to read stories and novels and stuff. (*Getting warmer.*)

Finally, after their brains were exhausted, somebody in the back of the room said, "Because you like kids." (*Finally, a winner.*)

At that moment, I started referring to myself as "Your teacher who loves you." Every time I passed out a worksheet, I'd say, "Your teacher who loves you made this worksheet for you, to help you learn something new so you can be a successful person." At the end of each exam paper, I added the note: "This exam was brought to you by your teacher who loves you and wants you to be successful in your life." At the end of each class, I'd stand in the doorway and say, "Thank you for coming to class today. It has been a distinct pleasure being your teacher. I look forward to the next opportunity to spend time with you. Y'all come back now."

Sometimes, during lessons, when somebody asks the question, "Why?" I freeze and point and say, "Why? Because I LIKE you." Invariably, my students laugh. They roll their eyes and shake their heads—but they smile as they shake and roll. Why? Because they like to hear that I like them.

Maybe you wouldn't feel comfortable referring to yourself as "your teacher who loves you," but you can communicate the same message in your manner. I do recommend plainly stating that you like your students, because I believe they do need to hear you say it, as well as see you do it.

2. Seeing is believing.

Regardless of how many times you tell them, some kids won't believe you like them, because they don't believe they're likable or have been told for so long that they aren't. So how can you convince them that you truly do care about them? As I suggested earlier, one way to demonstrate your caring is to do assignments with your students—especially in remedial classes. I used to have a terrible time getting my students to write. My most uncooperative class was a group of twenty-seven remedial readers, all freshmen, although some were seventeen or eighteen and repeating freshman English for the third or fourth time. Those freshmen hated writing, couldn't spell, insisted they couldn't think of a thing to say, and had a thousand excuses you've heard from your own students, I'm sure. Even when I wrote three or four different topics, including "Whatever you feel like writing about" on the board, they insisted they couldn't write a whole page.

One morning, after arguing for about fifteen minutes with one student after another, I threw my hands up and nearly shouted, "This isn't so hard. I'll show you. I'll do it myself!" I sat down at my desk, but they objected loudly, and one boy accused me of having the assignment already done, hidden in one of my desk drawers. I grabbed a few sheets of notebook paper and moved to the middle of the room where I sat down in an empty seat between two gangster wannabes. "Okay," I said. "Watch. I'll write my essay right here with you. If I can do it, you can do it." They snickered, delighted at the idea of me sitting with them, doing their work. For about ten minutes, they ignored their own journals and watched me. Some sneaked down the aisles and peeked over my shoulder. I pretended I didn't notice them. When the giggles grew too loud, I asked them to please be quiet because I was trying to concentrate. One girl accused me of "faking them out," so I offered to let her grade my essay—if she finished hers before the end of the writing period. She agreed and immediately started scribbling furiously in her journal. (She gave me a B on the assignment because my handwriting was too hard to read.) Eventually, most of the students were writing. A few holdouts still sat watching me. Every couple of seconds, I'd stop, frown, look at the ceiling, and think very obviously. Then, I'd return to my writing. Soon, I saw students mimicking my behavior, writing and thinking, thinking and writing. Eventually, the holdouts grew tired of watching me and wrote their own essays.

At the end of that writing period, for the first time, I had a full-page essay from every single student in that class. After I had collected their essays, one of the boys asked me why I was so happy just because they wrote "a bunch of stuff." I replied, "Because I honestly think it's important for you to learn to express your ideas and opinions in an intelligent and articulate manner." He seemed surprised by my answer, so I asked why he thought I had made that writing assignment. He shrugged and said, "To take up time until the bell rings, and make us shut up," as if that were the only possible answer to such an obvious question.

I learned several lessons from that experience. One, some of my topics were boring, others were impossible to write about. Two, I needed to allow more time for writing exercises, to give students time to sort out their thoughts. Three, those desks are uncomfortable. After that day, I let my students move around the room and write in other places, as long as they did the work and didn't interrupt others. Four, those students were much more apt to believe their assignments were important if I spent my own time doing the same work. Five, if I want students to behave in a certain way, I need to model that behavior—showing them how to "think and write," for example.

Now I do all of the assignments I give to all of my students, in class whenever possible, and at home if I give them homework. I let students take turns grading my papers. (Usually, they're tough but fair; they give me A's and B's.) When I first started this practice, I was amazed at how many of my assignments were either too easy or too time-consuming—not challenging enough or so challenging that students gave up without trying. Even when I have a cooperative class, I do every assignment with my students. Working with them keeps me on track and makes them feel important.

Perhaps you're thinking, "She's crazy. I have enough work to do as it is." Yes, you are right. Teachers have papers to grade and lessons to write, but students have assignments from five or six other classes, too. Sometimes I do run out of time and don't get my assignments done. In that case, I tell my students I didn't have time to finish the assignment— and I finish it for the following day. What I lose in time, I make up for by spending less time on discipline, because my students don't spend much time arguing with me or resisting my attempts to teach them.

Reward Positive Behavior

Imagine that your supervisor approaches you, first thing Monday morning, and warns, "If you don't do everything I tell you to this week, you can kiss your paycheck good-bye on Friday. And if you really screw up, you can forget about coming to work next week." How motivated would you be to work hard? Now, imagine that your supervisor stops by on Monday morning and says, "Good morning. I see you're right on time, as usual, and working hard. I appreciate that. If you keep up the good work, you'll receive your paycheck promptly on Friday. In fact, there's a good chance that you'll receive a bonus, maybe even a promotion." Now, how motivated are you? You're the boss in your classroom, and your students are your "employees." Treat them right and they'll be loyal little workers.

Rewards for positive behavior are much more effective than punishment for misbehavior. In the classroom, this is especially true because we have such a limited amount of time. How we choose to spend our precious time sends a clear signal to our students about what we think is important. When we spend more time threatening and punishing negative behavior than we do rewarding good behavior, we make misbehavior seem more important. Children love attention, and many of them are so desperately in need of attention that they will act out, knowing that they will be punished, because at least they will get some attention. If we want our students to cooperate and behave, we must notice it when they do and reward them.

It is difficult sometimes to focus on good behavior, because good behavior doesn't demand immediate attention and resolution. Still, we must make an effort to ignore the bad and reward the good. Here are some suggestions.

1. Reward complete assignments and homework.

When you collect homework or classroom assignments, don't say anything about missing assignments. Don't ask, "Where is your homework, Jimmy?" or "Chelsea, why don't I have your paper?" Instead, look over the papers you've collected, find one that looks particularly neat or complete, and say, "This looks great, Jerome. Thanks for working so hard. I appreciate it," or "Camilla, you are a treasure. You haven't missed a single assignment. I think I'd better give you 10 bonus points in my grade book for being such a wonderful student." After you've complimented one or two individual students, thank all those who turned in their work. "This is good work, ladies and gentlemen. Thank you. It looks like I'm going to have a lot of good grades in my book this term." By focusing on the positive, you will not only reward and encourage those students who are working hard, but you will get your students' attention—especially those students who forgot their homework or didn't complete the assignments.

Children love stickers, but sometimes we forget that teenagers are children, too. They enjoy seeing a cartoon character or a gold star on their papers, although they may pretend not to notice. (Remember, the harder they pretend not to notice, the more they care.) When I have a class of students who hate homework, I start by giving stickers to anybody who turns in a paper. After a few weeks, I raise my standards and give stickers only to students who earn C's or above. Eventually, only truly outstanding assignments receive stickers, although I reserve the right to decide what constitutes outstanding. One student's best work may only be average for another student, so I reward them on the basis of their individual effort and achievement.

If your students are terrible at turning in homework, why not give out random rewards for those who turn in their work? Without warning, for example, collect the assignments and announce that you're going to write down the names of all the students who did their homework. Your students will want to know why. Don't tell them. Instead, make a big production of cutting a sheet of paper into small slips and writing down the names on the homework papers. Then, put the names into a hat or box, and ask for a student volunteer to draw one name. Give the winner a prize—a piece of bubble gum, a candy bar, a mechanical pencil, 5 bonus points in your gradebook, a waiver for the next assignment. Once per quarter I give a bigger prize, such as a disposable camera or an inexpensive radio with headset. The prize isn't as important as the attention you will be giving to the students who have completed their homework. Don't schedule prizes, and don't tell the students when you will hold drawings. Do remind them that the more homework they complete, the better chance they will have of winning a prize.

2. *Call or write to parents with good news.*

As an experiment, I sent notes home to the "problem" students in one of my classes. I folded the notes but left them unsealed, and asked the students to deliver them to their parents or guardians. Naturally, the students assumed I was writing to complain. You can imagine their surprise when they opened the notes, as I knew they would, and read good things about themselves. Initially, I wrote about ten notes, but after I saw the response, I wrote to the parents or guardians of every student in the class. Here are two examples from the first batch of notes:

Callie was a bright young lady who enjoyed making jokes at my expense and using her brains to think of innovative ways to irritate me, such as glancing at the clock every five minutes and loudly sighing. On her note, I wrote, "Callie is a very bright young lady with a wonderful sense of humor. I enjoy having her in my class." Jason, a restless boy who wriggled and jiggled and drummed on his desk, received this note: "Jason is one of the most energetic young men I have ever met. He is also one of the most well-mannered students I have ever had the pleasure to teach. Thank you for doing such a wonderful job of raising him. I wish I had more students like him."

Callie rushed into my room and told me that her mother had hung the note on the refrigerator so all the relatives could admire it. "Do you really think I'm smart?" she asked. I assured her that I did. She stopped watching the clock and started paying more attention to her work. Jason told me that his father decided to let him borrow the car after receiving the note about him. "That was hella cool, Miss," Jason said. "He almost had a heart attack."

Several parents came to Open House that year and told me that they had never received a note about their children's good behavior. "All we hear is bad news," one mother said. "It's gotten so that if I answer the phone and it's a teacher, I can feel my heart sink because I know it's going to be bad news."

Make a point of spreading good news. Once each week, pick up the phone and call a child's home. Tell Mom or Dad or Grandma or Auntie that they have a star in the family. Don't mention grades. Talk about the student. Find something good about your least motivated student—good manners or beautiful handwriting, artistic talent or sharp wit, boundless energy or a neat appearance. Your students may not say anything to you, but they will tell their friends, and they will be less inclined to misbehave in your class—not because they're afraid you'll tell on them, but because it's hard to resist somebody who likes you.

3. Create monthly awards.

Give awards in your classroom for whatever behavior you want to encourage—punctuality, perfect attendance, kindness, helpfulness, sharing, volunteering. Try to include awards for nonacademic categories. Report cards reward good grades, and if you give awards only for the best grades, some students will be excluded from consideration. Some teachers give playful awards, such as Best Excuse for Being Late, Snappiest Dresser, Most Original Thinker, Best Back-of-the-Room Dancer.

If you have access to a computer, there are a number of software programs that allow you to create fancy award certificates, with elaborate fonts and artwork. If you don't have computer access, make your own certificates out of construction paper. The students will be just as delighted to receive a homemade award as they would be to receive a computer-generated certificate.

4. Give bonus points.

Award bonus points for the behaviors you want to encourage in your classroom. If student squabbles are a big problem, for example, give bonus points to every student who goes a day or a week without fighting. Encourage punctuality by giving one point per day to every student who is seated and ready to work when the bell rings.

Don't worry about giving too many positive points. You can raise the number of points required to earn a specific grade, if necessary. Or you can keep track of bonus points in a separate book and award prizes for them, instead of grades. If you have trouble coming up with a good system, ask your students for suggestions. They often create very good plans, and you can count on children to be sticklers for fairness.

5. Thank your students every day.

Thank your students, as a group, every day for coming to your class, for cooperating with you, for completing their assignments, for working hard, for taking school seriously. Thank them individually and often. If you teach older children, you might want to make your personal thank-yous confidential. In some schools, good students are targets for verbal and physical abuse, and there is tremendous peer pressure to resist being recognized as a good student.

Read to Your Students

Good readers tend to be good thinkers. And good thinkers tend to be successful students. No matter what subject you teach, your best students are the ones who comprehend the material you present, who can read a textbook assignment without struggling to understand every sentence, who know how to use books as research tools. I have taught thousands of at-risk teens, and I would estimate that 75 percent of their problems in school stem from either poor reading skills or lack of interest in reading. Instead of viewing books as sources of entertainment, information, or inspiration, many young people, especially teens, consider reading to be punishment or hard labor. If you teach young children, they are more likely to be enthusiastic about reading, but as they grow older, their enthusiasm very often wanes or disappears.

Why don't kids like to read? I've asked myself that question so many times. I've read many reasonable answers: they are media babies, raised on TV and video; they are lazy because the standard of living in this country has made their lives too easy; our public schools have strayed from the fundamentals of education.

There may be some truth in those claims, but I think young people hate reading because too often we have made reading a chore, or a test to be graded and failed. We have taken the easy road, sticking to the same classics by the same European and American men, in spite of the many wonderful books by men and women of many different colors and ethnicities who more accurately represent our multicultural country. We have allowed various community groups to censor books to the point that anything the least bit interesting or thought-provoking is banned.

Also, I think modern children have a different sort of brain storage than children used to have. When I was a child, if I read about something that took place in Central Park in New York City, or in Paris or India, I had no mental picture to go with those names, so I had to rely on the author's description to paint me a picture. Children today have what I call "CD brains." They have seen so many pictures in magazines, so many images on television and videotape, that they have incredible visual libraries inside their heads. If you mention Taj Mahal, they call up a picture. They don't need to read a lengthy description of the palace, and if a story does contain a description, they become bored and restless with the detailed reading. If somebody else reads the description to those students, however, they are much more likely to slow down and pay attention, because they can concentrate on watching the "movies in their heads," instead of reading words on a page. That's why I read to my students, regardless of their age.

Even adults enjoy having a story read aloud. It allows our imaginations to work as nature intended. Before I read the first page of the first story, I ask students to imagine "the most beautiful scenery in the world." Then I ask them to picture in their minds "the scariest, most horrible monster in the universe." Finally I ask them to think of the "most beautiful man or woman." I give them a few minutes to think about their visions, then I ask a few students to describe what they "saw." They are amazed at how different their pictures are, and often become involved in heated arguments about each other's descriptions. When they are sufficiently amazed or upset or both, I interrupt them and say, "That is the magic of books. When you read the words on a page, your own brain creates a mini-movie that nobody else can see and no special effects could ever match. When you watch a movie, you are seeing somebody else's vision, and you are letting somebody else think for you. I'd rather think for myself and then, if I'm curious, compare my vision to other people's pictures. I always like my own better."

Essay and short-story anthologies make good read-aloud books because they contain short pieces that can be read in five or ten minutes. Some short-short story collections contain thirty or more one-page stories that take only two minutes to read. Sometimes, I bring in a stack of my own books and read one sample paragraph from each one, then take a vote on which to read. If there is no single popular choice, I read the top three or four choices in order of their popularity.

For young children, I'd suggest *Where the Cinnamon Winds Blow* by Jim Sagel, *Falling Up* and *A Light in the Attic* by Shel Silverstein, *Pippi Longstockings* by Astrid Lindgren, or any of the Dr. Seuss books. For older children, your choices will depend on your own tastes and those of your students. Here are some of my own students' favorites:

The Hobbit and the trilogy by J. R. R. Tolkien
The Casebook of Hercule Poirot by Agatha Christie
short stories by Edgar Allen Poe and Stephen King
Lake Wobegon Days by Garrison Keillor
The Hitchhiker's Guide to the Galaxy by Douglas Adams
I Haven't Understood Anything Since 1962
   by Lewis Grizzard

The Bean Trees by Barbara Kingsolver
Welcome to the Monkey House by Kurt Vonnegut, Jr.
stories and poems by Dorothy Parker
The Elizabeth Stories by Isabel Huggan
Mirrors Beneath the Earth: Short Fiction by Chicano
  Writers, edited by Ray Gonzalez
Mama by Terry McMillan
The Secret House by David Bodanis
Do Penguins Have Knees? by David Feldman
Outrageous Acts and Everyday Rebellions
  by Gloria Steinem
The Canterbury Tales by Geoffrey Chaucer
  (I'm not kidding!)
any book of quotations
Spiritual Sayings of Kahlil Gibran

Expand Your Students' World

Unfortunately, the world is a more dangerous place than ever before, and many parents have responded to the increased danger by decreasing the size and scope of their children's world. Sometimes financial situations discourage exploration. Sometimes lack of English-speaking ability makes people afraid to venture outside familiar boundaries. School boundaries also have shrunk. Transportation and insurance costs, along with concerns about student safety, have nearly eliminated educational or recreational field trips from many school curriculums. Therefore, it's especially important today for teachers to bring the world to their students, via electronics, books and magazines, audio and videotapes, guest speakers, and pen pals.

1. Introduce new subjects.

People are intensely interested in themselves. Take advantage of that natural interest by introducing your students to subjects they might otherwise never explore, such as handwriting analysis, palmistry, numerology, astrology. Make sure your students understand that you don't advocate all of the ideas and theories involved in the subjects you explore, that you learn about them just for the fun of learning, just to tickle your brain cells.

2. Bring in the experts.

Although you may be a dynamic speaker yourself, I still recommend bringing in guest speakers whenever possible, for a number of reasons. An expert adds credibility to the topic. You can talk yourself blue in the face about the dangers of smoking, but you won't be as effective as a speaker from the American Cancer Society who arrives with brochures, photos, statistics, and little jars that contain preserved pieces of a smooth, pink, healthy lung and a black, pitted smoker's lung.

Having an outsider in the classroom generates excitement and interest. Students in one of my freshman composition classes moaned and groaned constantly about how much they hated writing. When I invited an amateur handwriting expert to visit our classes and informed my students that the woman needed several samples from each of them in order to analyze their handwriting, they suddenly became prolific writers. By the time our handwriting expert visited our class, each student had completed more than ten two-page essays. She graciously spent a few minutes with each student and focused on their positive attributes. For months after her visit, my students bragged about their creativity, foresight, versatility, optimism, empathy, ambition, and adaptability. In addition to inspiring them to write, the visit provided a challenging and practical vocabulary lesson.

Inviting members of the community into your classroom strengthens community support and involvement in education. As my juniors and seniors worked on writing their résumés, it became clear to me that they desperately lacked job-seeking skills. I contacted the employment directors at several local companies, including major computer corporations, banks, employment agencies, and hospitals, and asked if they would be willing to come to my classroom and conduct mock interviews. Every single company sent at least one representative, and some sent three or four. On the day of the interviews, the interviewers arrived with employment applications for the students to fill out while their résumés were being reviewed. Each student received at least one critique of his or her résumé and tips for improving job interview skills. In addition to giving my students valuable practice, and allowing the companies to contribute to the education of local students, the mock interviews led to several real interviews for seniors—and many of them landed good jobs.

Another advantage of guest speakers is that they allow you to sit among your students and gain a different perspective on their personalities. Too often, we see only one side of our students, and we are unaware of the dynamics that occur in our classrooms. By sitting in the midst of them, you see a different side of your students, which gives you a better understanding of their personalities and characteristics. The better you know your students, the better you can teach them.

In addition to well-known agencies, such as The Humane Society, Planned Parenthood, and the American Cancer Society, there are many smaller organizations that provide speakers and individuals who will visit your class without charging a fee. Fire fighters, paramedics, nurses, beauticians, police or probation officers, biologists, musicians, artists, auto mechanics, architects, computer scientists, and carpenters can all provide information about careers, as well as introduce students to different occupations. Colleges and public libraries often carry lists of speakers or information about the nearest speaker's bureau. You also might check with the public relations or human resources office of your state or district education office.

3. Conduct informal sociology/psychology experiments.

Children tend to view themselves as the center of the universe, which can cause problems because they aren't aware of the effects of their actions on other people. By introducing them to sociology and psychology, you can help your students see "the big picture" and realize that they play a small but important role in a large society. Here is one example of exercises that my students voted as their favorites.

Ethics in Action. Students answer the following questions individually in their journals:

1. If the clerk in a store gave you back too much change, would you return the money or keep it?
   a. yes   b. no   c. maybe

2. If you answered a or b, please explain why. If you answered c, what would affect your decision—the amount of money, whether anybody else saw you, etc.

3. If your answer would depend on the amount of money, where would you draw the line, what amount would it take before you felt it necessary to return the money?

After students answer the questions privately, they form small groups (three to five students) and discuss the question for ten minutes. After the discussion, students return to their desks and write down their thoughts about the discussion, particularly if they have changed their minds and what prompted them to change. Finally, we take a vote in the class, and write the number for each response on the board, and students can see where they fall along the "ethics spectrum."

You can slant these exercises to fit your subject. Using the ethics exercise in a social studies class, for example, after your discussion, you could assign the project of researching crime statistics for ten, twenty, and thirty years ago, and have students chart the trend. Math students could figure the percentage of people who would keep the money or return the money, and the percentage of change before and after the discussion. Computer students could generate charts or tables to display the results of the votes. Art students could make drawings or posters showing the comparison. English composition students could write essays about their thoughts on ethics in general or stealing in particular.

4. Set up pen pal projects.

Now that so many schools have computers, many teachers have created pen pal projects using e-mail that allows students to correspond with other young people across the country and even overseas. But even if you don't have access to computers, you can design a pen pal project to motivate and educate your students. Pen pal projects lend themselves to any subject; students can share information about geography, population, history, and local customs. They also can exchange artwork, essays about controversial topics, reviews of books or movies, and debates about the merits of various musical or athletic groups. One of the best things about pen pal projects is that after you have designed and launched your project, the students do the work. Quite often, students will agree to design and coordinate the projects themselves, which is even better. To locate other teachers who are interested in pen pal projects, ask for volunteers at district staff meetings or state and national conferences. Also, state education departments compile directories of schools, complete with addresses and telephone numbers. A good source that many teachers overlook are community colleges and universities; college students in education, English, and sociology departments are excellent candidates for pen pals.

5. Make music.

For most students, music consists of songs they hear on radios, audiocassettes, or CD players. Even if they participate in band or orchestra, their exposure to musical instruments from different cultures and countries is limited. You can expand the musical horizons of your students, and motivate them to study the people, customs, history, and geography of the U.S. and other countries, by bringing in instruments such as steel drums, bongos, mandolins, dobros (U.S./Czech), harps (probably Greek), harmonicas (developed by Benjamin Franklin), maracas (Brazil), and castanets (Spain).

If you have friends or relatives who play instruments, invite them to perform for your students, and discuss the history and background of their chosen instruments. Undoubtedly, there are talented musicians sitting in your classroom, but students often refuse to play for their peers (with good reason). Some of those shy students will change their minds, however, after a guest musician visits your classroom.

6. Computerize your classroom.

If your school budget does not include money for classroom computers, find a sponsor to donate a computer for your classroom. Sometimes a local company will donate a computer, or the money to purchase one, in exchange for publicity via a press release from the school to local media. Create a curriculum for your subject that requires a computer, and write a grant request. Contact the public relations department of large computer firms and ask if they donate used computers. Put an ad in your local newspaper and on bulletin boards at the nearest college or university asking for a used computer (many hi-tech people upgrade their systems every two or three years). Ask your students to design a fund raiser to buy a computer for your classroom. Even if you can't access the Internet, you still can take advantage of the thousands of educational software games and programs.

Lighten Up

I think we often forget today that children are indeed still children because they are so much taller, so much more sophisticated and worldly than children used to be. I've had high school freshmen who were two feet taller and a hundred pounds heavier than I am, and students who started working full-time when they were twelve years old. My junior high school students know more about sex than I did when I got married at age twenty, and most elementary students know more about drugs and weapons than I'll ever know. Sometimes I feel as though my students are older than I am—and I started teaching when I was old enough (thirty-five) to be the mother of most high school students! But, no matter how old they act, children are still children, and they need to laugh, to play, to create, to stretch their imaginations and tickle their brains.

Make no mistake—I am serious about teaching, and my students know that their education is important to me. They also know that I like to see them laugh because laughter heals the body, soothes the soul, and stimulates the brain. It also makes a long school day much more enjoyable. If you're too serious to waste time telling jokes, don't tell jokes. But do include some lessons that make learning fun. Here are a few examples, to inspire your own creativity.

1. Timed responses.

Write a controversial statement on the board: *Boys have life much easier than girls do. Only high school graduates should be allowed to have driver's licenses. If I were King or Queen of the Universe for one day, I'd change a lot of things, starting with . . .* Give students ten minutes to write their responses to the statement. Collect responses and read them aloud, taking care not to reveal the authors' names.

2. One-minute speeches.

Write down thought-provoking questions on slips of paper. Put the slips into an envelope, and select a volunteer (or draftee) to go first. He or she draws a slip, and must speak about the topic for one minute, after which time the topic will be open to class discussion. The first speaker chooses the next victim. Sample questions: *If you had the choice between being very good-looking and dying at an early age, or being very ugly and living to be 125, which would you choose and why? If you could create one law for this country, what would your law be and how would you enforce it? What is the nicest (or meanest) thing you've ever done for somebody else, or that somebody has done for you—that nobody knows about? What are you afraid of that nobody would guess?*

3. Whiz quiz.

Create a quiz containing trivia questions on your subject or a variety of subjects. Give your students fifteen minutes to find the answers. Include multiple choice questions that are impossible to guess. Sample question: *What is an ort? (a) a small toad (b) a type of cactus (c) a Russian monk (d) a table scrap*

4. Library treasure hunt.

Make arrangements with your local public or college library to bring your students in one hour before the library is open to the public. (If your school has a ban on field trips, schedule a Saturday visit and ask parents to bring students—or use your school library, which isn't as exciting.) Divide your students into teams of four or five. Give each team a Library Treasure Hunt worksheet tailored to your subject area. At the end of the hour, the team with the most complete worksheet wins a prize (I usually give pencils or bookmarks).

5. Magic.

One of my friends and fellow teachers is an amateur magician, as well as a special education instructor. Through magic tricks, she can capture the attention of the most apathetic students, and squeeze in some math and physics without students ever realizing that they are learning while they are being entertained. Ask around. I'm sure there is at least one aspiring magician in your neighborhood. If not, find a book on simple magic tricks at your local library or bookstore and try a few tricks on your students.

6. Brainpower books.

Check the Self-Help section of your local library or bookstore. Mensa is one of many organizations that publishes workbooks that explain how we learn and offers tips for increasing memory and thinking skills. My personal favorite is the *Big Book of Games,* which has some wonderful fun brain teasers, puzzles, and word games that you can use as samples for creating worksheets and puzzles for your own subject.

7. Handy dandy research paper guide.

Because so many students either buy or steal research papers, or turn in a bunch of drivel that was tossed together the night before the deadline, I give my students the option of either researching and writing a real paper or creating a handy dandy research paper guide for future reference. Students who are college-bound usually opt to complete the paper, while those who are undecided or definitely headed directly to work after graduation usually choose the guide. If they change their minds later and decide to go to college, or find themselves in school courtesy of their employers, they will know how to conduct research. To create the guide, students must become familiar with the tools and process of research, although they don't have to become involved in an in-depth investigation. (See the sample Handy Dandy Research Guide Instructions at the end of the chapter.)

GRADUATION CHECKLIST

Note: This form is set up on a semester schedule. You may need to alter it.

Very important: Check your transcript against your report card to make sure you received proper credit for every course completed. If there is an error, or if you failed a class, make a note under the "Remarks" section and be sure to follow up.

Each X = ____ semester credits. Place an X on the blank for each semester you pass.

Grade:	9	10	11	12	Remarks
Semester	1 / 2	1 / 2	1 / 2	1 / 2	
English					
total (__)	__/__	__/__	__/__	__/__	_____
Math					
total (__)	__/__	__/__	__/__	__/__	_____
Science					
total (__)	__/__	__/__	__/__	__/__	_____
Soc. Studies					
total (__)	__/__	__/__	__/__	__/__	_____
Phys. Ed.					
total (__)	__/__	__/__	__/__	__/__	_____
Fine Arts					
total (__)	__/__	__/__	__/__	__/__	_____
Electives					
total (__)	__/__	__/__	__/__	__/__	_____

(_____) total number of credits needed for graduation

List Elective courses below, with date completed:

_____ _____ _____
_____ _____ _____
_____ _____ _____

(Find out if you must take Driver's Training, Safety Ed, Drug Abuse Awareness, etc.)

HANDY DANDY RESEARCH
GUIDE INSTRUCTIONS

Although you have chosen not to complete a research paper at this time, you must become familiar with the proper format for writing research papers—if you expect to graduate. Read the chapter in your textbook about using and acknowledging sources. Based on your reading, and your library research, complete the following exercises. (For this assignment, if you have a choice between MLA or APA format, please use the MLA [Modern Language Association] format. Thanks.)

Note: This is a heavily graded assignment and is due on _____. No exceptions. If you choose not to complete this assignment on time, and you want to pass this course, you must submit a standard 10-page research paper by _____.

1. Prepare a list of Works Cited (see example in your text). These must be actual works, not ones you have made up. Your list must include each of the following:

    a. a book by a single author

    b. a book by an agency or corporation

    c. a book by more than one author

    d. an article in a reference book

    e. an article from a daily paper

    f. an article from a monthly magazine

    g. an article from a scholarly journal

    h. a musical record, tape, or CD

    i. a personal or telephone interview

    j. material from an information or computer service

2. Select 5 of the 10 works cited above and for each of these 5 works, copy one paragraph from the original document. (Obviously, you can't use a record, tape, or CD for this one.)

3. Write 2–3 pages of an imaginary annotated "research paper," making references to the works on your list of citations. You may use the paragraphs you copied for #2 in this imaginary paper. Your paper doesn't have to make sense. It doesn't have to be logical or factual, but it must use proper format and include the following elements (see your text or one of the research paper guides for examples to follow):

    a. a title

    b. two in-text quotations

    c. two block quotations

    d. two examples of paraphrasing or summarizing

    e. two parenthetical citations in text

When you are finished, you will have your very own *Handy Dandy Research Guide to Writing Excellent Research Papers*. You are prepared! File your guide for future use.

Potential Problems

If You Can't Avoid Them,
Be Prepared

An ounce of prevention is worth a ton of cure when it comes to the classroom. Being prepared may not prevent problems from occurring, but you will be much more likely to solve them swiftly and with the least amount of disruption if you have a plan of action in mind before problems raise their insistent hands and demand your attention.

Gangs

Unfortunately, it's unusual today to find a class of students that doesn't include at least a few gang members. Many teachers panic when they see tattoos, bandanas, and other signs of gang insignia. Teachers need to use caution and care, as we all do, to protect ourselves from harm, but we also need to be reasonable. We need to remember that although we are not their advocates, we are not the enemies of gangs, either. They have no reason to attack us.

You can't eliminate the possibility of gang violence erupting in your classroom, but you can reduce the chances if you make it clear to all of your students at the start of the school year that your classroom is neutral territory, not gang turf. Explain that you expect them to respect your neutrality by declaring a permanent truce while in your classroom, so that all students in the room can concentrate on receiving the best possible education.

Although I do think it's important for teachers to let their students know that we don't condone gang activity, because many students base their own opinions on those of the teachers they admire, I think it's a mistake to lecture older students about the senselessness and stupidity of gang membership. Surely you remember being lectured as a teenager, and how unreceptive you were to the advice of adults who were too old to understand what life was really like for you. Lecturing teens about the evils of gangs is about as effective as lecturing adults about the evils of alcohol and cigarettes. Instead of condemning gangs, concentrate on teaching your students to think intelligently and independently, to analyze themselves and their choices, as well as their lessons. Focus on their future, and encourage them to consider how their actions and choices today will affect their educations, their careers, their professional reputations, and their personal relationships. Encourage them to set goals and work towards achieving them. Believe in them, so they will believe in themselves. Gangs are attractive to students who feel alone, confused, with little hope for the future. If we can teach our students to believe in themselves, to look forward to the challenges of life with confidence that they can succeed, they will have the strength to resist the lure of gangs.

Challenged Students

The first time a student arrived in my classroom in a wheelchair, accompanied by a special aide, I was unprepared and had to scramble to rearrange desks so we could place the chair where the student could see the board clearly. In my overcrowded classroom, there wasn't room for the chair to fit along the outside row or behind the last row of student desks. Fortunately, Frankie was good-natured, patient, and able to catch up with the lesson. After Frankie's first day in class, the other students volunteered to move their desks to make room for his wheelchair and replace their desks at the end of each class period. Other than that, Frankie needed no special arrangements.

A few years later, a couple of weeks after classes started, a knock interrupted my lesson, and when I opened the door, a classroom aide wheeled two students into my classroom. Unlike Frankie, these two students were unable to move their arms; they couldn't write or turn the pages of their textbooks. My other students took the arrival of Kerry and Lynn as a matter of course and graciously accepted them into the class, but I had a hard time trying to figure out how to include them in many of the activities I had planned, and I was at a loss when it came to adapting some of the longer written assignments for them. Kerry missed at least two days a week due to illness, and often suffered such severe coughing spells that she had to be taken directly to the hospital from my classroom. Eventually, I worked out a plan for grading that I felt was fair and equitable, but I would have been much better prepared had I known in advance that Kerry and Lynn were going to be placed in my class.

Be alert for signs of delayed mental or emotional development in your students, and don't be fooled by students who look and act "normal." If you notice any discrepancy between a student's verbal and written ability, for example, check the student's records. On two different occasions, I mistook a student's lack of ability for lack of motivation, and pressed the student to perform skills that were beyond his scope before I realized that the lack of progress might be due to some development problem and not simple laziness. In one case, a boy earned A's on half his assignments and failed the other half, and was so cooperative and responsive to my instructions that I assumed he only did the work he felt like doing. I subjected the boy to several lectures about responsibility and self-discipline—to which he listened politely—before I found out that he had suffered brain damage from a childhood injury and was not able to perform certain mental activities.

My experiences are not uncommon; administrators and counselors often overlook the needs of teachers when it comes to preparing them for special students, so we must prepare ourselves. Check with the counseling or scheduling office to see whether students with physical, mental, or emotional disorders or problems have been placed on your rolls. If so, ask what special programs or services are available to help you accommodate your students. Review your lesson plans and exams to see where you will need to make adaptations. If possible, find out the names of any classroom aides or special counselors who can give you advice or assistance with your students. Sometimes an aide who is assigned to your classroom will insist on restricting his or her attention to the special needs students in his or her charge, but often aides welcome the opportunity to participate as an instructor or assist other students when time and circumstances allow.

Also, become familiar with the procedures you need to follow to recommend testing or evaluation, so that if you notice a student in your class who seems to be suffering from some problem other than attitude, you can refer that student to the proper person.

Group Dynamics

Once upon a time, teachers could assign students to work in small groups, or assemble the entire class for an open discussion, without worrying about students trying to throttle each other, literally. Today, life is not so simple. If you randomly assign students to work in pairs or groups, you may inadvertently be placing rival gang members together, or pairing an openly gay student with an openly homophobic student. If you place the desks in your classroom in a large circle, to encourage free discussion, you may find some students unable to concentrate because of the provocative clothing or behavior of the girls or boys seated directly across from them.

Go slowly. Get to know your students and their personalities before you assign them to work together in any group activities. I've found it helpful to ask my students during the second or third week of classes to write down on a slip of paper the names of three or four students they would enjoy working with in groups. I also ask them to list the names of any students they never want to work with. If a student lists one or two students as nonpartners, I respect his or her wishes. If a student lists several names, it usually turns out that the student is either shy or antisocial. In that case, I call the student aside and explain that it's important to learn to work with all kinds of people and that I can only allow each student to name two students as nonpartners.

Inadequate Etiquette

"It's not my job to raise these kids," teachers often complain. "Their parents should be teaching them good manners. Not me." I disagree. If parents don't teach good manners, or if children ignore their parents' attempts to teach them, then it's up to us to teach them, if we ever expect them to learn. My first attempts at teaching etiquette failed, because I lectured my students and insisted that they should be polite because it was the thing to do. Eventually, I happened upon a more effective approach. I tell my students that I include etiquette and social graces in my lessons because I don't want people to think they are ignorant—I want them to be able to go anywhere, talk to anybody, and be confident that they will be viewed as intelligent, educated people.

Perhaps you have faced the same problems I've faced when showing movies or videotapes to your classes. Students shout encouragement at the characters on screen, or feel compelled to critique the program in loud voices. The first time I showed a movie, I was appalled by my students' behavior. Several times, I stopped the tape and asked them to be more polite. Each time, their courtesy lasted about thirty seconds. Finally, in the midst of a feature film, after several stops and starts, I realized that my students didn't know how to be polite. I stopped the tape and switched on the lights.

"What's the matter?" they wanted to know.

"How many of you talk out loud when you're watching a movie in a theater?" I asked. Nearly every hand in the room shot into the air.

"I hate you," I said. "And so does every other polite person in our society." They were dismayed and clearly confused.

"Why?" they wondered. "What's wrong with talking? Everybody does it."

"I don't mean this as an insult to your parents," I explained, "but perhaps nobody taught them how to behave as polite members of society, so they didn't teach you. It is common courtesy, when you are in a group, to be quiet and considerate of other people, especially when they have paid their hard-earned money to hear a concert or watch a movie or listen to a speaker. Enjoying some form of public entertainment is not the same as watching a movie at home, where you can rewind the tape if you miss something. While you are shouting at the screen, the person next to you may miss a good joke or an important line of dialogue that helps explain the plot."

My students actually seemed interested in what I was saying. I asked them if they wanted to be considered ignorant and ill-mannered. No, they certainly did not, although a few holdouts in the back row shrugged to show that they didn't care (although I have studied enough psychology to know that a person who doesn't care doesn't take great pains to show that he doesn't care). This time, when I turned on the videotape, my students were quiet for nearly ten minutes before they forgot the etiquette lesson. I switched off the movie during an exciting moment.

"What are you doing?" one boy shouted.

"The movie is off. Now you can talk," I said. They didn't

want to talk; they wanted to see the movie. I turned on the tape and said, "Now you don't talk." A few seconds into the action, I turned off the tape again and said, "Now you can talk." After six or seven times, they finally learned to stop talking when the tape started. We practiced that lesson a few more times, but by the end of that year, my students knew what I meant when I asked them to be polite—and sometimes they even showed me they could do it.

We need to remember that children don't want to be disliked or criticized. They are immature, irresponsible, and inconsiderate because they are children, not because they are bad people. We must teach them to be the people we want them to be.

Open Discussions

Perhaps your students behave beautifully, like the students in the instructional videos my college professors showed us in our education classes. Perhaps they sit with their hands folded, listening intently to each other's comments, and waiting their turns to speak, so that holding group discussions is a pleasure and a thought-provoking exchange of ideas. If so, you may go directly to Park Place and collect two hundred dollars. If your experience is anything like mine, when you announce that it's discussion time, your students either slump in their seats with their arms crossed, unwilling to risk the ridicule of their classmates by voicing their own opinions, or they are too busy trying to shout each other down to listen to anything anybody else has to say. At best, a handful of model students participate while the others sit and watch.

1. Teach students to listen before they speak.

If you want your students to participate in scintillating discussions, you must teach them how to discuss. You must create a system for choosing topics, staying on topic, taking turns speaking, adding to another person's comments, actively listening. Your system doesn't have to be elaborate, and it may require revision, but you do need to establish a definite procedure to follow. Whether you use *Robert's Rules of Order* or a few basic guidelines will depend on your students and your objectives for holding a discussion. I've seen teachers use everything from official gavels, to talking sticks, to stuffed animals to indicate which speaker has the floor. If your system doesn't work well, ask your students for suggestions. Find a book that outlines different procedures for holding effective meetings and adapt the procedures to suit your needs. Or you might consider holding a discussion about how to hold an effective discussion and have your students take notes and vote on the best suggestions.

Whatever course you choose, be patient. Give your students time to learn the new skills involved. Don't expect them to become effective listeners in less than an hour. If listening is a problem for your students, and they wriggle in their seats, concentrating on what they want to say next instead of what the speaker is saying, you might consider having students keep a notebook open on their desks. When somebody finished speaking, give your students one minute to write down the most important point the speaker made. Then, require thirty seconds of thinking time before anybody is allowed to respond. After several practices, listening and thinking will become habit, and you can close the notebooks.

2. Teach students to argue effectively.

The most important point to stress during class discussions is that an argument is not a fight. An argument does not have to have a winner and a loser. An argument is a discussion, wherein two people share their different opinions on some topic, and each tries to get the other person to see his point of view. Nobody has to win an argument. One person may change his mind. Both people may change their minds. Or, perhaps, neither person will change his mind—but both people leave the argument with new information, with a new way of looking at something. When you argue effectively, both people win because they know more than they did before their argument. In order to keep an argument from turning into a fight, both people must focus on the topic and avoid making personal insults or accusations. It is acceptable to say that a comment does not make sense, or does not seem logical, and to ask for clarification or an explanation. It is not acceptable to call somebody stupid.

If arguments in your classroom tend to become fights, ask your students to act as moderators. When somebody makes an inappropriate comment—calling somebody stupid, for example—the moderators intervene and stop the argument. They remind both parties that an effective arguer sticks to the topic. With a little practice, your students can become adept at arguing. Be forewarned, however. They may practice their newfound skills on you.

Nerds and Bullies

Nerds sometimes need our help to survive. Often they are targets of ruthless ridicule and physical abuse by other students. You may not be able to stop the ridicule, but you can help your nerdy student build self-confidence and strength by giving him or her added responsibilities in your classroom. Enlist him as an aide to help you grade papers or log grades in your grade book. Ask her to suggest exam questions or help you make copies of worksheets for your classes. As you work together, reassure your student that there is life after high school, and that some day, when he or she is in college or working, what seems to be a disadvantage may very well become an advantage.

In some cases, your studious students may need more than words of encouragement. They may need your help with the logistics of life. Reza, a boy in my freshman class, earned the highest grades in my class for the first quarter of the school year, then stopped turning in his homework. When I insisted that he explain his actions, Reza confided that several bigger boys in class had been accosting him on the bus, demanding his homework. If he refused, they threatened to hurt him, and he believed them. So did I. I told Reza to stop bringing his homework to class. Instead, he bought a supply of business envelopes and mailed his homework to me each night. It arrived a day late, but I gave him full credit. In the meantime, Reza convinced the other boys that he had stopped doing homework because his grades had dropped so far that he couldn't pass my class and he no longer cared. He earned an A on his report card, but by then his classmates had given up on him.

Another boy, a junior, was also very bright but earned mediocre grades because he refused to do homework. He traveled to and from school with a group of five boys from his neighborhood who were proud of their reputation as "too cool" for school. None of the other boys was in Sergio's class of at-risk students who had volunteered for our special program. Sergio wanted to earn good grades, but his friends and his reputation were equally important to him. When I threatened to visit Sergio's parents and ask for their help in encouraging him to do his work, he explained that he couldn't do homework because his friends would stop liking him and might even beat him up. I suggested a compromise. Sergio agreed. He began doing his homework, but he didn't turn it in during class. Instead, he rolled up the papers and stuck them in the back pocket of his jeans, where they were hidden beneath the oversize plaid flannel shirts he wore to school. Before or after class, when nobody was looking, Sergio would sidle up to my desk and drop his crumpled paper into the wire In basket. His grades improved, but his friends never knew. (Sergio has held an excellent job for the past five years and has received two promotions during that time.)

Most of us are less inclined to help bullies than model students, but bullies also need our help. The most important thing to remember is that bullies are cowards at heart. They are afraid, and they are weak. If they weren't weak themselves, they wouldn't spend so much time looking for other people's weak spots. Don't ignore bullies, because they— and the other students in your class—perceive your ignoring their behavior as tacit approval. Because so many young people look to teachers as role models when forming their own attitudes and opinions, I think it's important for teachers to challenge inappropriate behavior and make it clear that we do not respect or like people who hurt other people intentionally.

Take a tip from your classroom bully; find his or her weak spot, then expose it, privately, of course. Perhaps he feels less powerful or competent than the other boys in class. Tell him that the mark of a true man is the respect with which he treats weaker men. Perhaps she is jealous of girls who are more attractive or popular. Tell her you understand how it feels to envy girls who are beautiful or popular, but that true beauty comes from inside, and picking on people won't gain her any friends, including you.

Your bully may ignore you, but the rest of the students won't. Sometimes, just having your undivided attention for a few minutes will be enough to tame your bully—he or she may simply crave attention, and for some students negative attention is better than none at all. If a bully makes your class uncomfortable for you or your students, make an appointment with a counselor, a respected athletic coach, or the principal to meet with you and your bully. Ask the other adults to help you explain the importance of getting along with other people, and look for positive character traits to praise in your student, so he can see for himself how much better it feels to receive positive attention.

If nothing works, warn your bully that threatening or intimidating other students—even nonverbally—will not be tolerated in your classroom. When you catch him in action, make him stand outside the room until the rest of the class has completed the current activity. While he's outside the room, ignore him. Don't reward his bad behavior by giving him more attention. If he chooses to continue, and spends most of his time outside of your room, it might be time to consider a change in his class schedule or a parent conference. If he is stubborn enough to continue tormenting others and spends so much time out in the hall that his grade suffers, remind him that you are not punishing him, you are allowing him to make the choice to cooperate and be polite or to fail your class.

Depending on your personality (and your fear of law-suits), you might try giving your bully a dose of his own nastiness. I happened to see one of my students knock down a fellow classmate who was wearing a cast on a broken ankle and kick the boy's cast. I had seen the same student taunting the injured boy, among others, in my classroom on several occasions, and I was enraged. Without stopping to consider the possible consequences, I grabbed the attacker by the collar of his shirt and said, "I hate bullies. They are the worst kind of coward. If I ever see you do anything like that again, I'll show you what it feels like. I'll whack you with a stick." Of course, I had no intention of hitting the child, and I wouldn't have threatened to if he hadn't been smaller than I am, but it worked. He stopped tormenting his classmates, and they told me that he had stopped picking on them outside of my room, as well.

Peer Pressure

Peer pressure is a given for children, and it takes time for them to develop the strength of character they need to resist doing things they know are wrong. We can help them develop that strength by lending them some of our own. I remember telling my mother that I sometimes did things I didn't want to do because I didn't want to risk losing my friends. My mother told me to use her as an excuse when-ever I needed to. If she wasn't around, I was to tell my friends that my mother had already expressly forbidden whatever it was they wanted to do, and that if she found out, she would send me directly to reform school. If my friends asked my mother for permission, as they often did, my mother told me all I needed to do was wink at her and that would be the signal for her to deny permission. Eventually I was able to stand up for myself, but until then, I appreciated having my mother's secret support.

When one of my students, Tamika, confided in her jour-nal that her best friend had been pressuring her to have sex on a double date and had threatened to stop being her friend, I took a cue from my mother. I called Tamika in for a chat and told her that true friends don't hurt each other. "I think you need to think about what being a friend means," I told Tamika, "but I know you've been best friends with Patti for years and you really care about her. So, you can use me as an excuse. Tell Patti that I know you very well and I could tell something was up, and I guessed what the problem was. Tell her that I said if you had sex, I would be able to tell just by looking at you, and I would tell your mother. Your mother would tell her mother immediately, and then you'd both be in a bad pickle."

"Perfect!" Tamika clapped her hands. "Patti knows you're always in my business." It worked. Patti stopped pressuring Tamika, and eventually the two girls drifted apart, as they developed different priorities in their lives.

Usually, when I think of peer pressure to have sex, I think of girls being coerced, so I was surprised to learn that many of my male students faced the same pressures. One sophomore boy stopped in my room after school and shuffled his feet for several minutes before he worked up enough nerve to ask my advice about a girl he had dated a few times and who repeatedly asked him to have sex with her.

"She's had a lot of experience," Bo said, "and I don't have any. My friends say I should go for it, because I'll know what's up after this, but I'm not too sure. She says if I loved her, I'd do it. I guess I love her, in a way, but in another way, I don't." I pointed out the obvious fact that a girl who had lots of experience at a young age was likely to move on to another boy soon, leaving him feeling heartbroken and used. I also reminded him that, statistically, a sexually active teenager was at high risk for sexually transmitted diseases, and I listed several that Bo had never heard of, although he'd completed sex education classes. Finally, I suggested that Bo wait until he was sure he loved a woman before he shared his most intimate feelings with her. "Sex without love might seem like fun at the time," I told him, "but I think you would regret it afterwards, and you'd feel empty and ashamed of yourself."

Because so many other students wrote about similar situations in their private journals, I made a sign to hang in the front of my room, along with the inspirational quotes I displayed for motivation. "If somebody insists that you do something to prove your love, tell him (or her) that people who love you don't try to make you do things you don't want to do." When I hung up the sign, several students applauded, and some took out slips of paper and copied the sentence down for future reference.

Crushes on Teachers

It happens all the time. Patients fall in love with their doctors, and students develop crushes on their teachers. Don't panic if a student declares his or her undying love for you. Such feelings are perfectly normal, and eventually they will go away. In the meantime, acknowledge your student's feelings, but explain that they are inappropriate and unreciprocated. If a student writes you a note, whatever you do, don't humiliate the student by reading the note aloud to the class, correcting the grammar, or sending the note to the principal or home to parents. Tell the student that you appreciate his or her honesty and are flattered, that you like him or her, but your feelings are entirely platonic. Stress the point that writing love letters to a teacher is not appropriate. You must both respect your positions as teacher and student, and act accordingly. If the student persists, remind him or her again and allow time for reality to sink in. If a student develops an alarmingly unhealthy attraction that continues for more than a few months, do seek advice from the school psychologist or counselor.

Humor might be your best tool, depending on your personality and that of the student who has the crush on you. One high school sophomore persisted in flirting with me in front of the other students, even after I met with him three or four times to explain why his behavior was inappropriate. Ty was a confident, good-natured boy, popular with both boys and girls. Their amusement at his amorous antics encouraged him, and he became more and more bold. Finally, one morning, after Ty had interrupted my lesson several times to ask whether I had a hot date for the weekend, I walked quickly to his desk and bent down so that my face was about six inches away from his. "I'm old enough to be your mama, sweetheart," I said, "and that's how I think of you, as my lovable child. I'm sure you'll fall in love with some pretty young thing before long, but if you don't, and if you survive to the ripe old age of twenty-one, then you call me up and we'll go the movies. In the meantime, you'd better check yourself because I'm afraid you're looking at a lot more woman than you can handle right now."

"Oooh, you're busted," the other kids cried, delighted. Ty joined in the laughter, then stood and took a bow—but he stopped asking me out on dates.

Racial Tension

Don't assume that there is no racial tension in your classroom just because you don't see any visible signs. If you teach in a multiethnic school, there is a potential for problems based on ethnicity or race. Don't assume that your students know how you feel about racism. Make it clear that in your classroom, you will not tolerate any racial or ethnic slurs, including nonverbal putdowns, because you believe that all people deserve to be treated with the same basic respect and courtesy. Point out that you aren't demanding that they like each other, but you do expect them to keep their prejudices private.

"You don't have to hold hands with the people sitting next to you," I sometimes say. "You don't have to kiss them or marry them—you don't even have to like them. All I'm asking you to do is treat them with basic respect and talk to them occasionally. That should be possible for intelligent, civilized people such as yourselves."

Good Morning, Class

Make the First Week of Class a First-Class Week

We all know what's supposed to happen on Day 1 of the new school year. The teacher covers the ground rules, hands out the syllabus, takes roll, and gets with the program. It sounds so simple, and it would be simple—*if* students were assigned to the correct classes on the first day, and no schedules had to be switched around, and everybody showed up on time, and your roll sheets were accurate. Stop laughing! It could happen. But it probably won't, especially if you're a new teacher.

What actually happens is closer to this: The bell rings. Kids continue to trickle into your classroom. As you take roll, you are interrupted several times by extremely important announcements over the intercom, such as a reminder that any students who blow up the school will be severely reprimanded. Finally, you get to your list of rules. Halfway through rule number one two kids realize they are in the wrong classroom. They should be in B103, not C103. You send them on their way and start again. You're on rule number two when a knock on the door interrupts and you open the door to find a scared-looking young girl, who blushes and stutters that she thinks maybe perhaps somebody told her she is supposed to be in your class. You hurry to your desk to retrieve your roll sheet and find that she is, indeed, listed. You direct her to an empty seat and call the class to attention. They respond reluctantly, and you resume your recitation. Another knock. This time it's a boy and a girl; neither of them is blushing. They glare at you and thrust their schedule cards in your direction, as though it were your fault that there is a typo on their schedules and they won't be in the same first-period class with their best friends. Again, you check your roll sheets, hoping that the names of the two newcomers won't be there. But they are. And so it goes. You check your watch and say a silent little prayer that the next four class periods will be better. Dream on.

Dynamic Day 1

What's a teacher to do? First, hang on to your list of rules and your syllabus. Have them ready—it's good mental preparation, and you may be required to file them in your main office. But don't launch into them the first day. Why not? My niece Lila, a ninth-grader, explained it much better than I could. Excited about going to high school, she confided that she couldn't sleep for two days before classes started. I called her after the first day and asked how she liked being one of "the big kids." She responded with a long, melodramatic, teenage-girl sigh.

"It was soooo boring," Lila said. "All we did was listen to a bunch of rules six times in a row. It was just like kindergarten. I thought it was going to be different. Now I don't even want to go back tomorrow."

Aside from alienating your students, reading the rules the first day can cause other problems. When new students join your class, you'll have to repeat the rules for their benefit (which will really bore the other kids who have already heard 50 million rules). Or you could hand them a printed copy of the rules (which they may glance at before they toss them into the trash). You could ask them to stay after class (which will irritate them because they have better things to do, and, besides, they heard the rules yesterday from the other teachers). Or you could cross your fingers and hope they'll behave.

You may think I'm splitting infinitives, but it has been my experience—and the experience of the many successful teachers who generously shared their ideas with me—that the first day of class sets the pace for the rest of the year. The amount of disorder you have during the first day is approximately equal to the amount of disorder you will have during the last few days of any particular term. On Day 1, concentrate on grabbing your students by their overactive adolescent brains. Get a good grip. There will be plenty of time to talk about rules later.

1. Kick butt and take names.

There is an old Navy saying, "Kick butt first, take names later." Boot camp instructors use that technique to keep new recruits on their toes and to quickly establish who is in control. I use a modified, gentler version of that boot camp strategy, but my purpose is the same—I want the students to understand immediately that they are welcome in my classroom, but that it is *my* classroom and I am in charge. Depending on your personality and philosophy, you may choose to do something entirely different from what I do. What you do isn't as important as whether it works. Until you have the students on your side, you can't teach them anything. Getting them on your side isn't that hard. I have yet to meet a child who wanted to be a failure, who wanted to be disliked. That isn't natural. But many children, especially teenagers, act obnoxious and unlovable when they are afraid. They're afraid of so many things, but in school they have two particular fears—that people won't like them and that they won't be able to pass your class. Even smart kids worry about those two things, so I address their fears immediately. As soon as the first bell rings, I check the hallway for stragglers, then close the door and take a good long look at my students. Usually, they become very quiet because they don't know me well enough to test me yet. I try to make eye contact with each student before I begin my introduction, which goes something like this:

"Welcome to my classroom. My name is Miss Johnson and I'm very happy to have you in my class because I like teaching school. I want to help you become more effective students. I'm not here to pick on you or try to flunk you or to boss you around. But I will expect you to think. It won't kill you to think, but if you do happen to die from it, I'll take full responsibility for your death. I give you my word that I will never embarrass you on purpose. Now, how many people would rather go to the dentist than read out loud? Raise your hands, please."

There are always hands. "Relax. You never have to read out loud in my class, so you can quit worrying about that right now. I don't want you to hate coming to my classroom. I want you to enjoy reading and writing and discussing the books and stories and essays we're going to read this year. I want you to learn to analyze other people's ideas, compare different ideas, and learn to express your own ideas in an intelligent and articulate way. The more command you have of your language skills, the more successful you will be in school, in your work, and in your personal life—especially your love life.

"I'm serious. Think about it. We use words to get many of the things we want in life. Of course, you use words to answer questions on tests in school. But you also use words to ask somebody for a date. Or to explain to somebody why you don't want to take drugs or take off your clothes. Or to convince your parents to let you shave your head or borrow the car. And later on, you'll use words to make your future mother-in-law like you—and if you don't think that's important, you're in for a big surprise.

"But before we start talking about what we're going to do this term, and all the rules and regulations and official stuff, we have something very important to do. I am going

to learn everybody's name right now. You are not just numbers to me. Each one of you is a special and unique person.
I'm going to go over the roll sheet now and I want you to
raise your hand when I call your name. Please correct me if
I mispronounce it, and let me know if you prefer to be
called by a nickname." (I can't count the number of students
who have thanked me for learning to say their names correctly.)

As I call each name, I take a moment to look at the student who responds, to give my brain time to match the face
with the name. Then, I go down the list once more. This
second time, I try to find the students before I call their
names.

Next, I pass out 3x5 index cards and ask the students to
provide some information. Because so many kids are visual
learners, I write the instructions on the board:

Name:
Full address:
Phone number:
Birthday:
Name of parent/guardian:
Student ID #:

2. *The 3x5 card trick.*

As they fill out the cards, I write the names of any absent
students on blank cards for them to fill out if and when they
show up. Then, I walk around the room, between the aisles,
with my roll sheet in hand. I mentally test myself to see
whether I can remember the students' names. If I get stuck,
I sneak a peek over that student's shoulder at his or her
index card. When they are finished filling out the cards, I
ask them to turn them over and provide a little bit of extra
information on the backs.

"I want you to tell me anything I need to know to be a
good teacher for you," I tell them. "If you have dyslexia or a
speech problem, or epilepsy, or you just hate reading, let me
know. If you have a job, I'd like to know where you work. If

there is something special you'd like to do in this class, let me know. And something very important—I had one of those fathers who would smack me in the teeth if I got in trouble in school, even if I was accused of something I didn't do. If you have one of those fathers or mothers or guardians who go bananas and forget how to act, let me know so I won't get you in trouble accidentally.

"Speaking of trouble, there is something you need to know. If I have a problem with you in this class, I want to call you, not your parents. You're big boys and girls and you are responsible for the things you say and do. I want your real phone number on your card—not the number of the local pizza delivery—so I can call you if we need to talk. If you and I can't settle things, then I'll have to call your parents, but I'd prefer to work things out between you and me."

I give them a few minutes to make notes on the back of the cards (and for me to memorize their names), then I collect the cards. Instead of letting them pass the cards up to the front, I walk down the aisles and take each card individually. This serves two purposes: it brings me closer to them, which makes them nervous and more likely to behave, and it gives me another chance to match each name with the student's face. As I accept each card, I say, "Thank you" and repeat the student's name aloud. Then, when I have collected them all, I go to the front of the room and flip through them quickly, mentally testing myself. If I can't identify a particular name, I ask the student to raise his or her hand. Then it's time for the Big Test.

3. The name test.

I tell the class it's time for our first test. Invariably, they gasp and groan and mumble. "Relax," I assure them, "this test is for me. I am going to go down the roll sheet and see if I have learned everybody's name. If I get them all right, I win. If I miss one name, then you all get an automatic A on your first test, and you don't even have to lift a writing utensil."

Of course, I have no test prepared for them, but they don't know that. And I have grabbed them. Even the cool kids are intrigued. Sometimes a sharp student asks what I will win if I remember all the names correctly. My response, "I win everything," delights them. They can hardly stand the excitement as I work my way down the roll sheet, identifying them one at a time. They are certain that I'll miss and they'll get an easy A on that imaginary exam.

So far, I have managed to pass the name test every time. Usually, somebody asks me how I can do it. I love it when they ask that because I love to tell them, "I remember your names because you are important to me. When I look at you, I see you, because I care about you." Even if nobody asks, I usually tell them that because it's true and I want them to know. I don't care whether they act cool and pretend they aren't impressed. I know that they are secretly thrilled to be considered so important. Who wouldn't be?

Sometimes I forget half the names as soon as they leave the room, but they don't know that and it doesn't matter. I have another chance to relearn them the next day. When I do make a mistake and forget a name, as I know I will someday, it won't be a disaster. The students will be delighted at earning a freebie A, and even more delighted at having caught a teacher making a mistake. It'll be a good lesson for them—that adults make mistakes, too, and the world goes on.

You may be thinking, "What a waste of time! My job is to teach, not to show off my memorization skills." I would argue that you will be able to teach much more effectively if you take the time to know your students before you begin your lessons. Names are much more than words—they represent us. In many cases, children come to school emptyhanded. All they have to bring with them are their names.

Or perhaps you're thinking, "But I could never learn 100 kids' names in one day!" If that's the case, give your students sheets of 8x10-inch construction paper and pass around a few felt-tip markers. Ask them to print their first names in large letters and then fold the papers in half to make name cards that will stand up on their desks so you can see them.

Spending time on names is worth your time and effort because it pays off. First, it demonstrates to the students that you care about them because you are willing to take the time to get to know them. Second, people are much more apt to misbehave if they are anonymous members of a crowd. If you say, "You boys in the back settle down now," or "You girls stop that giggling right this minute," the boys are likely to go on punching each other's arms and the girls may put their hands over their mouths and go right on giggling. But if you say, "Jimmy Saunders, please keep your hands on your own desk," or "Shamica Abdul-Haqq, please be quiet so the others can hear me," Jimmy and Shamica are much more likely to obey.

Learning everybody's name sometimes takes the entire period if I have a big class. When that happens, I don't try to squeeze in any other activities. Just before the bell rings, I say, "It has been a distinct pleasure being your teacher. I look forward to my next opportunity." Then, I stand in the doorway and smile as my students file out. I wave and drawl, "Y'all come back now." They roll their eyes and laugh at me, but they leave my room smiling, and a group of laughing teenagers is a lovely sight.

4. Getting to know you.

If we get through my introduction, the index cards, and the name test with ten or fifteen minutes to spare on the first day, I pass out a worksheet entitled "Getting to Know You." If we don't have time, I make it the first item on the agenda for the second day. (See the end of the chapter for the Getting to Know You worksheet.)

This worksheet may seem like a silly assignment to the students, but it accomplishes some serious objectives. First, it makes my students laugh, which breaks the tension that often occurs when they are placed into a room with peers they don't know or don't like. Second, it occupies them while I check out their hair, clothing, jewelry, facial expressions, interactions with each other, and body language—things that give me clues to their economic backgrounds, attitudes, social groupings, and so on. Third, it reveals quite a bit about their personalities:

- Some students can't think of a single good thing about themselves (question 6), which alerts me to possible confidence problems.

- Question 3 may give me valuable information about learning styles.

- Kids who choose d for question 11 may have reading problems or dyslexia.

- Responses to question 12 often indicate personal problems or concerns.

You don't have to be a psychologist to recognize the anger in this boy's response: he said he'd like to be invisible so he could kill his parents without getting caught. I interpreted his response as an attempt to shock me, a joke, or a cry for help. As it turned out, it was a cry for help. He continued to write about his family in his private journal and eventually agreed to talk to a counselor who helped him learn to cope with his life.

5. Do anything—except what they expect.

What you choose to do on the first day doesn't matter as much as whether it's interesting. Welcome the students to your classroom and tell them how much you look forward to working with them. (If you don't look forward to working with them, I urge you to find another job.) Tell them how much you like your particular subject—and why you chose to teach it. Tell them what they are going to learn during this term, but don't go into great detail about what you will cover during the course. Keep it short and simple.

Now, grab their attention somehow. Entertain them with a slide show, shock them with statistics about things that affect their lives, tempt them with a word puzzle, challenge them with a difficult question, inspire them with a motivational pep talk. Do anything *except* what they expect you to do. They expect you to talk about rules and regulations and course requirements and standard procedures. So, talk about something else, anything else. Catch them off guard.

If you're a scholarly type, pass out copies of a recent newspaper editorial on a topic that is related to the subject you teach. Ask them to read the editorial and jot down their response in one or two brief paragraphs. This quick assignment will give you a lot of information about their academic skills: reading rates, reading comprehension, and composition skills. It also will give you information about their personalities: their confidence in expressing their own opinions, their attitudes and opinions, their willingness to cooperate with your requests.

If you're an English or drama teacher, or a ham, recite Hamlet's "To Be or Not to Be" soliloquy and ask your students what it means. Music teachers, English teachers, social studies teachers could all quote a popular rap song and ask students what they think of the lyrics. A history teacher might ask them to write down a list of the three most important inventions ever created by humans. In art class, ask them to sketch their self-portraits as they think they will look when they are seventy years old.

Tips from Some Pros

Before I became a teacher, I mentioned to a friend that I was thinking of entering the field. Shortly thereafter, she invited me to her home for a dinner party. She didn't tell me until dessert was served that all of the other guests were teachers. She said she wanted to give me a chance to hear them talk about their profession without trying to influence me. What I heard was entertaining, and instructive. At one point, somebody asked the question: *What is the first thing you do on the first day of school?* The answers were wonderful.

One man, rather small and slim in stature, said that he stands in the doorway of his classroom and shakes the hand of each student who enters. He introduces himself by name and welcomes them to his classroom. "They know right away that I am the boss and it is my classroom," he said, "but they don't feel threatened." (*Yes, I used his example.*)

Another teacher, a rotund woman, said she enters the

room armed with a Polaroid camera. "As soon as the little stinkers are seated, I go up and down the aisles and take their individual pictures," she explained. "When they're developed, I write their names on them and tack them to the bulletin board next to my desk. I tell them, 'I know who you are, and don't you forget it.' They remember, all right." (*I used a version of her example, too.*)

One of the younger women said she used to have problems because of her youth, slim figure, and soft voice. "The first year, I had a hard time getting their attention and respect," she said. "So I got smart. Now, on the first day of class, I wear a suit and carry a briefcase. I wait until the bell has rung and the students are seated. Then I fling open the door and stride into that room with an air of urgency. I slap the briefcase down on my desk and write my name on the board in big letters before I ever say a word. They pay attention." (*She gave me the incentive to try different personas.*)

Be Prepared for "Test the Teacher"

Your students may begin to test your tolerance during your first class period. A couple of kids in the back row may begin talking or passing notes while you're addressing the class. Somebody may get up and walk across the room to talk to a friend. What will you do if those things happen? Your reaction will set the tone for the rest of the year. Remember, you are still establishing your teacher persona. If you want to be seen as a no-nonsense, strict disciplinarian, by all means come down hard and fast. But if you aren't comfortable with a Teacher vs. Student environment, don't let them draw you into a confrontation so easily. You will have to do something, but you don't have to let your students dictate your behavior.

It takes time for your students to trust teachers, and true respect can't occur without trust, so give them some time to get used to the idea that you are a wonderful person. Don't take it personally if they don't cooperate during the first days of class. There are a lot of reasons why they may act disruptive or challenge your authority, but the odds are very good that you aren't the reason. Here are just a few examples of student behavior in my own classes. I wouldn't have guessed the reasons in any of these cases.

- A boy leaped out of his seat, overturned his desk, and started shouting and shaking his fists, then ran out of the room. He refused to explain his behavior, but one of his friends told me, in confidence, that a girl had been sitting across from the boy who jumped out of his seat, crossing and uncrossing her legs seductively, and the boy wanted out of the room because he was becoming physically uncomfortable.

- A girl hit the boy seated next to her and then refused to explain her behavior or come out into the hallway with me to discuss the problem. Thinking perhaps the boy had taunted her, I told her to sit down and behave herself. Her response was to hit a different boy in the head. I saw no choice but to call the office and ask for somebody to come and escort the girl out of my room. Much later, after she learned to trust me, the girl confided that she had wanted to be sent home from school that day because she had to use the bathroom and was afraid she would be assaulted in the school bathroom (she had previously been assaulted twice by older girls).

- A boy threw a dictionary at my head. (If you read *My Posse Don't Do Homework*, you'll recognize Emilio.) He wanted out of my classroom because he couldn't read and was afraid I would find out his secret.

- A girl walked into my classroom, took one look at me, and flopped into a seat with bad attitude scrawled across her face. She refused to do anything I asked her, except to leave my room. After several visits to the counselor's office, the girl admitted that her parents were recently divorced and she had been sent to live with her father and stepmother, a woman she detested. Unfortunately, I looked very much like her stepmother and it upset her to be around me. (When she discovered how lovable I am, she agreed to overlook my appearance and stay in my classroom.)

I could go on, but you get the picture. Don't take your students' behavior personally. Don't assume that every challenge to your authority is an intentional sign of disrespect. Unless a student insults you specifically and personally, assume that it is your status as teacher, adult, or authority figure that is the target of the disrespect. Continue to demonstrate the kind of respect you want your students to show you.

Let's Get Acquainted

Sometime during the first few days of class, take time to introduce your students to each other. I think it's sad for children to sit in the same room with each other for a few months, much less an entire year, and not know each other's names. There's another reason why I think they should know each other. Just as they are less likely to raise a ruckus if they know you can identify them by name, they are more likely to treat each other well if they know each other.

1. Getting to know you—from a safe distance.

Games designed to help people get acquainted work much better for small children and adults than they do for older elementary and secondary school students. Why? Because little kids are usually too innocent to be truly cruel, and adults are usually too polite or too dependent upon their paychecks, but kids in between are expert at humiliating each other. Another consideration, which breaks my heart, is that many of our children today are involved in, or targets of, gangs. What may seem to you to be a simple game designed to give students a chance to become acquainted may create an uncomfortable or dangerous situation for some of them. I would not recommend pairing students or forming small groups until you know them well enough to be sure that your grouping won't cause problems.

2. Interviews can be traumatic.

One of the most popular introductory games in school (and college) is Interviews. You've probably played it more than once. The teacher instructs the students to pair off and interview each other, then introduce their partners to the class. This exercise appeals to teachers because it's quick and simple. It doesn't take much time and requires only pencils and paper. But for many students, this activity is an exercise in embarrassment and agony. Here are just a few reasons:

• A handful of students is always left out—nobody wants to be their partners. They feel rejected and unlovable. If the teacher forces people to join them, they feel even worse, even if their partners are polite.

• Some students are so shy that having to speak in front of the class is a major trauma, especially on the first day when they don't know the other kids. Students are quick to pick up on weaknesses such as lisps, accents, stutters, blushing—and often will use them to taunt the quiet ones.

Preadolescence and puberty cause all kinds of physical conditions that embarrass children: budding breasts, acne, sudden voice changes, random facial hair, uncontrollable physiological responses to stimuli. Sometimes the worst thing you can do to a child is make her or him the center of attention.

3. The Adjective Game is a winner.

If you decide to use a game to give the students time to get acquainted, try to select a game that doesn't require speaking or standing in front of the group. One of my college professors used a game that worked very well—the Adjective Game. He asked each student to give his or her first name and an adjective that best described his or her personality at that particular moment. The outgoing students chose rhyming or alliterative names—Delirious Debra or Marvelous Marvin. The more private students gave quick, simple responses such as Tired Jerome or Quiet Miranda. We all got an idea of the other students' personalities without focusing a lot of attention on them.

I've used the Adjective Game in my high school classrooms with great success. I add another element, however, to help the kids learn each other's names. As each student gives an adjective and name, I jot them down on a sheet of paper. After the first five people have given their first names and adjectives, I point to the first student and ask the class, "Who is this?" They call out the adjective and name, and move to the second student, and so on. After each group of five students, I go back and start with number 1 and work my way back to the last student who has been introduced. When we reach the end of the line, I start with number 1 and go all the way around the room, asking for the name of each student. Then I instruct the students to get out a pen and paper, number it from 1 to 30 (or however many students are in the class), and get ready for the Adjective Exam. Reading from my name list, in random order, I give an adjective and ask the students to write down the correct student's name. (I number my list so I know which names I've used and in which order.) When I have read all the adjectives and the students have listed all the names, I quickly go over the list, giving the correct names. Then I ask to see the hands of the people who got them all right, or who missed one or two. I award boxes of Animal Crackers or spiffy pencils to the students who correctly identify the most names.

Aside from being fun and giving the students a chance to learn each other's names and a little about their personalities, this game also gives me important information. The students who remember the most names are the auditory learners in your group, the ones who will learn most quickly from oral instruction and who probably will do the most talking during class because they need to hear themselves speak in order to learn.

Don't be put off by kids who roll their eyes and shake their heads at your silliness. If they have enough sense of humor to laugh at you, they'll probably go along with the game. But if you have a truly tough class, as I have had, and you see that the ringleaders are going to ruin the game or refuse to play, you'll have to make some quick choices. You can ignore the party poopers and play with the kids who cooperate, which sends the message that the students who cooperate are going to get more attention from you than the ones who don't—not a bad message. You can ask the non-participants to step outside the room until you are finished, which is risky because they may refuse to go and that would give them two free points because they would have succeeded in their goal of getting you to abandon your plans and fight with them—not a good precedent to set. You can stop the game, without explanation, and move on to the next item on your list, preferably a worksheet or a reading assignment, which might be a good response because you will have made it clear to everybody that if they don't want to play, you have plenty of work for them to do—not a bad message. Trust your instincts.

After the Names and Games

1. What do your students need?

I give the counselors three or four days to straighten out student schedules before I review the rules or present any material that students will need in order to complete future assignments. But I don't waste time. I use those first days to find out what I need to teach. I've had remedial freshman English classes where students had much higher reading levels than I had been told to expect. And I have had accelerated classes where students needed considerable instruction in basic grammar and composition.

Now I begin every class with a diagnostic exam. I include sample questions from chapter tests, semester reviews, and final exams, to find out how much my students already know. If the results show that the majority of the class needs to back up and cover some old ground, I plan accordingly. On the other hand, if nobody misses more than one or two grammar questions, I eliminate the easiest lessons I had planned in that area.

Responses to reading are a good way to find out what your students know about your subject. Find an essay, an editorial, a feature article in a newspaper or magazine, and make copies for your students. Have them read the article and write a response to the content (for younger students, I may require a paragraph or a page; for senior high school students, I require two pages). This not only gives you information about students' analytical thinking and com-position skills, it also gives them good practice for the kinds of writing they will be expected to do if and when they attend college. At one time, I taught freshman composition at a four-year university. My freshmen, all high school honors students, had a terrible time coming up with their own theses—they wanted me to tell them what to say. When I returned to the high school classroom, I immedi-ately added many more open-ended writing assignments to my lessons.

2. Review your rules.

Two or three days into the semester or quarter, when you're relatively certain that most of the students sitting in your classroom belong there, it's time to review the rules. If some-thing is important to you—punctuality, for example—then make a rule about it. If something isn't extremely important, why give the kids ideas?

A few big rules are much easier to enforce than a long list of little ones (and easier for your students to remem-ber). As I explained in the previous chapter, I provide one single rule that expresses the lesson I most want to teach my students: *Respect yourself and the other people in this room.*

3. Give students your game plan.

Remember the first day of your college courses—when the professor would distribute copies of the course outline and syllabus and then dismiss the class so you could get started on the reading assignments? I use a modified version of that approach with my students. They're too young to be sent home to work, so I hold them hostage, but I try to instill the habit of using long- and short-term planning. I use a monthly planning calendar form and fill in important dates, such as major exams or due dates for graded essays. I distribute the calendars and instruct them to keep the calendars in their English notebooks so they can add other important dates and progress checks.

My basic course outline and objectives, a requirement for many school districts, is only one page. (See the sample Outline and Objectives at the end of this chapter.) I include my phone number; some teachers prefer not to. Perhaps I'm lucky. Once in a while, a student will call, just to find out whether I gave them my real number, but I've never had a problem with inappropriate phone calls—even when I teach "bad" students who live in "bad" neighborhoods.

4. Use Maslow's theory to help students understand themselves.

Young people are more interested in themselves than any other topic. They are also most confused about themselves, and that confusion often leads to problems in school. (Excuse me. I just heard somebody think out loud, "Oh, right. I need one more thing to add to my already overcrowded curriculum. Between school holidays, pictures, pep rallies, assemblies, and administrative busywork, I don't have time to cover the textbook, much less try to teach psychology." You're absolutely right. It isn't your job, so you may decide to skip over this section. But . . . if you have problem students who make you want to change professions, then you might consider discussing Abraham

Maslow's theory with your students. It will only take a few minutes, and it may save you many hours of aggravation.)

At some time during your teacher training, you probably had a quick course, maybe two, in child psychology, so you've probably read at least one interpretation of Maslow's Hierarchy of Needs. I'd like to add my version to your repertoire. I first discussed this idea with a class of students who had serious problems resisting the lure of gangs, drugs, shoplifting, and sex. We began talking about why people do what they do, and I told them that during my college studies in psychology, I learned that we often do things because we need to belong to something. No matter how many times we promise ourselves that we will be independent and stand our ground, we end up giving in and doing things we regret. Then we hate ourselves.

"That's me. That's me." One of my students waved her hand in the air. "I'm always going shopping with my sister and her friends and they always steal stuff from stores and I say I'm not going to do it, but then I go right ahead and do it and I always wish I didn't. I swear I won't go with them again, but the next time they ask me, there I go, doing what I said I wouldn't and I feel so bad, especially when I go to church and sit next to my grandma and think about how ashamed she would be if she knew."

I assured Tyeisha that she wasn't horrible, simply human, because it's human nature to want to belong and be accepted by a group of people. That's why we join clubs and social organizations, including gangs. We just need to belong and feel accepted for who we are.

"How many of you have a family, people who love you, but you still feel like you don't really belong?" I asked my class. More than half of the students raised their hands. "You aren't the Lone Ranger," I told them. "Lots of people feel left out, even in their own families. But we're human beings and we need to belong to something. So you need to find something to belong to—a sports team, a hobby club, a karate studio, a church, a garage band, a choir, a group of sidewalk musicians, an actor's theater, even just a group of two or three kids you eat lunch with or walk home from school with every day."

I explained that if they belong to some group that is important to them, they would be less inclined to join negative groups such as violent gangs, vandals, or shoplifters. My students seemed so interested in the concept of belonging that I decided to introduce them to Abraham Maslow's theory called Hierarchy of Needs. Briefly, I outlined his theory on the board, and we talked about it. That night I made a chart for them to take home and keep where they could check it periodically to remind themselves to keep growing and moving up the ladder of happiness.

Maslow's Hierarchy of Needs

Physical Needs—food, water, shelter, etc. If you are starving, you aren't worried about whether you're wearing cool shoes. Until these needs are met, you can't move on to bigger and better things. Take care of yourself. If you need help, ask for it.

Safety—Once your physical needs are met, you can think about things like keeping warm, avoiding harm.

Social—People (and lots of animals) need to belong to a group and to feel loved. You can have a family but still feel unloved. That may be why you hang around with people you don't really like or do things you know are wrong—because you want to belong. Find *something* good to belong to—a team, a choir, maybe just a couple of kids you eat lunch with every day. Create your own personal club if you have to, but join something.

Ego—Once we know we're loved, we start to look for ways to increase our self-respect because we all need to feel important and appreciated.

Self-actualization—You have food, shelter, people who love you, and self-respect. . . . Now you're cooking! You don't have to waste your time on unimportant things. You're ready to develop your talents, learn things just for fun, invent new things, help other people. Follow your dreams!

For an older group, I may use more sophisticated vocabulary and more complicated examples, but I've never had a group that didn't get it. In fact, the "worst" classes seemed most interested in these ideas.

5. Use Bloom's Taxonomy to help students think about thinking.

One day a high school junior challenged my assignment. He asked me what the point was. I asked him what he thought it might be. He said the point was to waste time and give me something to grade. I was tempted to hush him up, but decided instead to give him such a complete explanation that he'd never ask such a question again. As it turned out, the discussion was a lively one and everybody in class sat up and paid attention. The next day I presented the same lesson to my other classes and they all responded positively.

When I write "Bloom's Taxonomy of Cognitive Domains" on the board, I can hear the whispers behind me. "What's that?" "I dunno." Eventually, somebody asks: "Hey, what's that mean, Miss J?" I tell them to try to figure it out. Usually, they recognize the word "domain" as a kind of kingdom, but "taxonomy" stumps them. I grab a big textbook dictionary from the shelf and announce that I am "looking it up in my handy dandy pocket dictionary." Freshmen usually giggle, older students roll their eyes and make disgusted *tsk*ing sounds when I grab my dictionary. I ignore their ridicule. I wink and say, "You gotta have big pockets." I don't do those things just to be a clown, but to model the behavior I want them to practice. (It works. Before long, they are grabbing their handy dandy pocket dictionaries to look up words they don't know during class.)

After I define the terms, I tell them that I'm going to share with them a lesson that teachers learn in college but don't usually pass on to their students. I tell them I think they should know why we ask them to do the things we ask them to do. So I explain the different levels of thinking, giving one or two examples. I ask them for additional examples from different subjects for each level, and I give them my first chart, titled "Bloom's Taxonomy of Cognitive Domains—English Applications."

Bloom's Taxonomy of Cognitive Domains—English Applications

Recall—Remembering information: reciting your ABCs, listing the parts of speech, giving the definitions of the words "fact" and "opinion."

Comprehension—Understanding things, such as the difference between a noun and a verb, or between a fact and an opinion.

Application—Using the things you understand: filling in the blanks with verbs or nouns to complete a list of sentences; writing a list of facts or opinions.

Analyzing—Comparing different things: underlining all the nouns in a paragraph, then circling all the proper nouns; or deciding whether a particular sentence is a fact or an opinion and explaining why.

Synthesis—Making up your own sentences that contain action verbs. Writing a paragraph that states your own opinion. Composing a factual report.

Evaluation—Comparing three different sentences and deciding which uses nouns and adjectives to give the best description; reading two different opinions on the same subject, deciding which makes more sense, and supporting your choice with specific examples from the statements you read.

After we discuss the first chart, and I'm sure they understand the concepts, I give them another chart that has examples of using different levels of thinking in daily life. My students are amazed to see that all that "boring, useless stuff" they are learning in school—even analyzing Shakespeare—actually will help them when they begin their "real lives."

Using Bloom's Taxonomy:
<u>Your Own Life</u>

Recall—Remembering all the words to a song or all the foods on your grocery list; reciting the stats of your favorite baseball team; listing all the parts of an engine or a stereo system.

Comprehension—Understanding the difference between a receiver and an amplifier; knowing how a gasoline engine or computer works; realizing that some people are shy.

Application—Installing a stereo or changing the spark plugs in your car; making your own guacamole; filling out a job application with proper grammar; asking a shy person for a date without scaring him/her; fixing a toaster without electrocuting yourself.

Analyzing—Deciding which job to accept; picking the best college for you; deciding whether to get married now, whether to open a credit card account, whether to send your kids to private school, join a gang, quit smoking, start using drugs, do your homework . . .

Synthesis—Making a plan for your life and putting it into action; creating your own heavy metal band or rap group; starting your own business; building a house; making a budget based on your monthly income; raising healthy children.

Evaluation—Deciding whether your current job offers the kind of future you want; reading the news and deciding whether it was presented truthfully; figuring out the best way to discipline your kids; deciding what will be best for your children if your spouse asks for a divorce; figuring out what went wrong and how to make things work better.

The day after we discuss levels of thinking, I bring in items from newspapers for them to analyze. We read an editorial commentary, a movie review, a review of a new music album. I ask the students to see how much they can tell about the writers from reading their work, and whether they accept those writers' opinions. We look at all of the ads in a particular magazine, and then I ask the students to decide what kind of people are the target audience of that magazine, what political point of view the publisher is likely to hold, and what kind of people write the articles. This kind of analytical, critical thinking comes naturally to some students, but for others, this will be a new and exciting introduction to their own brain power.

6. *Demonstrate the power of choice.*

When I was a college student, my psychology professor, Dr. Kenneth Brodeur, once gave our class the simple assignment of completing these two sentences: *I have to . . .* and *I can't . . .* After urging us to write down the first things that came to mind, and giving us a few minutes to complete the sentences, the professor told us to cross out the word "have" and replace it with "choose." Then we were to cross our "can't" and replace it with "don't want to."

I objected, as did everybody else in class, but the professor persisted and, finally, we admitted that he was right— there are very few things in your life that you truly have to do or that you can't do if you really want to. That was the most powerful lesson I ever learned in school and one that I try to teach to all my students. We complete an exercise similar to Dr. Brodeur's during the first week of classes. Even students who have already done the exercise can benefit from this lesson because it's one that most of them need to learn several times before we finally "get it."

If you decide to use this exercise, make sure that the students understand your purpose. Reassure them that it isn't a test, they don't have to read their answers out loud, they won't be graded on what they write, and they won't have to turn in their sentences to you. It's important for them to understand that this exercise is for their benefit, to help them understand themselves better and to make them stronger people. (Of course, it will help you work with them, but some of them may not be interested in helping you, so why mention it?)

Here are some typical sentences from students:

I have to do my homework. I can't get an A in math.
I have to clean my room. I can't wear my hat in school.
I have to go to school. I can't cut classes.
I always have to baby-sit. I can't lose weight.

When you tell your students that they *choose* to do their homework and clean their rooms and go to school, they will object. They'll insist that parents or guardians or teachers make them do those things and hundreds of other horrible chores. Your response: What would happen if you chose not to do those things? What would the consequences be? You don't want to face those consequences, do you? Unless somebody physically forces you to perform an action, you make the choice to perform it. Even a gun to your head or a knife to your throat allows you the choice of not acting and being injured or killed. We do the things we do because we choose to do them. The only things we truly have to do, in order to live, are eat, breathe, and sleep.

When you tell them that they *don't want to* earn A's or wear hats or cut classes, they will most certainly argue with you. And in some cases they will be right. If they give examples of goals that have legitimate limitations (a girl with severe astigmatism cannot become a commercial jet pilot) or physical impossibilities (a boy cannot have a baby), then accept those answers as valid. But the majority of "can't" will not hold up to these objections: Is there any possible way you could accomplish this feat? What would you have to do in order to achieve this goal? Are you willing to do all those things? If you could achieve this goal, given that you were willing to spend the time and energy required, then you don't want to do this particular thing badly enough. In order to take responsibility for ourselves and our actions, we must begin by telling ourselves the truth: we choose to do what we do, and most of our dreams can be achieved if we are willing to do all that is required to make them come true.

You don't need to use a worksheet for this exercise, but if you'd like to use a handout, there's a sample at the end of this chapter. After everybody has completed the sentences, ask them to cross out *have* and write "choose" above it, and to cross out *can't* and write "don't want to" above it. Give them a few minutes to write down their thoughts. Ask them to take the worksheets home with them and reread them from time to time.

Once your students understand and accept the truth of this lesson (be prepared—for some it will take time and repetition), then they will understand that when they misbehave or fail in your class it is because they *choose* to misbehave or fail. They don't have to let somebody copy their homework. They don't have to respond to another student's insult by offering an insult in return. They don't have to come to your class if they don't want to learn. And if they have a problem learning the required material, they can ask you for help or arrange for a tutor or spend more time on homework. Unless they have a true learning disability, there is no valid reason why they can't pass your class, graduate from school, and be successful people.

One Down, Thirty-Something to Go

Not bad—by the end of the first week of school, you know the names of all your students, they know all your rules, you have a good idea of what you have to work with, they understand that you will hold them responsible for their actions, and they know what they will have to do to pass your class. With a little luck, they also understand themselves a little better, and have at least a basic understanding of the different levels of thinking and how they will be called upon to develop the highest-level skills.

Now, you can create lesson plans that suit your classes— but don't get too specific. If you plan your teaching days down to the minute, the administrative tasks and unavoidable interruptions (inoculation day, picture day, career counseling day, college day, armed forces information day . . .) will drive you crazy—and that's your students' job. You wouldn't want to spoil their fun.

GETTING TO KNOW YOU

Name:_____Class period: _____

DIRECTIONS: Fill in the blank or circle the best answer for you. This is NOT a graded exercise, but it is important to me. The better I know you, the better I can teach you.

1. My favorite flavor of ice cream is:_____

2. If I could meet a famous person (living or dead), I'd like to meet: _____

3. Given the choice, I would rather: (a) watch a movie (b) listen to good music (c) play a sport or game

4. If a wizard bopped me with a magic wand and said he was going to change me into an animal, and I got to choose the animal, I'd choose to be a/an:

   _____

5. I'd choose to be that particular animal because

   _____

   _____

6. The best thing about me is:_____

7. My favorite sport/game to play or watch is: _____

8. If I had to choose just one, I'd rather be: (a) good-looking (b) popular (c) smart (d)talented in art/music

9. Which best describes your homework habit?

   (a) I do my homework quickly and get it over with.

   (b) I put off doing my homework until the last minute.

   (c) I sometimes forget all about it.

   (d) If I don't have time, I just copy off my friends.

   (e) I just ignore it and hope it will go away.

10. I like the following kinds of music:: (circle as many as you like) (a) rap (b) heavy metal (c) rock (d) jazz (e) ranchero (f) salsa (g) country (h) classical (j) oldies

11. I would rather (circle one): (a) read silently to myself (b) read out loud (c) listen to somebody else read out loud (d) do just about anything in the world EXCEPT read

12. If I could be invisible for one day, I would

_____

_____

_____

_____

P.S.: Thank you very much for taking the time to complete this worksheet which was created for you by Your Teacher Who Loves You. (That's me!)

COURSE OUTLINE AND OBJECTIVES
L.A. JOHNSON

This English class is designed to help you improve your communications skills through reading, writing, vocabulary, and grammar exercises. We will read a wide variety of literature including short stories, plays, and essays. Our emphasis will be on developing critical thinking skills, particularly in the area of analyzing and evaluating writing. Assignments will include timed responses, journals, essays, and critiques. Of course, we'll learn spelling, grammar, and vocabulary—I know how much you love them!!

THE RULE in this room: Respect yourself and other people. No insults based on ethnic background, skin color, gender, sexual preference, or religion will be tolerated. It is unfair to erase somebody's face. We all have the right to our human dignity and self-respect.

ATTENDANCE: I think it's important, and I promise that I will do my best to make this class interesting. I will never intentionally embarrass you in front of your classmates. My job is to make this class a place where you enjoy learning. Your job is to come to class.

PROCEDURES: I expect you to be seated and ready to work when the bell rings. Likewise, you should expect me to be ready to teach.

TARDY: Tsk! Tsk! Don't you hate waiting for people? I do. Don't be rude!

HOMEWORK: We won't have it every night, but we'll have it and your job is to do it—by yourself, using your own personal brain (although it's perfectly acceptable to get help and share ideas with your friends). If you have problems or questions, call me: 555-6101.

ABSENCE: If you know you are going to be absent, please let me know so I can give you the assignments ahead of time. That way, you won't be overloaded when you return.

MAKEUP WORK: When you return to class after any absence, it is your responsibility to check the Makeup Folder on my desk. You will have three days, in most cases, to complete the work for your grade.

DISCIPLINE: I prefer to deal directly with you when we have a problem, instead of calling your parents/guardian to tell on you. You are responsible for your own behavior.

STUDY MATERIALS: It is your job to bring the necessary materials to class. That's one of the things we're here for—to learn responsibility. So, bring your books. What would you think if you made an appointment to have your car fixed and when you took it to the shop, the mechanic said, "Oh, gee, I forgot to bring my tools today. Sorry."

FUN: It is important to have as much of this as possible. When you were little, itty bitty, teeny tiny children, you loved to learn new things. Learning can still be fun.

"I HAVE TO" AND "I CAN'T"

In the spaces below, finish the two sentences. Don't spend a lot of time thinking about them. Just fill in the first thing that comes to your mind. You will not be required to share your answers with the group unless you volunteer, so don't worry about being personal.

I have to _____

I can't _____

When you have completed the two sentences; put down your pencil or pen so the instructor will know you are ready for the next step.

After we've finished this exercise, take a few minutes to jot down your reaction to what you wrote. What was your first response? Did you change your mind after the discussion? How do you feel now about your sentences?

_____

_____

_____

_____

_____

Time & Energy Savers

Tips for Making Life a Little Easier

Teaching can steal your time and sap your physical and emotional energy very quickly, so it's important to conserve your precious resources whenever possible. Some of the following tips will save you only a minute or two, but you will be much more effective if you spend those minutes teaching your students instead of plodding through mundane, repetitive chores. And, between classes, a minute can go a long way toward helping you recharge your mental batteries before your next group of eager scholars arrives to hear your words of wisdom.

Lesson Plans

Many education textbooks advise new teachers to make detailed lesson plans, so that each minute of class time will be used productively, and your classes will progress smoothly through the required curriculum. That concept sounds good—on paper. When I first began teaching, I planned each class period to the second. I'm serious! I was so nervous that I didn't trust myself to remember what I wanted to cover during class. I imagined myself facing my students and not being able to think of a single intelligent thing to say. So, I planned and outlined and made hourly, daily, weekly, monthly, quarterly, and semester calendars, all filled in neatly and in complete detail, down to the last spelling quiz. I was prepared to walk into the classroom and be the super teacher I knew in my heart that I could be. Unfortunately, I hadn't planned time for reading the daily announcements, calls from the administrative office, buses delayed by traffic, announcements over the squawking intercom, picture day, pep rallies, district testing days, and a hundred other interruptions. I also hadn't planned for the human variable—my students. Often, they would whiz through a worksheet that I thought would take thirty minutes with twenty minutes to spare, or they'd labor for an entire class period over what I thought would be a simple fifteen-minute assignment.

At first, I spent hours revising my lesson plans, but something always seemed to happen to throw my classes off schedule, and I finally realized that I was far more likely to lose my mind than to create a lesson schedule that wouldn't have to be changed frequently. Now, I make a very rough schedule of what I want to cover during a given school year, dividing the units into semesters and quarters. After I meet my students and get a feel for their abilities and personalities, I alter the plan to fit their needs. My daily and weekly plans are very general and flexible, with optional activities and exercises that can be added or deleted as time allows.

Of course, I try to cover the required curriculum, but I have found that I teach much more effectively, and my students learn far more (and do better the following year with the next teacher), if I concentrate on teaching each unit well, instead of rushing them through the material just so I can say we covered the curriculum.

Many schools require teachers to turn in lesson plans for each class at the start of the year, and they sometimes list mandatory units or topics for inclusion. I file the required plan, but I don't lose any sleep worrying about implementing it exactly as written. It has been my experience that administrators collect the lesson plans as a matter of course, and not always because they are interested in reviewing them; they collect them so that they can rest assured that they have complied with district and/or state requirements.

1. Keep some short assignments on hand.

For those days when your scheduled lesson runs short or students finish assignments early, keep a file of short assignments that can be used to fill (not to waste) time. If half the class finishes an exam early, for example, let them work on the assignment in class and allow the others to take it home and turn it in the following day. If you decide to use a game or fun assignment, don't pretend it's important or pertinent to the material you've been studying—tell the truth. Tell your students you're giving them some brain candy because they're smarter than the average bears. If you find yourself running out of material quite often, your assignments may be too simple, or you may be underestimating your students.

2. Assign independent projects.

Assigning students to work independently has many advantages. Independent assignments free you to roam the classroom and act as a guide, instead of the leader. Students learn to take more responsibility for their learning, and they have the opportunity to practice valuable skills such as setting priorities and managing time. Independent exercises also allow students to work at their own pace, instead of having to hurry or slow down for other students. And, probably the most important, by placing more responsibility on your students, they understand that you have faith in their abilities and trust in them as people.

Review your textbooks and curriculum materials with an eye towards independent assignments. Instead of handing students information, assign them the task of discovering a new concept or developing a new skill. Depending on the maturity and enthusiasm of your students, you may want to provide a detailed outline of the steps needed to complete an assignment, or simply state their goal and let them figure out how to reach it.

Note: I have found that students work harder and turn in higher-quality work if I require individual contracts for any major independent project, one that requires two weeks or longer to complete. Contracts eliminate confusion about deadlines and requirements, and reduce the chances of a student failing to earn credit for the work. Your contract needn't be elaborate: the objective, deadline, benchmarks (if any), and student signature should be enough. I also schedule an interim check, midway between the starting date and the deadline, at which time I check to make sure nobody is confused or lagging too far behind to finish the project.

Don't give up if your students flounder on their first attempt at working independently. If they have problems working without direct supervision, then they need such assignments more than students who handle them with ease. Provide a timetable for them to check their progress, and give them credit in your grade book for completing each step of the assignment, so they won't worry about failing.

If you misjudge the time or complexity of an assignment, don't panic. Explain the problem to your students and ask them for suggestions. Students are often better judges of their abilities—and much less forgiving—than their teachers.

3. Share the wealth.

Some teachers are reluctant to share their best lessons, afraid that they will become overused or that some other teacher will steal their thunder by using them with the same group of students. Some teachers, however, will be delighted to swap winners with you. Sharing lesson plans, and tests, gives teachers a new perspective on their assignments and lets them see whether their lessons are easier or harder than those of other teachers in the same grade or subject level. If you find generous teachers at your own school, do extend them the courtesy of checking your roll sheets to make sure that you won't be using the same lesson with students who attend both your classes.

Absences

Although roll sheets provide an official record of absences, I prefer to make my own attendance log in the back of my grade book, which allows me to check attendance at any time and keeps me alert to extended or frequent absences. Also, in my grade book, when a student was absent for a particular assignment or exam, instead of leaving the space blank, which could indicate incomplete or late work, I write a small "a" (in pencil) when I record the grades, to remind me that the student needs to make up that assignment. When the work is turned in, I erase the "a" and insert the proper letter or number grade.

1. Make students responsible for make-up work.

Absence doesn't make the teacher's heart grow fonder; it makes the teacher's life difficult. Few things are more frustrating than walking into your classroom prepared to begin an exciting new assignment or unit and finding six or seven students absent. Keeping track of the assignments missed by absent students, and making sure the work is made up in time for the next exam, adds more frustration. My advice: make students responsible for their own make-up work. For each class period, buy one of those accordion-type file folders that has sections labeled alphabetically. Label the folder "MAKE-UP WORK" and place it on your desk where it is clearly visible to your students. When you distribute worksheets or assignments, write the name of each absent student across the top of the paper, and place the paper in the Make-Up file under the first letter of the student's last name. Tell students that when they return to class, they are responsible for retrieving their work from the Make-Up folder and for scheduling a conference with you to discuss any questions they have about the work. Unless otherwise noted, all assignments are due within three class days of the student's return. This system eliminates the problem of trying to remember which students missed which assignments, and transfers the bulk of the responsibility from your overworked old shoulders to their sturdy young shoulders.

2. Be prepared for your own absence.

You will save time and trouble if you are well prepared for your own absences as well as your students'. Most schools require an emergency data card to be filled out and filed in the office or kept in your desk to provide information for substitute teachers. In addition to the basic information about where keys are kept and when lunch is served, your substitute teacher will be much more effective in teaching your lessons and maintaining discipline if you provide some specific information about your lesson plans and students. If you have a particularly rambunctious or studious class, for example, let the substitute know in advance. I make a brief fact sheet for each class period, giving the names of students who are dependable and responsible, as well as those who need extra attention to ensure their cooperation. I also give the names of one or two teachers in nearby rooms who know my students and can be called upon for help if a question or problem arises.

Create a folder for your substitute teacher, with a fact sheet for each class period (grade level, student info, name of textbooks, etc.), a few short assignments that can be completed if students complete the regular assignment ahead of time, your home telephone number, a copy of your classroom rules, and any special instructions. Also, include a note asking the substitute to let you know about any problems with the lessons or discipline, what was completed or left incomplete, and any information that will help you make a smooth transition when you return to your classroom.

Substitute teachers come in a wide variety of flavors, from the overzealous drill sergeant to the laid-back camp counselor. Unfortunately, random assignment of substitute teachers often creates serious mismatches between those teachers' personalities and teaching styles and the personalities and learning styles of your students. Having a regular substitute has many advantages: the students respond better to a familiar face and are less apt to try to take advantage of a sub who knows them; the sub will be familiar with your classroom, materials, and students; knowing your students are in capable hands gives you some peace of mind when you are absent. Check with your district office to find out whether you can request a specific substitute teacher. If so, ask other teachers on your staff to recommend good substitutes (you may need to have the social security number to request a specific teacher). If possible, get the home telephone number of your chosen substitutes and call them, in advance, when you know you will be absent to see if they are available.

When you know you will be absent—for a doctor's appointment, a conference, or some personal matter—let your students know. Of course, you run the risk of some students cutting class or skipping homework if they know you won't be there, but most of your students will appreciate your consideration. Remind them that their behavior reflects upon you, and that you don't want them to embarrass you by misbehaving when you are not there. You might have a few students who become quite upset at the thought of you not being in your classroom where you are supposed to be when they need you. For example, I had two freshman students, a boy and a girl, who acted terrible whenever I had a substitute—not because they were bad children, but because they liked me very much and hated any kind of change, especially unexpected change. When I was absent, I made arrangements with one of the guidance counselors to call those two students to his office for a brief conference, to let them know I was absent and to assure them that I would be back very soon, before sending them to my classroom. He also suggested that they could help me by helping my substitute. Instead of tormenting my substitute, those two students became the official classroom helpers on the days I was absent.

3. Take a mental health break.

In an effort to safeguard our sanity, another teacher and I made arrangements to give each other a "mental health break" once each month, by teaching each other's classes during our free (planning) period. (I know. I know. Many of us dream about having a free class period. One of my teacher friends estimates that her free period begins somewhere about midnight.) If you have no break during the day, arrange with another teacher to merge your two classes for a group lesson—outside, if your classrooms are too small. Large groups require extra planning and discipline, but your students will appreciate the change and two tired teachers are better than one burned-out teacher.

Student Help

1. Enlist student helpers.

Some schools have a policy whereby students can earn credits for helping teachers, but if your school doesn't offer that option, create your own classroom clerk program. Enlist a few students to help you before and after school, and during lunch hours. I also enlist a clerk for each class period, to take roll, distribute and collect materials, and answer the phone or the door during lessons. Both you and your students benefit from a student clerk arrangement—they get good experience and a dose of confidence, and you get much-needed help with time-consuming chores.

Select the clerks yourself and sign up students for one quarter or one semester if you have several good candidates. Making a general announcement that you are seeking volunteers may create problems; you may be inundated with requests and end up hurting the feelings of the students you don't choose. I sometimes accept clerks who are not enrolled in my classes, but I try to give my own students priority.

When selecting student clerks, don't overlook those students who have weaker study habits or social skills—as I said earlier, often my "problem children" turn out to be the most responsible, dependable workers. Don't be afraid to give real responsibility to your clerks, such as grading exams or recording grades in your book, but make it clear that any information they see about other students must remain confidential or their status as student clerks will be terminated immediately.

2. Create individual portfolios.

At one time, students took copious notes and kept them in notebooks—at least they did a hundred years ago when I was young. In my recent experience, the A students carry notebooks and use them; most students rely on their memories and take their chances (they also frequently complain that the questions on the exam were about things that were never discussed during class). Some teachers require students to keep notebooks for their classes and assign grades for the notebooks when they are turned in at the end of the grading period, but I have seen too many students borrow notebooks at the last minute and copy all the notes.

My method for making sure my students have the information they need to study, and helping them learn how to develop good study habits, is to provide each student with a manila file folder at the start of the school year. They label the folders with their names and I allow them to decorate the outside of the folders if they choose, although I don't allow gang graffiti or obscenities. The folders stay in my classroom, and students must sign them out if they want to take them home overnight. Whenever I present an important lesson, students must take notes and store them in their folders. All graded assignments and exam papers are also kept in the folders. Prior to exams, we go through the folders during class and students note which materials they will need to study. They are allowed to take the materials home to study but must return them to their folders on exam day. At the end of each grading period, we go through the folders and discard any information that won't be needed in the future. Some students opt to retain all of the contents of their folders; in that case, I give them a new manila folder for the new grading period and they are permitted to take the old one home or file it in my classroom for future reference.

Smaller portfolios, for specific projects or study units, also help develop student responsibility and independence, along with good study skills. Instead of assigning one exercise at a time, a portfolio assignment allows students to work at their own pace, take advantage of their individual strengths, and spend time on the areas that interest them most. And portfolio assignments allow you to act as a guide instead of the leader, which encourages your students to develop good critical thinking skills, such as setting priorities and time management. (See the sample portfolio project assignment at the end of the chapter.)

Teaching your students to build portfolios helps them develop good study habits, and they provide tangible proof of student progress—students can see for themselves how much they have learned in your class, and they can review their work to check their level of progress.

Standard Procedures

You can save time and energy and prevent confusion by outlining specific procedures for various classroom activities. For example, when your students must leave your classroom and travel across campus or through the building, for school pictures or a group library visit, do you want them to walk in single file or in pairs? Do you want them to stay closely grouped? Are they permitted to talk during the trip? Will you allow them to make detours to visit the restroom, drinking fountain, or hall lockers on the way? What consequences will you assign if a student disrupts other teachers' classes or disappears temporarily during the journey?

For every activity, there will be a similar lengthy list of questions—and you are far better off answering the questions before they arise than trying to instruct students while they are involved in some activity. After you've created your list of standard procedures, make several copies. Post one copy on the bulletin board or near the doorway of your classroom, and give a copy to each student for future reference. Your own list will depend upon the ages of your students and your local school policy, but here is a sample list that might be helpful.

Library Visits (Individual). Students who complete classwork or exams early may request a pass to the library. A maximum of five students may visit the library at any one time. All students must return to my classroom with a pass signed by the librarian before the end of class. Students who fail to return passes will not be eligible for future passes.

Library Visits (Group). Students will stay close together, and walk quickly and quietly to the library. No talking in hallways or near windows outside classrooms. Any student who intentionally disrupts a class will be required to locate a library book on the topic of etiquette and write a two-page essay on the subject. This procedure also applies to any group travel on campus.

Parties. Students are responsible for clean-up of all parties. Music and talking must not disturb students or teachers in nearby classrooms. During any party, if a fight occurs, physical damage is done to any school property, or complaints about noise are made by any staff members, all future parties are immediately canceled.

Restroom Privileges. The bathroom bear is located on my desk. If you need to use the restroom during class, you do not need to raise your hand and ask permission—come and get the bear to use as your hall pass. Walk quietly and do not disturb other students as you leave or enter the room. Only one student may use the restroom pass at any one time. Any student who uses the bathroom bear for a purpose other than visiting the restroom will lose his or her restroom privileges permanently.

Hall Passes. Only one student may be absent from the classroom on a hall pass at any given time. Students who abuse the privilege by visiting sites other than those listed on the hall pass, or who are reported for disruptive or improper behavior, will lose their hall pass privileges permanently.

Homework and Assignment Baskets. Completed classwork and homework must be placed in the appropriate wire basket on my desk—one is labeled Homework, one is labeled Assignments. You also may place gifts and large sums of money in the baskets. Five points will be deducted for each day homework is turned in late—unless you request an extension ahead of time.

Student Visitors. If you have a friend or relative visiting you, and you want to bring that person to school, you must obtain a visitor's pass from the principal's office.

New Students. When a new student is added to our class, it is everyone's responsibility to make that person welcome. The last seat in the first row is reserved for new arrivals. If you would like to sign up as a mentor for new students, see me.

Time-Outs. Occasionally, I may ask you to step outside the classroom for a Time-Out. A Time-Out is not intended as punishment, but to give you time alone to regain control of your temper or reconsider your present behavior. If you are asked to step outside the classroom, you must remain standing or seated near the door, and are not permitted to leave the immediate vicinity. When time permits, I will step outside to talk to you. Students who leave the area will be considered as cutting class and will face the consequences.

Private Journals. Journals must remain in the classroom, unless you notify me that you intend to take your journal home. Journals are private property, and no student has the right to read another student's journal without his or her express permission. Violators will be prosecuted to the full extent of Miss J's anger.

Interruptions

You can minimize the effect of interruptions with a little forethought and planning. If you have a telephone in your room, for example, teach students how to answer the phone and take proper messages. I keep a message pad from the stationery store by the phone, to get students in the habit of recording the date, time, name and phone number of the caller, and a brief message. Instruct students to inform callers that you are busy and will return their calls as soon as possible, unless it is an emergency (or your principal).

To save time and minimize the distraction when students need hall passes to visit their lockers, the office, the nurse, or other legitimate places, have a supply of partially completed passes on hand, ready to issue. Fill in student names, dates, and times in ink to prevent tampering, and make sure that your supply of passes is kept in a secure place where students won't be tempted to help themselves. Some schools issue each teacher one plastic framed pass to eliminate the problem of fraudulent passes.

Assign the student seated nearest the door to act as door monitor and respond when anybody knocks during class. Instruct your door monitor to step outside quietly and find out what the visitor needs, then relay the message to you, if necessary. If a student messenger has been sent to request that you release one of your students from class, you will have to decide whether the request takes priority over your lesson. Of course, I release students for valid reasons, such as receiving a phone call from a parent, but in most cases, I hold my student and send him during the last ten minutes of class, instead of sending him in the midst of whatever activity is ongoing in our class.

Your students will follow your lead, so don't panic when your principal or other administrators visit your classroom to observe you for periodic evaluation. Unless you have been notified about a problem, the visit is most likely routine. If you are prepared for unexpected visitors, you won't have to scurry about trying to find a place for them to sit—you can greet them calmly, direct them to the visitors' seats, and get on with your lesson. They probably will be so impressed by your professional demeanor and organizational skills that they'll give you an A+ and move on to the next victim.

Grading

1. Go hi-tech, if you can.

If you have access to a computer and software for creating a grade book, learn how to use it. Although you may have to spend several hours learning how to use the software, and more hours typing in the necessary information, such as student names and a list of every assignment for every class, the benefits of computerized grading are well worth your time and effort. Once your data base has been created, all you have to do is enter new assignments and student grades; the computer does the mathematical computations. In minutes, you can print out a grade sheet for each class, showing each student's overall grade and grades for the different categories you have chosen. You also can print out a single student's grade report, which allows you to provide frequent and accurate feedback to your students.

You can use the computerized grade book to motivate students. When I have a student who needs to exert just a bit more effort to raise his or her grade a notch, I call the student into my office and display his or her grade report on the screen. Then I change two or three grades by only a few points, to show the student how easily a C could become a B.

If your school requires teachers to turn in their grade books at the end of each report card period, you can print out the grade reports for each class, staple them together, and have your grade book ready to submit within a few minutes, as opposed to several hours of manually computing (and rechecking) grades with a calculator.

2. Good old-fashioned manual grading.

Even when I have a computerized grade system, I record grades in a standard spiral grade book, as a backup in the event of computer failure and so that I can keep a grade book in my briefcase for handy reference at home. There are as many ways to maintain a grade book as there are ways to maintain a checking account. Some teachers keep immaculate records and can quickly check any student's grade, while others are always a week or a month behind in recording grades and respond with ambiguous answers when students ask about their grades. If you can work out a system that allows you to stay closer to the well-balanced end of the spectrum, you will save yourself considerable time and frustration when report cards are due.

You will want to design a system that works well for you, but if you are starting from scratch, here are a few suggestions.

Take your time. Don't be too quick to enter student names in your grade book. You may find yourself erasing and rewriting names several times, or else adding names at the bottom of the page out of alphabetical order. Wait at least a few days until schedules have been arranged and students have been shuffled to the proper classes. In the meantime, make a Xerox copy of your roll sheets and use the copies to record grades that can later be entered in the permanent grade book.

Indicate absences. To eliminate student claims that they never received assignments and to avoid penalizing absent students, use blue or green ink to outline the squares in which grades for those absent students will be recorded at the time you distribute an assignment. If a student doesn't have a box beside his or her name, that means the student was present to receive the assignment and should turn it in on time. When a student fails to turn in an assignment, pencil in a zero in the square until the deadline has passed for that assignment—then replace the penciled zero with a red zero to indicate that the work was not completed in time to be graded. (You will have to decide whether to let students make up the zeros at the end of the grading period, when they begin begging for mercy.)

Include interim grades. Leave a blank column after every ten or twenty assignments, depending upon how many graded assignments you make, so that you can insert the student's percentage, point total or letter grade at that time. This will allow you to provide accurate interim grade reports for students and will alert you to potential problems and failures.

3. Use Scantrons sparingly.

Automated grading machines save time by allowing you to grade hundreds of exams or quizzes in just a few minutes— but because such machines are limited to multiple-choice or true/false questions, they require exams that use only lower-level critical thinking skills. Even if you use the ten or fifteen spaces at the end of the exam for short-answer questions, you still restrict yourself to the three or four lowest levels (recall, comprehension, application, analysis), when the higher-level skills (synthesis and evaluation) are necessary to truly evaluate student knowledge and skill development.

Two or three well-written, challenging exams that you grade by hand will provide a more accurate assessment of your students' learning—and your teaching—than fifty quick and easy quizzes that can be whisked through the Scantron or other machine.

4. Grade papers immediately.

The sooner you provide feedback on assignments and exams, the more interested your students will be in analyzing their work. Exchanging papers and letting students grade each other's work (or their own) also saves time for you and allows your students to receive immediate feedback so they can correct misunderstandings or confusion. If a week or more passes before a student receives a grade on a worksheet or exam, the student is very apt to have learned or memorized misinformation and either will have forgotten or will have trouble relearning the information that he misunderstood.

When exchanging student papers, many teachers instruct students to pass papers ahead or behind, or across rows. I prefer to collect papers and distribute them myself, for a number of reasons. Friends often sit together and may be tempted to try to help each other by changing answers. Students sitting next to each other may dislike each other enough to try to sabotage each other's grades. If I have a sensitive soul who does not earn high grades, I try to give his or her paper to a student who has the maturity and tact not to laugh or discuss the student's mistakes with other classmates. And, finally, I sometimes ask students who earn low grades to mark the papers of students who earn high grades, in the hope that the good grammar, spelling, handwriting, and quality of the answers will serve as a good example for those students who need to improve their study skills.

Common Courtesy Pays

Although I was raised to believe that good manners are their own reward, I have learned that people often will reward courtesy and consideration in more tangible ways. At one school, we had a single copy machine for the entire staff, and as low woman on the teaching totem pole, I rarely had an opportunity to use the machine. Because I often came to work early and stayed late, I became well acquainted with most of the people on the custodial staff. One evening, as I was chatting with one of the custodians, I mentioned that I planned to stop off at a local copy shop to make copies of an article I wanted my students to read. He offered to open the office and allow me to use the copy machine, instead. I didn't abuse the privilege, and I never exceeded the number of copies permitted per teacher, but I did take advantage of the opportunity to make copies after hours from time to time.

Secretaries, receptionists, and other administrative personnel also appreciate being treated with dignity and respect. I have worked as a secretary and as a receptionist, so I know how difficult their work can be, and I know that the boss is often the last person who knows what is happening on her staff. The administrative staff can make your life easier by providing information and assistance in dealing with parents, making or receiving long-distance phone calls, tracking important mail, locating information and materials, and scheduling appointments with administrators.

Treat the teacher in the room next to yours as you would a neighbor at home. Be friendly and helpful, but don't be a pest. Do stop by to chat occasionally, and offer to supervise his students if he has to make a quick trip to the teacher's lounge or the office during class. Also, offer to keep an eye on his room when he is absent and come to the rescue of the substitute teacher, if necessary. If your next-door teacher is a cynical old fart, then forget him and find another teacher a few doors down to be your friendly neighbor.

Security personnel can give you information about students that you would not have otherwise, since they see your students under different circumstances. If you have a problem student who you believe might pose a physical threat to you or other students, you might check with security to find out whether the student has had problems in the past. You might find out, to your surprise, that the student is a good citizen who plays the part of tough guy or girl to deter physical or verbal assaults by other students. At one school, I made friends with a security guard who taught kung fu during his off-duty hours. When I was recruiting mentors for my students, he volunteered to befriend a few of my "problem" students. He was an excellent mentor and role model, and I saw a marked difference in the students' attitudes after they spent a few weeks in his company.

Introduce yourself to the monitors of your school detention room, and find out what procedures are standard in their classroom. If monitors are receptive, I often ask them if they will permit my students to complete assignments during detention, instead of twiddling their thumbs or completing inane assignments. (I do believe students must face serious consequences for misbehavior, but most problem students are delighted to be removed from classrooms where they must use their manners and their brains.)

Department chairs tend to be either extremely organized or desperately trying to keep up with the added workload. In either case, you can benefit from spending time with your department chair. If he or she is organized and on top of things, you will learn valuable time management techniques. If he or she is drowning in a sea of paperwork, you can offer to help and, in the process, learn more about the administration of your department and your school.

You Didn't Hear This from Me

Occasionally, I have been known to bend a rule or ignore instructions—but only in the interest of being a better teacher. The following are not suggestions or advice. They are included simply to provoke thought and perhaps inspire you to stage your own quiet rebellion against stupidity, irrelevance, and time-wasting.

Staff meetings. Doughnuts don't speak to me, and in my experience, eating doughnuts seems to be the primary focus of most regular staff meetings. When attendance at staff meetings is mandatory, I go. I arrive early, make sure the administrators see me, find a seat near the door, and cross my fingers that something of import and interest will be presented. If so, I stay and contribute what I can. When the doughnuts prevail, I wait about twenty minutes, then glance at my watch, look extremely dismayed, grab my briefcase, and rush out the door. Nobody, including the most strict principal, has ever asked me where I went. (I didn't play hooky. I went directly to my classroom, where I spent my time grading papers and creating exciting, inspirational lesson plans for my students.)

Phone calls. Phones in a classroom are often more trouble than they are worth. When we're reading Shakespeare or working on some other complicated assignment that requires concentration and quiet, I take the phone receiver off the hook and place it in a nest of papers inside the trash can. At the end of class, I replace the receiver. In the event of a true emergency, a messenger will be sent from the office. Occasionally, I forget to replace the receiver immediately after class. If anybody notices it, I pretend to be surprised to see it sitting in the trash can and rush to rescue it.

Office requests for students. When messengers arrive at my doorstep asking me to send my students here or there, I sometimes send my students, if the request is for something important that can't be scheduled at some other time—a phone call from parents, a summons from the principal, an appointment with the nurse. When my students are busy working, and I receive requests to take them out of class for minor matters that can be handled during lunch hour, between classes, or before school in the morning, I take the messages and "forget" to deliver them until after class. If I'm not sure about the importance, I call the students aside and ask whether they want to leave the room. When they say no, that they would rather work on their lessons, I keep them. In any case, I give my students permission to blame me for forgetting to deliver their messages, and I offer to write a note taking full responsibility for the error, so they won't get in trouble.

Pointless paperwork. My first supervisor in the U.S. Navy was a master chief journalist named Hubie Black. JOCM Black was a tough cookie, a no-nonsense swabbie. Every Friday afternoon, he picked up his In basket and dumped it in the trash. The first time I witnessed the dumping, I gasped, appalled. "Don't worry about it," he told me. "There's nothing rated Secret or Confidential in there, just garbage from all the paper pushers around here. If there's something really important in there, they'll send me another copy. If they don't, then I'm glad I didn't waste my time on it."

Although I've never managed to work up enough nerve to dump an entire basket of paperwork in the trash, I did take a tip from Master Chief Black. When I am overwhelmed and struggling to cope with the normal stresses of teaching, and I receive what appears to be pointless paperwork, I stuff it into the middle drawer of my desk and forget about it until the person who sent it contacts me to find out why I didn't comply with the instructions. If somebody does call, I apologize profusely and get right to work on the task. About half the time, nobody ever calls, and I file the paperwork in its proper location at the end of the school year.

Detailed curriculum outlines. I used to make one very detailed curriculum outline, until I realized that nobody reads them and I can't follow them because my students are human beings, not robots who can be required to learn at a certain pace. Now I create a beautiful outline, with lots of details and asterisks, that I submit to the administrative office for the official records. Then I make another, more realistic outline, to use in my classes.

Detention. As I stated earlier, I don't like detention. I especially don't like blanket detention wherein a student who misbehaves in one class is removed from all his or her classes for one or more days. I don't think another teacher has the right to make a student fail my class. Detention is not an effective deterrent to misbehavior and it certainly is not an effective motivator for disenchanted students. Yes, I do believe students need to face serious consequences for their misbehavior, but most of them consider detention as a reward, not a punishment, because they don't have to attend classes they don't like. Furthermore, I don't see how making students miss classes and assignments, which means lower grades, can help them learn to be better students.

Detention doesn't address the real problems—student who lack the skills to complete their classwork and hid their ineptitude behind disruptive behavior; students w have personal problems that they can't handle, but who too proud or afraid to ask for help; students who ar angry or hungry or ill or confused that they can't concentrate on schoolwork. We would be much more successful in changing student behavior if we addressed these problems through remedial classes, tutors, effective counseling, and consequences that actually address the misbehaviors in an effort to improve behavior.

When I find out that one of my students is sitting in detention, I go get him or her. I explain to the teacher or monitor on duty that I will take full responsibility for my actions if the principal or anybody else complains. To date, I have removed dozens of students from detention and, sadly, nobody has ever complained; apparently, nobody even noticed that they were gone.

THE AMERICAN EXPERIENCE

Name:_____
Portfolio Project – Grade 11

DIRECTIONS: You must complete each task on the list, but you may do them in any order you wish. As you complete each task, have Miss J initial the appropriate blank on this sheet. This portfolio counts as ½ your grade for this quarter.

___ 1. Read "The Historical Setting," pages 2–3 in your text. Be prepared to summarize it.

___ 2. Go to the school, NMSU, or public library and find information about Native American tribes in the U.S. during the 1500–1600s. List your main source below.

(title of publication)_____

(author)_____(pages consulted)_____

___ 3. Complete at least ONE of the following tasks (you can earn extra credit by doing more).

a. Write a brief comparison of two different tribes. Describe similarities and differences in their social organizations, customs, housing, clothing, art, etc.

b. Draw your own illustrations of two different tribes, showing their clothing, customs, housing, art, etc.

c. Prepare a brief (3- to 5-minute) minute presentation on two or more tribes, describing their lifestyles, customs, clothing, art, music, etc.

___ 4. Read the "American Events/World Events" timelines on pages 4–7. Select three entries on the timeline (i.e., 1609 Gallileo builds first telescope) and research more information about these topics in a literature text or at the library. List your sources here:

(title of publication)_____

(author)_____(pages consulted)_____

(title of publication)_____

(author)_____(pages consulted)_____

___ 5. Using the source(s) above, write one paragraph summarizing each event.

___ 6. Create a timeline for your own life. Illustrate it with your own drawings or pictures cut from magazines.

___ 7. Write a short (one-page minimum) essay that explains the religious beliefs of the Puritans and compares those beliefs to your own. (Do you agree or disagree with the ideas of "original sin" and the Puritan "work ethic," for example.)

___ 8. Read "The Earliest American Literature," pages 9–12. Be prepared to discuss with Miss J.

___ 9. List the names of three U.S. states that come from Native American words. List the names, tribes, and meanings of the names/words.

State	Tribal Origin	Meaning
a._____	_____	_____
b._____	_____	_____
c._____	_____	_____

___ 10. Read "Upon the Burning of Our House," and write your response to this poem.

___ 11. Read and write a brief summary, in your own words, of the following:

"Delaware, Navajo" ___   "The Iroquois Constitution" ___

"The Walam Olum" ___   "Pima, Chippewa, Sioux"   ___

"The Navajo Legend"___   "From the Houses of Magic" ___

___ 12. Create your own myth with pictographs like those in "The Walam Olum" to describe your own theory of the origin of life.

___ 13. Write your own legend like "The Navajo Origin Legend" to describe the origin of your own ethnic group. Try to use animals, nature, or other symbols to tell your story.

___ 14. Write your own Constitution stating the fundamental laws and truths that govern your life and actions. OR Imagine that you are the leader of some people and you must create a Constitution that will best govern their lives.

___ 15. Chose at least one task below (you may do more, for extra credit):

   a. Write a song or poem to express your feelings about nature.

   b. Write down the lyrics to a favorite song or poem that expresses your feelings about nature and explain why you chose this particular song/poem.

   c. Make a drawing or painting that expresses your feelings about nature.

   d. Take photos (or clip from magazines) and create a nature display. Write your own captions for the photos.

___ 16. Place all of the above assignments into a portfolio. Design a cover and a Table of Contents.

___ 17. Give your portfolio to Miss J on or before _____. (Don't be late.)
   One day late = minus one letter grade.
   Two days late = minus two letter grades.
   Three days late = no credit. Sorry, Charlie.

**Feel proud that you are so responsible
and creative!! You are a treasure.**

The Big Kids

Parents, Teachers, Administrators

Parents

Because teachers tend to be good students, and most of us enjoyed going to school, we sometimes forget that parents used to be students, too, and that not all of them have fond memories of their school days. School is a traumatic, painful experience for many children, and when those children grow up and become parents, they may try to avoid anything associated with school because the moment they step into a school building, those painful childhood memories come flooding back. I have seen parents outside the principal's office waiting to be called in for a conference, sitting with their backs straight, feet together, hands folded, eyes cast down, looking for all the world like children who know they are in trouble and are waiting for the inevitable punishment.

When we approach parents to discuss their children's

problems or progress in school, we need to be tactful and sensitive to the parents' reactions. If they are uncooperative and defensive, we should assume that their attitudes are a response to their own experiences, and not because they dislike us or are uninterested in their children's education.

1. A little PR can work wonders.

Your first contact with any parent or guardian should be positive, not a phone call to complain about Stephanie or Luis. Call and introduce yourself as Luis's teacher, and tell his parents what a pleasure it is to have such a well-mannered child in your class, that you wish you had fifty more like him. Thank them for raising him to be so polite and respectful of other people. Tell Stephanie's parents how happy you are to have her in your class, since she is a delightful child. (If she isn't delightful, say that you're happy to have her in your class. Period.) The point of this introductory phone call is not to lie, but to make a connection and pave the way for future communications about their children. Later in the year, if you have to call for help with discipline, for example, those parents will understand that you aren't blaming them for the problem, or criticizing their child rearing. They will know that you realize their child's behavior may not coincide with their instructions.

Call two or three parents per week, just to introduce yourself and compliment them on their wonderful children. During these chats, don't focus on academics, focus on the child. Let the parents know that you like the child as a person. Find something positive—good manners, a sense of humor, cheerful personality, kindness to other students, helpful attitude. Although many children act differently in school than they do at home, remember that you are talking to people who know your students intimately. Don't concoct wonderful personalities for your students. If you try, you can find something good in even the most difficult child. A nonstop talker, for example, could be described as an energetic child who is full of life. A child who challenges you constantly certainly has a strong personality.

Don't let language barriers stop you from communicating with parents. If you have students in your classes who come from homes where English is not spoken, tell your students when you plan to call their homes, and ask them to translate for you. If you have an ear for languages, you might ask the students to teach you one or two phrases. They will appreciate your effort, and so will their parents. You might want to follow up your phone call with a written note, so that the parents who don't speak English can have the note translated as proof that their children are as wonderful as they suspected.

2. Write notes to parents of "bad" kids.

Pay special attention to the parents of your "bad kids," the uncooperative students who make your job more difficult. Parents of these children are used to hearing negative things about their children, and they will assume, as soon as you say you are a teacher, that you have one more complaint to add to the long, long list. After you call these parents to introduce yourself, keep an eye out for something good to tell them. If their child completes a test ahead of the class, earns an A on a quiz, writes a thought-provoking essay, participates in a class discussion—anything that you can brag about—send a note home to Mom and Dad. Ask the student to deliver the note. Even if the student pretends not to care, and the parents don't respond, they will pay attention to you. But they may be so used to negative feedback from schools that they may find it hard to believe your positive message, or they may suspect a trick. More likely, though, they will hang your note on the refrigerator door in their home for all the world to see.

3. Keep parents informed.

Not all parents have the time or inclination to attend Open House or Visitor's Night, or to schedule conferences with teachers, but you still can keep parents informed. At the

start of the year, I send a form letter home to parents, outlining the material we're going to cover during the year. I
invite them to sit in on our classes as observers, or to participate if they have some special knowledge or skill that my
students might enjoy. One mother who is a personnel direc-
tor accepted the invitation and gave a brief presentation
when my students were writing résumés and practicing for
summer job interviews. Whenever one of my classes begins
a special project that may require extra time or parental
assistance, I send home a letter explaining the project and
inviting the parents to come to the classroom and view the
results when the project is completed.

Keep parents informed about student absences. Invite
them to call you if they have any questions about their children's attendance in your class. Even if your school has a
computerized system for reporting absences, mistakes may
occur, and students always figure out ways to circumvent
the system. One young man who had been in my classes for
two years in a row, and not absent a single day during those
two years, came to me after school one day and asked me to
help him. He said his father had beaten him because there
had been a message on their answering machine saying that
Raul had been absent from school one day. I checked my
roll sheets. Raul had been present. We checked with his
other teachers, and he had been present in every class on
that date. I called the Attendance Office to report the error
and was told not to worry, that the machine sometimes
dialed numbers incorrectly, but that it didn't happen often.

Attendance reports are a quick and easy way to keep
parents informed and deter students from cutting classes.
(See the sample Attendance Report at the end of the chapter.) Students can deliver the completed forms, or parents
may opt to pick them up at the office or have them mailed.
If you do mail attendance reports or other communications
about students who have discipline or attendance problems,
don't use envelopes that bear the school letterhead, and
don't type the address on the envelope. Instead, use a plain
envelope and hand-write the address. This tip comes courtesy of one of my students who informed me that he opens

any letters from the school and destroys any that contain information about his misbehavior. He was impressed that I had managed to slip a note by his surveillance—by accident. In a hurry one day, I wrote a note to his mother on pink paper and sent it in a personal-size envelope with no return address.

Beware of leaving messages for parents on answering machines. The same student who told me about intercepting letters told me that he makes sure that he arrives home ahead of his parents every day, so that he can erase any messages on the answering machine that might get him in trouble. After talking to that student, I now ask parents if it is acceptable for me to call them at their workplaces and if I might send mail to them there, in an emergency. Whether the mail is addressed to home or work, when I send an attendance report or an important note to a parent, I use an off-size envelope, such as those that come with greeting cards. And I call parents at work or at home during evening hours, whenever possible.

4. One parent's point of view.

While paddling about the Internet one day (I'm not up to surfing speed yet), I happened upon a Web site for parents who home-school their children. Interested in what motivates parents to take their children out of public schools, I read several messages and reports. I was particularly intrigued by a link that led me to a page entitled "Top Ten Mistakes in Education." Each of the ten mistakes on the list begins with the questionable wording "Schools believe," and some of the arguments are downright silly ("Studying is a waste of time. No one ever remembers the stuff they cram into their heads the night before the exam, so why do it?") Still, I found some of the comments thought-provoking, especially the idea that schools should not assess how well they perform their own work. "Products ought to be assessed by the buyer of those products, not the producer of those products. Let the schools do the best job they can, and then let the buyer beware. Schools must concentrate on learning and teaching, not testing and comparing." Two other statements in the list deserve our attention. On the subject of grades: "Age-grouped grades are one of the principal sources of terror for children in school, because they are always feeling they are not as good as someone else or better than someone else." On the subject of discipline: "The threat of a ruler across the head makes children anxious and quiet. It does not make them learn. It makes them afraid to fail, which is a different thing altogether." (If you are interested in reading more, I found it at this Internet address: www.ils.nwu.edu/~e_for_e/nodes/NODE-283-pg.html)

Teachers

1. Do unto other teachers.

Treat the other teachers on the school's staff as you would like to be treated. Don't criticize other teachers in front of students; aside from being unprofessional and inappropriate, criticizing your colleagues behind their backs sets a bad example for your students, who are likely to repeat your comments, and who may use your criticism as an excuse for misbehaving in other teachers' classrooms. And remember that a student's perspective may differ from yours. Unless you observe another teacher interacting with students, you cannot be certain what actually occurs in another teacher's classroom. If you become concerned about a teacher's conduct, give that teacher the courtesy of tactfully discussing the situation with him or her first. After your discussion, if you are still concerned, talk to your department chair or administrators. Be discreet in your conversations with other staff members. False accusations may permanently damage the credibility, morale, and effectiveness of a teacher, even if the accusations are publicly discredited and disproved.

Don't interfere with your colleagues' teaching. If you must take students out of classes for a field trip or special event, print a list of student names, along with the date and reason for the absence. Put a copy of the notice in every teacher's mailbox so they will know about the student absences in advance and won't schedule special projects or exams on those days.

2. Share the load (and the fun).

You can add interest and complexity to your assignments if you find another teacher to work with you to design projects that fulfill requirements for both your classes. Some compatible pairs are obvious—an English teacher can work with almost any other teacher on an essay or report, with the English teacher grading the assignment for composition, grammar, and spelling, and the other teacher grading the assignment on content and accuracy. But you might be surprised at some of the less obvious pairings. Here are just a few possible pairs, to get you started.

- *Athletic coach and Art teacher: student paints portrait or draws scene from a game*

- *Athletic coach, Computer teacher, and Math teacher: student creates a graph showing percentage of team wins and losses during a specific time period or a chart that compares statistics of three favorite teams or players*

- *Athletic coach and English teacher: student writes essay describing a game*

- *Computer teacher and Math teacher: students design and create graphs to track their "investments" in stocks and bonds*

- *History teacher and Science teacher: students research newspaper accounts to see how media and public responded to some invention or discovery*

- *History teacher and Art teacher: students create visual representation of some event from history text*

- *English teacher and Art teacher: students create posters to advertise movies based on Shakespeare's plays*

3. Create your own lunch club.

Perhaps you have the good fortune to work with a group of experienced teachers who have managed to maintain their enthusiasm and sense of humor. Unfortunately, that is not always the case. Teaching drains people, physically, emotionally, and mentally—it makes people tired. Many new teachers are disheartened and dismayed when they hear the conversations between veteran teachers that take place in staff lounges and lunch rooms. Instead of hearing the veterans discussing ways to capture the interest of the disinterested student or how to inspire creativity, they hear those teachers lamenting the ignorance and disrespect of the cretins they are expected to teach, suggestions for getting rid of students to reduce class sizes, gossip and innuendoes, and the all-too-common (and valid, unfortunately) complaints about being overworked and sorely underpaid for their efforts. Tired old teachers are like anybody else. They may be dedicated professionals who love their work, but they enjoy complaining about how hard they work and how little they are appreciated. Unfortunately, instead of being inspired by the energy and idealism of new teachers, these veterans often shake their heads knowingly and warn the new kids on the block to back off and quit wasting their time on children who don't want to learn.

Don't spend your precious free time with negative people; they can sap the mental and psychic energy you need to maintain your enthusiasm about teaching. If the air in your school's staff lounge or lunch room is blue with bitter smoke, try taking your break and eating lunch in your departmental office, if there is one. Pack a brown bag and eat your lunch while taking a walk, or find another teacher who shares your attitude towards teaching, and eat in your classrooms. Most likely, before long, you'll find students peeking through the windows or peering around the door jamb, peaceful souls looking for a place to escape the pressure and negativity of the younger crowd.

4. Recruit a mentor.

Some schools have a mentor program for new teachers. If your school doesn't have one, ask your principal or department chair to recommend somebody who might be willing to serve as your guide and sounding post. Or when you are introduced at the first staff meeting, announce that you would appreciate a volunteer to be your mentor.

A note of caution: Take your time getting to know the other staff members. Personal and professional politics abound on school campuses, and you may find yourself unwittingly drawn into the midst of arguments, even feuds, if you aren't careful. Be courteous and friendly, but be wary of overly friendly staff members until you have a sense of the different social cliques and political groups that exist on your campus.

5. Conserve your energy.

Contribute to your school—but don't take on too many extracurricular activities or additional duties, especially at the start of a new school year. If you take on extra duties early, you may run out of time or energy before the end of the first grading period—and you may find it difficult or uncomfortable to disengage yourself, regardless of the validity of your reasons.

"A school is like a huge sponge," one veteran teacher explained to me. "It will absorb as much energy as you are willing to give. Nobody will thank you for running yourself ragged trying to help, and you can bet that if you end up having a nervous breakdown, people won't send you sympathy cards—they'll be mad because you aren't there, making their lives easier."

Until you know your students and their needs, you cannot accurately predict how much time you'll need to spend on lesson plans, special projects, or remedial work. If you find yourself with time to spare, by all means, volunteer to edit the yearbook, coach the girls' volleyball team, or create a chess club. Give as much as you can give without overtaxing yourself, physically or mentally, but don't feel guilty about drawing the line. Learn to say "no."

Administrators

Talk to your administrators. Find out their philosophies and attitudes about detention, expulsions, and other disciplinary tools. Know what will happen if you refer a student to the office. Will he be lectured and released? Will a staff member call her parents? Will he be suspended? Expelled? I once sent a boy to the office for threatening to hit me. I knew Alex wasn't serious; he was simply angry. He had been a student in my classes for two years, and we liked each other, but something went wrong that day. I sent Alex to the office to give us both time to cool down, and I assumed the principal would give him a good scare. The following day, I found out that the principal planned to expel Alex. Fortunately, I was able to convince the principal that a written apology, a parent conference, and a handshake would be sufficient punishment.

1. Tell your principal or dean what you need.

Don't assume that your principal or disciplinary dean knows your personality and teaching philosophy. Tell them how you operate and how they can help you. If you have a difficult class and need some backup support, or a class that needs motivation, ask the principal to stop by your room once a week, or once per month, to observe silently or to talk to your students.

If you find a principal who shares your outlook, you can work together to help your students. When I asked one principal if he would mind visiting my classroom and giving a short pep talk to my remedial readers, he surprised me and delighted my students by bounding into the room that afternoon and offering to host a pizza party at the end of the semester if everybody in the class earned a C or higher on their report cards.

"You look hungry," Mr. Melendez told my class. "I don't know if I can afford to pay for all that pizza, but a deal is a deal." He shook hands with several students who wanted to seal the deal. Thrilled at the thought of making the principal pay, those students applied extra effort—and they earned their pizza.

Mr. Melendez came to my rescue another time, when two older boys, one a known gang member, decided that they didn't have to listen to me or participate in class. One of them pulled a stack of photos from his pocket, and they began talking loudly, laughing over the photos. When I asked them to be quiet, they ignored me completely. I walked to the room next door and borrowed the phone to call the office and asked if Mr. Melendez would come and talk to the boys. He was there in an instant. A tall, husky man, Mr. Melendez threw open the door to my room and stalked inside. "Who needs to come talk to me?" he demanded. I indicated the two boys. Mr. Melendez pointed to the hallway and they meekly walked outside to wait for him. He glanced around the room. "Anybody else?" The other students stared, wide-eyed, and shook their heads. No, they were fine. They didn't need to go to the office for a talk.

That afternoon, Mr. Melendez told me that he had explained to the two boys that attending school was a privilege, not a right. If they wanted to return to my class, they had to come to me and ask me to admit them to my room. One of the boys returned the following day. The other waited a week before giving in. Mr. Melendez stopped by every now and again to make sure that those students appreciated the privilege of attending his school and my English class.

2. Ask to be included in decisions.

Some administrators insist on making their own decisions about student discipline, without any interference from teachers. Others may be willing to consider your ideas and suggestions. You won't know unless you ask. If you do find an administrator who is willing to listen to you, make sure you are familiar with district policy, and local and state laws;

in many schools, expulsion is mandatory for any student found in possession of a controlled substance, no questions asked, no excuses accepted. In cases not covered by laws, you might be able to suggest consequences that will address the problem and correct the behavior without suspending students or sending them to detention. A student who cuts class frequently, for example, is not likely to care whether she is suspended and her grades go down. A three-day suspension for a truant is a three-day television-watching vacation. Spending three lunch hours in your classroom writing reports on juveniles in prison would be much more effective and would have the added benefit of not hurting her grades.

3. Put yourself in the principal's place.

Sometimes I think teachers forget that, because of their responsibilities, principals have a different perspective from ours. Although they may be friendly and popular with staff and students, their job is not to be the students' best friend or to act as the staff cheerleaders. Their job is to maintain a safe and orderly campus, where students are protected from harm, and the staff teaches the required curriculum and complies with district and governmental policy and law. While you may focus on an individual student's needs and your desire to help that student stay in school, the principal may focus on the time and energy expended on that student, the effect that student has on other students' behavior and attitudes, and the risk that student poses to the safety of other students and staff. It may seem to you that the administrators at your school are more interested in creating a good appearance for the public than they are in helping students or increasing graduation rates—and that may be true, unfortunately. But it may simply be a matter of making safety the top priority and accepting the disadvantages that accompany that decision.

4. Offer your special expertise.

If you have areas of special expertise—music, desktop publishing, or martial arts, for example—why not offer to provide entertainment for the annual staff Christmas party or help publish a staff newsletter? Your principal may be able to suggest other teachers who might be willing to work with you to present a student assembly. At a local elementary school, several staff members dress up in 1950s costume every year and lip-sync songs by the Beach Boys, the Shirelles, and other popular groups. Rave reviews from students have made the concert an annual event.

5. Volunteer early for extracurricular assignments.

Check with your principal during the first few days of the school year to see whether staff members are required to volunteer for a certain number of hours of extracurricular activity. If so, find out where the activity list is posted and sign up for events that interest you, so you won't end up, as I did my first year, getting stuck with the most time-consuming and unattractive assignments.

SAMPLE ATTENDANCE REPORTS

Attendance Report for elementary student—one teacher:

ATTENDANCE REPORT for the week beginning _____

Student's Name_____

Home Telephone_____

Teacher's Name_____Room Number_____

	Monday	Tuesday	Wednesday	Thursday	Friday
X=Present **T**=Tardy **A**=Absent	X T A	X T A	X T A	X T A	X T A
Homework done	Yes-No	Yes-No	Yes-No	Yes-No	Yes-No
Behavior acceptable	Yes-No	Yes-No	Yes-No	Yes-No	Yes-No

Is student passing your class at this time? Yes-No

Teacher's Signature_____

Attendance Report for student with more than one teacher:

Attendance Report for the week beginning _____

Student Name_____

Teachers: Please mark Y (Yes) or N (No) for each day to indicate student's presence and completed work. If no homework was assigned, leave homework section blank. Please use ink.

Teacher's Signature	<u>Monday</u>	<u>Tuesday</u>	<u>Wednesday</u>	<u>Thursday</u>	<u>Friday</u>
			present/homework		
_____Period 1	/	/	/	/	/
_____Period 2	/	/	/	/	/
_____Period 3	/	/	/	/	/
_____Period 4	/	/	/	/	/
_____Period 5	/	/	/	/	/
_____Period 6	/	/	/	/	/
_____Period 7	/	/	/	/	/

If student's present grade is D or lower, please circle your class period: 1 2 3 4 5 6 7

Comments:

_____

_____

_____

Inspiration & Motivation

Resources from Here to the Internet

Teaching can be a lonely profession if you shut the door of your classroom and try to do everything yourself. No matter how hard you try and how well you teach, you will be a better teacher (and you will have the energy to teach effectively for a much longer time) if you take advantage of the experience, expertise, and generosity of other adults in your community, across the country, and around the world.

Start at Home

Your own school is the most obvious source of help for motivating and inspiring your students. If you have a handful of nonreaders, for example, ask a counselor to speak to your class about learning disabilities, tutoring programs, or other services designed to help students succeed. Or if you have discipline problems that you can't handle, ask other teachers for advice, and invite the principal or disciplinary dean to talk to your students—to scare them, motivate them, or both. Find out what special programs are available at your school, and take advantage of the assistance and expertise they can offer.

1. Staff members.

Counselors. Ask to see previous report cards for a student who has trouble in your class; a student who receives special tutoring in reading, for example, may not be able to understand the text and materials in your class. Request a guidance counselor to visit your classes right after report cards are issued, to help students learn to read their transcripts and find out how to correct misinformation. A guidance counselor also may be able to provide motivation by explaining how your subject will benefit them in future careers. Counselors sometimes may make schedule changes, separating troublesome pairs, for example, or moving one of your students to a different class period where he or she may feel more comfortable or find the level of work more challenging.

Psychologists. If you suspect abuse, neglect, or serious emotional distress, ask the psychologist to call your student in for an informal meeting, so that the student will know help is available. Depending on legal implications—in some school districts, for example, a teacher can be sued by parents for simply suggesting that a child may be using illegal drugs—you might want to word your request carefully, to indicate that you think the student may be having problems, although you are not accusing the child or the family of any inappropriate behavior.

If you develop a good relationship with your school psychologist, you may be able to discuss individual student problems informally and ask for advice that may help students. Sometimes, students will confide in a trusted teacher but will not feel comfortable talking to a psychologist or counselor because they are afraid of the consequences. A student who is mistreated at home, for example, may need somebody to talk to, but may not want to risk being taken away from his family, so he may refuse to talk to a counselor or psychologist. You may not be able to solve the problem, but you can offer emotional support, and sometimes that's enough.

Principals. If your principal has the time and inclination, invite him or her to visit your classes frequently, to encourage attendance and motivation, and to discourage misbehavior. In Chapter 8, I discussed a very helpful principal who motivated my remedial readers by offering them a pizza party if everyone in class earned a C or higher on their semester report cards. Your administrators may be willing to consider offering rewards to motivate and reward your students.

Teachers. Other teachers may be able to help you identify problem areas; a student who has trouble understanding abstract concepts in biology or English, for example, probably isn't doing well in math, particularly algebra. Once you have identified an obstacle, you can work together to help your student succeed.

Ask the teachers in your department to share their best lesson. (Beware. Some teachers won't share, for fear that you will steal their goodies.) At a staff meeting, make a brief announcement that you are soliciting suggestions for lesson plans or assignments that teach effectively and interest students.

Find out what teachers who teach the next higher level of your subject are teaching, so you can target your own lessons appropriately and motivate your students. Students often work harder when you explain that you are teaching specific skills in order to help them succeed in future classes.

Education office personnel. Your district or state education office should have a public relations or human resources officer who can provide information about publications, multimedia and other classroom materials, classes and workshops for teachers, conferences, and professional organizations. In many cases, your education office will maintain a professional library where you can browse and check out materials for use in your classroom.

2. Students.

Don't overlook people just because they are young; students are often the best, most reliable and enthusiastic helpers. At one high school, the guidance office created a peer counseling program in which students were assigned to offer a sympathetic ear, advice, and encouragement to other students who had been involved in fights with other students or teachers, who were truant or frequently sent to detention, or who simply needed to talk to somebody who understood them.

Students can offer valuable insight into discipline or motivation problems, and may suggest solutions that might not occur to you. Students with natural leadership ability make excellent mediators when arguments arise in your classroom. Students also make excellent classroom clerks, peer tutors, mentors for new students, messengers, paper graders, mediators, quiz makers, bulletin board decorators, party planners, worksheet creators, developers of questions for exams, and sounding boards for future projects.

Whenever possible, give your student helpers academic credit for their efforts, as well as paper certificates or awards to hang on their bedroom walls and file with their college or employment applications.

Look to Your Local Community

Don't be selfish. Share the wonderful feeling of knowing you've enriched a young person's life by recruiting adult members of your local community to help you inside or outside of your classroom. There are dozens, perhaps hundreds or thousands, of potential volunteers within a few miles of your school, but most of those people are at a loss as to how they can share their wealth (literally and figuratively speaking) with your students. With a little ingenuity, you can provide the necessary bridge between your school and your community.

1. Parents and guardians.

Far too often, teachers think of parents only when they need to discuss problems with their children, but parents have much more to offer. One mother who worked as a personnel manager spent an entire day in my classroom, helping each of my classes develop good interview skills. A father brought his guitar and sang a duet with his son, who dreamed of becoming a professional singer. Another mother collected good used clothing, laundered and repaired it, and placed it on a counter in the back of my classroom where students could take what they needed without feeling embarrassed.

Send a note home with each of your students, asking their parents or guardians to let you know if they are interested in helping the children at your school. To reassure them that you aren't asking them for a long-term commitment or extensive time, include a checklist that they can return to you. Include categories such as classroom helper, guest speaker, hall monitor, field trip chaperone or host, test grader, entertainer, and so on. Ask them to choose from the following: daily, weekly, bimonthly, monthly, or one-time volunteer. Then ask them to provide a work or home telephone and the best time for you to call.

Note: To avoid problems with unions or other official groups, refer to your parents and guardians as classroom volunteers, not as helpers or aides. Should you face problems or objections from administrators, take the matter to your local school board or parent-teacher association and urge them to support and enable parent involvement in your school. Remind them that students' whose families support their education are far more likely to succeed in school.

2. Adults of all ages.

Parents and relatives of students often are asked to volunteer at school, but we may overlook adults who do not have school-age children living with them. Young adults, full-time college students, and retired people often are eager to contribute to local schools, but they don't know how to go about it. You can give them the opportunity to help young people by enlisting them for one of the following programs.

Mentors. If no mentor program exists at your school, you might consider working with a team of teachers to create one—or make this a personal project for your own students. Draft a letter to your local chamber of commerce and ask them to distribute copies to their members, requesting volunteers to act as mentors for your students. Your plan doesn't have to be elaborate, but you will need to create a plan for screening volunteers to make sure they are suitable. As little as one hour a month can make a big difference in the life of a child. (More information about mentors is included later in this chapter.)

Gift donors. Ask local businesses to provide awards for your school, or your classroom, on a monthly, quarterly, or yearly basis. Even a small business can afford to supply a pen or an inexpensive gift certificate. You may be surprised at the generosity of the people you contact. One year I approached several small business owners and asked them to donate gifts to be given out as door prizes at an award ceremony for the students in our at-risk program. In one day I received ten used videos of popular movies, twenty certificates for free hamburgers and fries, five baseball caps, a dozen colorful binder notebooks, a portable am/fm radio with headset, and several small cash donations—and each of those donors offered to provide another gift for the next award ceremony the following year.

Workshop presenters. Recruit employers and employees to present workshops (with your help, if necessary) about their professions to give students insight and information about future careers. Firefighters, police and probation officers, nurses and dental technicians, personnel managers and human resources specialists, shipping and receiving specialists, insurance agents, independent sales representatives, computer technicians and programmers, day care specialists, social workers and psychologists, truck drivers, convenience store managers—all have valuable information and experience to share.

Tutors. If your school does not have a tutor program, you might suggest that a team of teachers and administrators work together to establish one. Place an ad in your local newspaper, and post notices on bulletin boards in community centers, colleges, high schools, and senior centers. Explain that teaching experience or advanced degrees are not necessary, but that a desire to help children succeed is the requirement.

If you decide to try to create your own tutor program for your students, check with your district or state office to find out if there are any guidelines you must follow. In any event, you will need to screen volunteers carefully.

Magazines and newspaper recyclers. Provide local businesses with a postcard listing your name and the address of your school, so they can send you the hundreds of magazines and newspapers that are discarded from their lobbies and waiting rooms. Dentists, doctors, hairdressers, insurance agencies, attorneys, accountants, computer companies, car dealerships, health food stores, and coffeeshops are all good candidates.

Good Samaritans. Both parents of one of my students worked as security guards at a big convention center, and they were appalled at the amount of quality, unused material that was discarded after conventioneers departed. They provided my students with hundreds of pencils, pens, ball caps, notebooks, clipboards, candies, canvas bookbags, and T-shirts. From just one convention, we received enough tablets to supply paper for two years of weekly spelling quizzes for five classes of students!

Note: If you have the good fortune to find a similar Good Samaritan, keep your arrangement confidential, to avoid complaints or legal problems; sadly, there are bureaucrats who would rather waste valuable goods than to donate them to children who could use them.

3. Local colleges and universities.

In addition to a library and a computer lab that may be available to the public, colleges and universities are good sources for volunteers to work as tutors, counselors, mentors, or classroom helpers. If your college has an education department, the future teachers may be interested in working with you to gain more experience before they begin teaching. Creative writing students may be willing to conduct mini-workshops with your students, helping them to write poetry, short stories, or plays—and may be able to arrange for your students to present their plays or skits on stage via the college drama department. Other departments—engineering, chemistry, mathematics, entomology, journalism—often have graduate students who will speak to your students about career options or the latest research in their fields.

4. Social service agencies.

Find out what services are available to children in your community—free counseling, recreational activities, programs to help young people stop smoking or drinking, for example—and post the information in your classroom where students can see it. Counselors or probation officers may be willing to visit your classes and talk about their job duties and to invite students to make use of program and facilities that are specifically designed to help them. Check your local phone book to see if there are any hot lines for teens. Many communities maintain special phone centers to provide counseling and assistance for runaways, suicide prevention, and drug abuse prevention.

5. Police and fire departments.

Your local police or fire fighting team may agree to "adopt" your class and make regular visits or act as mentors. If they don't have the time or inclination for that level of involvement, they may be willing to visit your classroom and discuss their job duties with your students.

6. *Other schools.*

Visit other public and private schools for ideas that you can use—from the layout of classrooms to special programs that work. Create a network of teachers in your area who are interested in sharing ideas for lessons and solving problems, and for giving each other a pat on the back when somebody's morale needs a boost.

Take advantage of district or state conferences to do some networking. Ask other teachers, not just the workshop presenters, for suggestions. Teachers have shared great assignments with me via e-mail and standard U.S. Post Office mail. (Samples from some super teachers are presented at the end of this chapter.)

7. *Local public library.*

Take your students on a field trip to the local public library. Ask the librarians to provide a very brief overview of the facilities, just enough to point your students in the right direction. Send your students on a treasure hunt for information, so that they become familiar with the various departments, from reference books to the latest novels. Provide applications for library cards and encourage them to become regular library visitors.

If no funds are available to support a library field trip, consider arranging a voluntary visit for your students, early in the evening, and send notes home asking their parents to provide transportation. If a class visit is simply not possible, don't give up; ask the library to come to you. When I taught in San Mateo County, one of the librarians from Redwood City visited our school frequently to present "book talks" to the students. She brought a number of novels and nonfiction books, and gave a brief synopsis of each book, sometimes reading a few paragraphs or pages to pique the students' interest. Your local librarian may be willing to provide book talks for your class—if not, why not do it yourself?

Beyond Your Neighborhood

1. Professional publications.

Read several professional publications for educators, not just the ones intended for your subject or grade level. The *English Journal*, for example, often describes lessons and programs that could easily be adapted for other subject areas. As you read, note the names of other journals and publications cited that may contain useful information. Here's a brief list of professional publications to get you started:

> *American School Board Journal*, Alexandria, Virginia
> *Educational Horizons*, Bloomington, Indiana
> *Educational Leadership*, Alexandria, Virginia
> *Middle School Journal*, Columbus, Ohio
> *Principal*, Alexandria, Virginia
> *T.H.E. Technological Horizons in Education*, Tustin, California

2. Commercial publications.

Check your local library for the following commercial magazines that are published for teachers. If your library doesn't carry them, write and ask for a sample copy, or ask your school librarian to order a subscription (take up a collection among your colleagues if the school budget won't cover the cost). Here is a short list of education magazines to get you started. Watch for ads announcing other publications and professional organizations.

The ATA Magazine contains articles about education and education-related topics, published quarterly by the Alberta Teachers' Association, 11010 142nd St., Edmonton, Alberta T5N 2R1 Canada.

Calliope and *Cobblestone*, history magazines for young people (ages eight to fourteen), are published monthly during the school year by Cobblestone Publishing Inc., 7 School Street, Peterborough, NH 03458-1457.

Class Act, published by Act, Inc., P.O. Box 802, Henderson, KY 42420, is a newsletter published nine times per year for teachers of high school language arts.

Creative Classroom is a bimonthly magazine published by Children's Television Workshop, One Lincoln Plaza, New York, NY 10023, that offers practical advice and activities for elementary school teachers.

Education in Focus, a semiannual newsletter published by Books for All Times, Inc., Box 2, Alexandria, VA 22313, focuses on articles that expose failures and celebrates successes in education.

Electronic Learning, from Scholastic, 555 Broadway, New York, NY 10012, is subtitled *Your Resource for Technology and School Change*, and advocates using technology to reform our school system. Scholastic also publishes *Instructor Magazine*, which offers practical suggestions and reports on projects for elementary grades.

Emerge, from Emerge Communications, Inc., 1 BET Plaza, 1900 W Place NE, Washington, DC 20018, is subtitled "Black America's Newsmagazine" and reports on a wide variety of issues that affect Black Americans, from health to sports to politics.

Home Education Magazine, P.O. Box 1083, Tonasket, WA 98855-1083, features articles that address concerns of parents who want to be directly involved in their children's education. Although intended for home-schooling parents, this magazine may provide insight and information that will enable teachers to deal more effectively with parents whose children attend public schools.

Jack and Jill, from the Children's Better Health Institute, P.O. Box 567, Indianapolis, IN 46206-0567, is designed to encourage children to read for pleasure and focuses on articles, stories, and activities that promote health, safety, exercise, and nutrition.

Learning, 1607 Battleground Avenue, Greensboro, NC 27408, focuses on innovative ideas and practices, firsthand personal accounts of successes and failures, and practical advice for middle school and elementary school teachers.

New Moon: The Magazine for Girls & Their Dreams, from New Moon Publishing, Inc., P.O. Box 3620, Duluth, MN 55803, publishes articles about girls, women, and working to make dreams come true.

School Arts Magazine, 50 Portland Street, Worcester, MA 01608-9959, is published nine times per year and offers suggestions for art teachers of grades K to 12.

Teaching K–8, The Professional Magazine, from Early Years, Inc., 40 Richards Avenue, 7th floor, Norwalk, CT 06854-2319, publishes ideas and techniques that have been proven successful in the classroom.

Teaching Tolerance, from the Southern Poverty Law Center, 400 Washington Avenue, Montgomery, AL 36104, is a semiannual magazine dedicated to helping K to 12 teachers promote tolerance and understanding between diverse groups of students.

Third Force Magazine, from the Center for Third World Organizing, 1218 E. 21st Street, Oakland, CA 94606, is a bimonthly covering news from communities of color, grassroots organizing, and low-income communities. Politics aside, this publication may provide insight and information about problems and challenges that our students face.

Wonderful Ideas, P.O. Box 64691, Burlington, VT 05406-4691, is a newsletter published eight times per year, with creative activities, games, and lessons (teacher-written and classroom-tested) for elementary and middle school math teachers.

3. Special programs.

Expand your knowledge base by investigating some of the thousands of special programs established by public and private schools and colleges, government agencies, and private foundations and corporations. Contact foundations and charitable organizations in your state for information about local and national programs that you can use as models for creating programs at your school. At a conference in Amarillo, I met a woman who was working to replicate a

Philadelphia Futures' program called Sponsor-A-Scholar (winner of the President's Volunteer Action Award in 1994).

4. Consultants and traveling teachers.

For training, information, or inspiration, consider inviting an educational consultant to present a workshop for teachers or students at your school—and take notes about techniques you can adopt for use in your classroom, such as magic and music, which are irresistible to children of all ages.

Your local library or education office should have information about consultants who offer presentations in your area, but don't overlook friends, family, and colleagues. They may be able to provide personal recommendations or referrals for consultants they have seen in action. My own list of personal recommendations includes two dynamic women, Diane Hererra Shepard and Marcey Walsh Johnson. Diane, a former college special education instructor, now works out of her home in Placitas, New Mexico, and travels the country as Diane the Magicienne, presenting magic shows for entertainment and education. Marcey, an educational performer and owner of Highly Contagious Education in Clarkston, Michigan, offers musically and visually exciting math and science programs for elementary and middle school children. Diane can be reached at (505) 867-6545, and Marcey's number is (810) 620-8863. (No, they haven't paid me a penny. I just think they're good.)

5. Motivational and inspirational books.

Haunt your local library and bookstores in search of inspiration. Mike Rose's *Possible Lives*, for example, is filled with success stories about teachers and administrators who are making a real difference in the lives of their students. Check the logical places, such as the Instructional, Educational, or Self-Help sections, but don't stop there. Browse the Art and Music aisles, too, for books that may inspire lessons. Learn to understand your students (and yourself) better by reading the latest psychology studies. Visit the Military History section to read about people with extraordinary leadership skills. Take notes from the books about super salesmanship, the art of persuasion, and effective public speaking.

6. *Videotapes.*

Many teachers make educational videotapes a regular part of their curriculum, and Language Arts teachers often use movie adaptations of novels to reward students who complete lengthy or difficult reading assignments. But don't limit your video selection to educational tapes. With a little ingenuity, you can find ways to incorporate music videos into your lessons (nonverbal communications, the psychological effect of music, persuasive and misleading advertising). Make a tape of TV commercials and ask your students to analyze them to see how the advertisers use sex and glamour to manipulate consumers.

Share your favorite motivational tapes with your classes. For years, I watched renowned motivational speaker Les Brown's tapes at home, while exercising, for inspiration and to spark my creativity. One day, it occurred to me that my students might be inspired by Les's stories. He had been erroneously labeled EMR—educable mentally retarded—during elementary school, but eventually became a popular disk jockey and an Ohio state legislator before going on to become a highly successful public speaker. For information about Les Brown, who is based in Detroit, call (800) 733-4226.

As I mentioned in Chapter 1, I believe all teachers can benefit from watching Craig Cameron's videotapes on horse training. If we adopted his psychological approach and used similar training techniques in our classrooms, we would have fewer wild students. Craig Cameron can be reached at the Double Horn Ranch in Bluff Dale, Texas, at (800) 274-0077.

7. *The Internet.*

If you have any experience on the Internet, you know that one Web site often provides links or leads to dozens of other sites. A good place to start is "Web Sites and Resources for

Teachers," which is maintained by two professors of elementary education at California State University Northridge, Dr. Vicki F. Sharp and Dr. Richard M. Sharp. This site provides links to hundreds of interactive activities and virtual museum trips (both U.S. and international). Lesson plans, projects, and other resources are available in eight categories (Language Arts, Social Studies, Math, Science, Art, Music, ESL/Bilingual, and Just for Kids).

Each category offers a number of options. Last night, for example, in less than an hour, I visited the Diego Rivera Art Gallery at one on-line museum (via the Art entrance), then traveled to one of several natural history museums (via the Science entrance) to view the latest information and an exhibit on dinosaurs in the Triassic period. Then, I retrieved lesson plans for elementary, middle, and high school students from teachers in England, Canada, and the U.S. To visit this site, type the following prompt on your computer screen exactly as it appears here: http://www.csun.edu/~vceed009

If you are unfamiliar with the Internet, the most important thing to remember is that you must type the Web site address exactly the way it appears on the Web page. Capital letters must be caps, and lower case must be lower case. Forward (/) and back (\) slashes are not interchangeable, and other symbols and characters must be included. Don't omit this symbol ~ if you can't locate it on your keyboard immediately. Take your time. Once you successfully arrive at your desired Web page, you will find information that is highlighted, printed in different color type, or accompanied by messages such as "Click here" or "Enter this door." If you double click on those locations, they will take you to a different Web site automatically. When you find useful information, copy down the Web site address so that you can find it in the future. If you end up in some undesirable place, select "Back" (if your program offers that option) to return to your previous Web site. If you get lost, close the program and start over, inserting one of the addresses for the pages you wanted to revisit. Many programs offer a "Bookmark" option whereby you can add different Web addresses to your computer's memory so you can automatically visit those sites.

If none of this makes sense to you, ask another teacher, or one of your students, to give you a quick lesson on navigating the Net. Even elementary school children may be surprisingly well versed in computer and software operations.

This following list is by no means comprehensive and will be out of date before this page is typed, because new Web sites are added every day. But this will give you a good start on your journey to the land of high-tech teaching.

http://www.newmoon.org If you've been looking for ways to motivate and inspire the girls in your class or include women's historical achievements in your lessons, visit this on-line version of *New Moon: The Magazine for Girls & Their Dreams*. A pro-girl publication started by the mother of twin teens, this magazine has no advertisements and is written by the girls who read it. In addition to feature articles and information, the magazine provides a wonderful list of links to other sites, including the National Women's History Project (http://www.nwhp.org), a nonprofit organization that promotes gender equity through education about women's accomplishments. The NWHP provides a clearinghouse for women's history, resources, and activities that can be used in your classroom. Other Web sites for girls include:

http://www.herspace.com
http://www.cybergrrl.com
http://www.girlpower.com
http://www.cyberkids.com (for boys and girls)
http://www.cyberteens.com (for older boys and girls)
http://www.teenvoices.com
    (an on-line magazine written by teenage girls)

http://www.teachnet.com Teacher's Edition Online Tools for Teachers offers lesson plans, a discussion group, five-minute micro-activities, employment info, humor, tips on classroom management. Some information changes weekly. This week, I found several Internet addresses where teachers can find free puzzles to use in their classrooms. The list of puzzle sites is too long to print in its entirety, but here are a few:

http://www.interlock.com.au
http://www.puzzledepot.com/contests
http://www.riddler.com
http://www.talkcity.com.gamers.gamestown
http://www.discover.co.uk/games/coffee/welcome.html

http://www.teacherpathfinder.syr.edu/School This site contains a plethora of information, with individual offices (Parent, Professional Development, Serving Teachers) that provide access to additional sites. Inside the Schoolhouse, you'll find information on Assessment, Subject Areas (all the basics, plus technology and human services), General Ed Resources, Immersive Curriculum, Integrated Curriculum, Library, Special Needs, School to Work, and Students Schoolhouse.

http://www.web66.coled.umn.edu Web66, from the University of Minnesota, is a project designed to bring technology into K-12 schools. This site includes an international registry of schools on the Net, a resource center, Web information, and help for educators who want to set up their own Internet home pages. If you've been wanting to take your school onto the information highway, here's your chance to hitch a ride with some experts.

http://www.youth.net/cec/cec.html Columbia Education Center and a consortium of teachers from fourteen states created this Web site to provide easy but high-quality lesson plans, particularly in math and science. In less than a minute, I had lesson plans for making a pinhole camera. Good stuff here.

http://www.bingwa.com Bingwa means "champion" in Swahili, and this site is designed to help kids become champion learners. Although the sponsor is a commercial software company, the site contains many links to free information and other Web sites. From the home page, you can select from a number of categories, including Education K-12 Worldwide, Hotlist Black History, Home School Resources,

Academic Institutions, and On-Line Geometry. I selected Hotlist Black History, which gave me more choices, including Faces of Science (an alphabetized list of African-American scientists, engineers, chemists and information about their contributions).

http://www.home-ed-press.com/wlcm_hsinf.html This will take you to the Homeschool Information and Resources Page, which provides links to information designed for parents who home-school. Teachers may find the resources and information useful, such as the article entitled "Learning Disabilities, Facts and Fictions," which contains anecdotes from therapists and doctors about working with children.

http://www.doubleclickd.com/Articles/sheddinglight.html This site contains an article linked to the DoubleClickd Web site, which promotes holistic wellness. The article "Shedding Light: Childhood Behavior & Learning Problems," includes input from several doctors—allergist, pediatrician, osteopath, speech pathologist, nutritionist, family therapist—in which they discuss their successes in helping children diagnosed with ADHD (attention deficit) and other learning disorders. These experts discuss possible factors such as sugar, food allergies, fluorescent lighting, pollution, and family stress, which may be responsible for many problems in school. A thought-provoking and well-written discussion.

IN-CLASS TELEPHONE SCAVENGER HUNT

Courtesy of Marc Vincenti, Advanced Communications Instructor, Palo Alto, California

An exercise in creative thinking, problem solving, locating information, telephone tact, social skills.

TEACHER DIRECTIONS: Find a company to donate (or lend) six or seven cellular phones to your school. Divide class into groups of 4 to 5 students. Students then designate group leaders and recorders to keep the written log. Brief the class on the existence of possible resources (clubs, societies, city or county bodies, libraries, businesses). Lay out "ethical" rules for this exercise: no lying, identify yourself as a high school student, be polite, thank people. Give each group a cellular phone with instructions for use and a list of scavenger hunt questions.

STUDENT DIRECTIONS: You have this class period to answer as many of your scavenger hunt questions as possible. if you can't find full answers, give partial ones.

Grade: 50 possible points towards your semester grade. 5 "extra-credit" points for the group that digs up the most info. Groups will be graded as groups, on the basis of the number of points earned and the accuracy and detail of the log sheet.

Log Sheet: Decide how you will keep this record of your calls. Be accurate and specific, and include complete information. This counts as part of your grade.

Ground Rules: You may use the phone, the phone book, and your brains. No outside help.

Procedure: You have four questions to answer. You may pursue them in any order or all at once. Questions are worth different numbers of points. Questions answered *in full* will gain you the full number of points indicated. Partial answers earn partial points. Smart pursuits and valiant attempts, *recorded in the log,* will gain points also.

Hints: Each group may ask for help only *twice,* to get past roadblocks. Just twice!

Disagreements: If your group can't resolve disagreements, the team leader decides how to proceed.

Phone Etiquette: You are working on a class project for which it is legitimate to ask for help from the community, within reason. Please remember: you represent yourself, your fellow students, your teacher, our English Department, and Gunn High School. Be polite.

Telephone Scavenger Hunt: The Phone Log

Group Number_____

Phone call made to: (person, title, or organization)	Time of call (beginning & ending)	Information sought	Result of call

SAMPLE QUESTIONS FOR IN-CLASS
TELEPHONE SCAVENGER HUNT

A. (5 points). On a Sunday, you are going to ride the local train from the California Avenue station in Palo Alto to San Jose. You must arrive in San Jose as close to 3 P.M. as possible. What time will your train leave the California Avenue station?

A. (10 points). You wish to hire a stretch limousine to drive yourself and nine friends to San Francisco, departing Palo Alto at about 5 P.M. on a Saturday and returning to Palo Alto at about 3 A.M. the following morning. Assuming you share the cost equally, and that you are satisfied that you have found a "reasonable rate" by doing some checking around, how much will this cost each of you?

B. (15 points). What is the rarest bird ever sighted within the city limits of Palo Alto?

B. (25 points). What is the most expensive piece of artwork for sale in Palo Alto and how much does it cost?

C. (25 points). Leland Stanford, Jr., is buried in a mausoleum on the Stanford campus. At first, though, he was laid to rest elsewhere. Find out exactly where he was first buried, and find out (in general) what was (or is) on the tombstone there.

C. (25 points). How many bagpipers live in Palo Alto? (A bagpiper is someone who owns and plays a bagpipe.)

D. (45 points). Suppose you want to propose marriage to your beloved by having an airplane tow a banner above Stanford Stadium on the day of the Big Game (football) against U. of California. Find out on what date you would be able to do this, how long you are permitted to have a plane circle the stadium, how to hire a plane to do it, how much it would cost, and how many readable letters (of the alphabet) you can get on the banner.

D. (50 points). Surely you have noticed the cows that from time to time may be seen grazing along Highway 280, somewhere between Page Mill and Alpine Roads. Who, *specifically*, owns these cows?

GREAT GAME IDEAS

from Deborah Carter,
Latin Teacher, Frederick, Maryland

Vocab Bingo: I keep a huge pile of photocopied bingo sheets on hand, with rolls of small candies to hand out as markers. Each sheet contains 24 boxes, with one Latin or English word in each box, and a free space in the center. I call out the same words that are on the sheets—but in the "other" language, so students have to know the meanings. When somebody has 5 in a row, he or she has to read back the answers in both languages to win a prize (candy or extra-credit points). In English class, I use the same game, giving synonyms or definitions for the vocab words, or using characters in a novel and giving their descriptions.

Roulette: Using a cheap cardboard roulette wheel that spins, I made a game that takes a few days to set up, but also gives a complete lesson plan for those few days. Divide kids into groups and give each group 39 blank index cards. Have them number the cards 1 to 39 in large numbers on one side, and write questions on the other side (and answers). The questions should get increasingly harder as the numbers increase, so that card #1 is worth 1 point for a correct answer, card

#39 is worth 39 points. If you have 4 teams writing questions, you will have 4 different questions for each point value. In a couple of years, you will have a huge bank of questions.

Let the kids form teams. They spin the wheel and try to answer the question that matches the number. If they get it right, give them points and put that question aside. If they get it wrong, don't give the answer—put that card back in the deck and continue. If a team lands on a number for the fifth time and there are no more questions, give them the choice of answering the next higher (harder) or lower (easier) question. If a team spins a 0 or 00, they lose their turn.

Seat Races: I do this several times a week, often using a vocabulary crossword puzzle. To review for a test or quiz, hand out your worksheet or exercise papers, face down, until every student has a paper. When I say, "Begin!" everybody starts to work. When they finish, they call out and I assign them a number. The first 5 students who complete the exercise *correctly* earn extra credit or some other prize.

Stump the Teacher: This works well with cultural or mythological reading, but any reading will work. Students read an assignment and write questions about the reading. Questions must be legitimate, not something silly, such as "How many words are on page 10?" Students also must have correct answers to their own questions. The next day, they get to quiz the teacher. They pay close attention during questioning because (1) if they repeat a question that has already been asked, they are disqualified, and (2) their questions will be used on the quiz the following day. If a student stumps the teacher, the entire class wins a prize (candy, points, whatever). Collect the questions and assign grades for the accuracy of the answers, then select the best 15 or 25 for your quiz. This exercise provides a homework grade, a quiz grade, and a darn fun activity—plus, the kids really read the material when you assign it in this way!

A slight variation on Stump the Teacher: Have students take individual notes during a reading, lecture, or video. Then, put them in pairs and have each pair write a complete quiz on the subject. The best quiz becomes the official quiz for the class—and the winning pair earn an A.

One on One

My Personal Advice to Kids Who Ask for It

"**O**ne of my students came to my room after school today," a teacher confided to me. "She told me she was pregnant and asked me what I thought about abortion."

"What did you say?" I asked, curious to know whether her response was similar to what mine would be in the same situation.

"I told her I was too busy to talk," the teacher said. "It's not my place, as a teacher, to discuss personal matters with students."

I disagree. While I do agree that we should not try to impose our own morals and values on our students, and that we should not try to influence their religious beliefs or undermine their parents' authority, I believe that we have a moral obligation to help young people articulate their own beliefs, locate accurate information, and develop good analytical and problem-solving skills. That teacher was right in not condoning or condemning abortion, but I think she was wrong to turn a pregnant child away without offering any help. At the very least, she could have encouraged the girl to talk to her parents or a counselor, instead of ignoring her plea for help. There are no correct answers to the difficult questions that children ask, but it is cowardly and wrong to ignore them.

Teachers have tremendous influence on the opinions our students form, and on the choices they make based on those opinions. Even our offhand remarks are taken seriously by children, simply because we are teachers. We cannot escape the responsibility that comes with the job—whether we try to or not, we shape young lives. Students notice everything we say and do, and model their own behavior and attitudes on ours. We can take advantage of our influence to help our students develop the strength of character and self-confidence that will enable them to "just say no" to drugs, sex, and the thousands of other temptations that beckon them every day.

Because so many students have asked me for advice, and because so many of their problems involve the same issues—power, fighting, sex and love, drugs, drinking, and smoking—I've developed six basic monologues based on the advice that caught their attention and helped them the most. You may disagree with my opinions, but perhaps they will help you better articulate your own, so that when your students ask questions, you'll have answers.

Power

You may recall the one-sided conversation that I have with my power players—the students who try to take control of my classroom by refusing to play school. During the school day, I don't have much time to make my point, and usually the short version works. But when I have a stubborn child who continues to challenge me, I call him in before or after school and try this long version. So far, it has worked every time.

(Please note that I am fully aware that girls can be as difficult and challenging as boys, although in my experience,

I've found that twice as many boys require this longer speech. I have used the masculine form here solely for the sake of brevity. Naturally, I would make some changes in the text if I were talking to a female student.)

You're probably tired of being treated like a child. You aren't a child. You're becoming a young man, and you want to make your own decisions and run your own life. But people won't let you. People keep telling you what to do, what to wear, what to say, what to eat and when to eat it, what to read, where to go and where to sit when you get there, when to go to bed and when to get up, who to be friends with, what to watch on TV, and so forth. I didn't like being told what to do when I was your age, either. It made me mad. I still don't like being told what to do. And I don't like telling you what to do, either. I'm not trying to boss you around just to show that I can do it because I'm the teacher. I'm not interested in making you feel bad or stupid or embarrassed. I am interested in helping you become a successful and happy person. I see talents in you that you can't see yourself. I'm trying to help you see your talents, so that you can be successful in school and in your job and your personal life. I want you to be a happy, healthy, responsible adult.

I want to treat you as an adult, but I can't do that if you continue to act like a child. Adults don't pout when they have to do something they don't want to do—that's part of life. I don't want to pay taxes or do the dishes or write reports or spend my nights grading papers. We all do things we don't want to do. The difference between an adult and a child, a man and a boy, is that a man accepts things he can't control and doesn't throw a tantrum. A man doesn't make life difficult for people who are trying to help him. A man doesn't challenge everybody all the time to try to prove that he's tough because he knows he is strong.

A man makes choices and accepts the responsibilities that go with those choices. You make choices, too. You are not powerless. Nobody can make you do anything. Think about it. The only things you truly have to do are eat, drink water, and breathe. The rest is optional. You may choose to do things because you don't like the alternatives—if you don't go to school, your parents may ground you or take away your allowance or hit you. But they can't make you go to school and they certainly can't make you learn. You choose that for your-self. I'm sure you know plenty of kids who cut classes or cheat or who don't go to school at all. They are making a choice. You are making a better choice than those kids just by being here where you have a chance to learn.

Your biggest choice, the most powerful one, is the choice you make about the kind of person you are. Nobody makes you a liar, a cheater, or a quitter—and nobody makes you honest or a hard worker or somebody who doesn't give up. Nobody can make you be friendly or make you have a nasty attitude. You choose those things. You choose who you are every second of every day of your life. You can choose to act like a man, or you can choose to act like a little boy. And people will treat you according to the choice you make.

I am trying to treat you like a man, and I expect you to act like one. That means you don't make my job difficult. You don't fight me just for the sake of fighting somebody—because I'm on your side. If you have an objection, an honest objection, to something I say or something I ask you to do, then all you have to do is tell me. It's all right to argue, because an argument isn't a fight. An argument is just a case of two people discussing dif-ferent points of view. There doesn't have to be a winner and a loser. A constructive argument produces two winners—both people learn to see something from somebody else's point of view.

Now, before we go back into my classroom, I'd like to know two things: whether you want to be in my class, and whether you want me to treat you like a man or like a little boy. I hope you choose to stay, because I like you and I think I can help you be a successful student. And I hope you choose to be treated as a man, because I would prefer to be able to talk to you honestly, as I am doing right now.

If you choose to stay in my class and you want me to treat you like a man, I want you to look me straight in the eye and give me your word of honor that you will try to act like a man. I don't expect you to be perfect, because everybody makes mistakes. But I do expect you to try. I expect you to treat both of us—you and me—with respect. And I will do the same. I give you my word of honor. And I want to shake hands with you on that.

I have never had a student refuse to shake my hand, and I have never had one renege on his promise to try to act like a man (or a woman). I think this approach works because it makes the students responsible for their behavior, and it also makes it clear that I respect them, I like them, and I have faith in them. I trust them to make the right decision in this case, and trust is one of the most valuable gifts we can offer a child.

Fighting

Every year I have several students—both boys and girls—who are repeatedly sent to detention or suspended for fighting on campus. In almost every case, the students insist that they must fight to protect their reputations or their honor, and that the other party instigated the fight. Students know they shouldn't fight; they've heard the same lectures since they were tiny tots. Instead of insisting that violence is wrong, I address the underlying psychological issues—power and control. Here's my Personal Power speech for fighters:

I am not going to try to tell you not to defend yourself or not to ever fight. Those are decisions every person has to make for herself. What I want to talk about is control—of your body and your mind. When you let somebody make you so angry that you have to hit her, then you have given that person control over your mind and your body. You are letting that person dictate your behavior. Let's say you're getting good grades, maybe you're going to college, or you're going to get a better job than I am. So, I'm jealous. When I see you looking like a winner, I feel like a loser. I feel like my life is going down the drain, and I want to take you down with me. So, what do I do? I talk some stuff about you to some other kids, because I know they'll tell you. I insult your mama, or I shove you in the hallway, or I come right up to you and get in your face. I figure out what will make you mad, and I do it. I keep doing it until I make you so mad that you hit me. I don't care if you rearrange my face or break my arm, because I'll still be the winner. You'll get in trouble, maybe you'll get suspended—and maybe your grades will go down, or the teachers won't think you're such hot stuff.

When you let somebody make you mad, you are handing that person control of you. It's hard, I know, to resist and not to get mad when somebody really puts on the pressure, but you have a good brain and you can use your brain to make yourself stronger. When somebody challenges you, you don't have to accept. You can choose not to fight—and it takes a much stronger person to walk away from a fight, to ignore the insults, and risk having other kids call you a coward. But the kids who are smart, the ones that you respect, won't think you're a coward, because they'll know that you are the winner, that you were too strong to let somebody else control you. They may not tell you, because they won't want to be the next target, but that's what they'll be thinking. There's a big difference between fear and respect. Kids may fear somebody who has a knife or a gun or strong fists—but they don't respect that person. They respect the person who has the self-confidence and the strength of character to resist letting ignorant, obnoxious people pull you down to their level.

When somebody teases you or taunts you, ignore it. If she persists, tell her you aren't interested in fighting. Don't play her game. Don't let her control your mind. Keep your mind on your own goal—to be a successful, strong person. If you can resist long enough, she will get tired and find another target.

SEX, LOVE, AND BABIES

1. Sex and love.

Teenagers are no different from adults—many of them confuse sex with love, or they think that if they offer sex, they will receive love in return. So, I begin my Sex Speech by discussing the difference between sex and love.

Don't expect me to tell you to have safe sex, because I'm not going to. I think you are too young to have sex. You aren't too young to have real feelings—you may be very deeply in love with somebody. I know couples who fell in love during high school, got married after graduation, and are still happily married fifteen or twenty years later. But I know many more couples who thought they were in love when they were thirteen or fourteen or sixteen, and they ended up miserably unhappy or divorced, usually with children they couldn't afford or didn't want.

I think you are too young to have sex because you don't have the emotional maturity and experience to avoid hurting yourself or other people. Sex is one of the most intimate and wonderful experiences humans can share, and when you engage in intimate acts, you make yourself vulnerable to hurt. I'm not talking about physical pain. Our bodies heal. I'm talking about emotional pain. Some people never recover from a broken heart. You know how much it hurts when somebody you trust lies to you or stabs you in the back. That is nothing compared to the pain of giving your heart and body to somebody who tells you they love you, and you find out later that they didn't care about you at all, they just wanted to have sex with you. And, if you are any kind of person at all, you will hurt even worse if you know that you have broken somebody else's heart because of your own selfishness. Most of us will have our hearts broken sooner or later, but heartbreak is easier to handle if you're an adult when it happens.

Don't let anybody talk you into risking your heart by having sex until you are ready. By "ready" I mean grown up enough to truly know yourself and what you want from life, and in a stable relationship with somebody you know very well, somebody you trust and love, somebody who loves you in return.

Maybe your boyfriend or girlfriend says, "If you really loved me, you'd have sex with me." My answer to them would be, "If you really loved me, you wouldn't ask me to do something I don't want to do. People who love you don't hurt you—at least on purpose. People who love you care about you and respect your feelings."

I'd like you to think about something for a minute. Think about who your best friend was five years ago. And think about what your favorite hobbies were back then. If you had a boyfriend or girlfriend, think about them, too. Now, ask yourself whether you have the same best friend, the same hobbies, or the same boyfriend or girlfriend today. Have your personality and tastes changed? Probably. And you're going to keep on changing for a long time. Some day you'll look back and see those people you think are sexy today—and they probably won't look so good to you. If they still look good, and you still love them in a couple of years, then you probably are feeling real love. Wait and see. Give yourself time.

Don't confuse sex with love. They are two very different things. If you think that somebody will love you because you have sex with him or her, ask yourself this: would you love somebody just because they were willing to have sex with you? There are lots of people in this world who would be willing to have sex with you, people who don't even know you, so they couldn't possibly love you.

Everybody feels lonely sometimes. Nobody else can make you feel good about yourself or make you stop feeling lonely. That's part of life. If you want to feel good about yourself, do things that make you proud, things that make you happy, things that make you grow as a person. Do something good for somebody else. Help somebody who is less fortunate than you are. You'll feel good—and it will be a genuine feeling.

When students admit that they are sexually active, I do recommend that they stop having intercourse, but not for the reasons they expect to hear. I try to make them think about why they are having sex.

> *If you like having sex because it makes you feel good, or because you want to have an orgasm, then you are using the other person and using people is wrong. When you have sex just to make yourself feel good, you are masturbating on the other person. You might as well stay home and enjoy your own company—that way, you won't get any diseases and you won't make any babies you aren't equipped to raise.*

When they giggle and cover their mouths and look aghast because I said the "m" word, I tell them:

> *You have just proved my point. If you were mature enough to have sex without risking your own or somebody else's emotional or physical well-being, you wouldn't laugh when I said masturbation or penis or breast. But you do laugh at those words because you are not a mature adult—and you are not mature enough to have sex.*

2. Babies.

Nearly every school offers sex education, often beginning in elementary school, yet most high school students are surprisingly ignorant or misinformed about the entire business. Girls are especially confused because they hear so much myth and misinformation about menstrual periods outside the classroom. Once, I had four freshman students who became pregnant during the same school year. These were not wild girls. They didn't smoke, drink, or take drugs. They were intelligent girls, good students, genuinely nice people—but they were also insecure about their attractiveness. They wanted to be loved, and they were willing to do what their boyfriends asked in return for what they thought was love. One of the girls wrote to me in her private journal:

*Miss J, you're the only adult I can talk to about this who
won't yell at me or treat me like a little kid. I know I was stupid
to have sex, especially without protection, but I couldn't help it.
I said I wasn't going to do it. I prayed in church that I wasn't
going to do it. I even told my boyfriend I wouldn't, but then I
went right ahead and did it. I wish I knew why I went and did
that. Do you know?*

My response was longer than Darcy's question, but I
wanted to write a good answer for her. I explained the menstrual cycle and the powerful effects that biology and hormones have on our behavior. When I handed back her journal
after school, Darcy grabbed it, glanced at my answer, and ran
out of the room. I thought perhaps she was embarrassed by my
frankness. A few minutes later, she rushed back into my room,
followed by three other girls. They sat down in the front row
and Darcy said, "Go ahead, Miss J, tell them the story, just like
you wrote in my journal."

I suggested that they read what I had written, but Darcy
insisted that I explain it in person. "It's so cool," she said.
"They have to hear it. Tell about Little Susie Uterus."

First, I drew four rows of X's on the white board in front
of my room, seven X's in each row. I circled the fifth X in the
first row and drew an arrow to the side where I wrote
"Ovulate." I circled the fifth X in the third row (which
would be two weeks later) and drew an arrow to the side
where I wrote "Menstruate." Then I told the girls about
menstrual periods and Little Susie:

*These twenty-eight X's represent the days of your menstrual
cycle. At least your cycle is supposed to have twenty-eight days,
but we all know that isn't usually the case. Some of us have a
period every thirty-two days, or every forty-five, or maybe even
every twenty-six days. Sometimes, we go thirty-two days one
cycle and fifty-three the next. We might have two periods in one
month, or we might skip a month altogether. The only thing you
can be sure of is that you will ovulate fourteen days before your
period starts. When you ovulate, you are fertile. That means you*

can make a baby. If your periods are irregular, as most of ours are, then you won't know exactly which day you ovulate, but you can bet that your hormones know. Hormones are chemicals that tell your body to develop breasts and have periods—and they are strong little chemicals. On the day you ovulate, your hormones take over your brain and say, "Shut up. I'm tired of listening to you. You spoil all my fun." And even if you know in your mind and your heart that you don't want to have sex, your hormones will talk your body into it. Your hormones are the best talkers in the world. "Ooh, baby," they whisper. "Just this one time. Please, please, please, please, please." And because hormones do their best talking on the day you ovulate, the day you can't resist is the day you are most likely to get pregnant. That's why so many girls say, "But I only did it once, and only for a few seconds, so how come I got pregnant?" Because the one time you couldn't resist was the time your body was ready to make a baby. It's biology. It's natural. Your body doesn't know any better. When you start having periods, your body is capable of making a baby, and that's what it wants to do. And it doesn't take long to make a baby, because sperm are faster than lightning.

While we're on the subject of periods, let me assure you that they are not horrible or nasty. They are not a curse, and they don't make you unclean or irrational. Having a period is the most natural thing in the world, but most of us are embarrassed to talk about them. Most men are embarrassed when we mention our periods, because they don't understand them, but neither do women. It's really very simple. Here's how it goes.

3. Little Susie Uterus.

Little Susie Uterus has a nice, cozy little apartment inside you. Just down the street from Susie's place, you have hundreds of tiny eggs in storage. Your body doesn't make a new egg every month, as some people believe. Your eggs are already there— that's why you have to wear a lead apron if you have an X ray at the dentist's office—so your precious little eggs won't be exposed to X rays that could harm them.

Every twenty-eight days, or whatever your cycle is, one of your little eggs—let's call her Ms. Egg—comes to visit Susie Uterus. Ms. Egg is lonely. She wants to make a baby. That's her entire purpose in life, but she doesn't have much time. She only has a few hours, a day or two at the most, to find Mr. Right and make a baby. Susie is a good friend. She's so excited about Ms. Egg and her potential baby that she redecorates the whole apartment—puts up new wallpaper, everything. Then, Susie and Ms. Egg sit and wait. Mr. Right isn't the most punctual or polite guy in the world. He's a sperm. He's little and wiggly and pushy and in a terrible hurry. If he shows up in time, Ms. Egg grabs him, hugs him, and they make a baby.

Usually, Mr. Right doesn't show up. Ms. Egg gets upset and leaves in a huff. Susie Uterus is disappointed, too, after all that work. She rips down the wallpaper and tosses it out—that's the tissue that lines the walls of your uterus in case you make a baby. The tissue is your period. Old wallpaper. No big deal.

Now you know why so many girls get pregnant the first time they have sex. So, here's my advice. Don't run out and get on the pill. Wait until you are emotionally and financially able to support a baby and give it the best possible life. Avoid situations where you will be tempted to have sex. I'm not telling you not to kiss your boyfriends. It's normal to want to share affection. But don't put yourself in a position where your hormones can talk your body into having sex. Don't hang out behind buildings or park in cars or go to parties where there will be alcohol or no chaperones.

Speaking of alcohol. Remember those eggs? Well, those little eggs are your potential future children. Take care of them. Nurture them carefully. Don't eat too much junk food that's loaded with chemicals or artificial sweeteners, and don't drink alcohol or take drugs—because those little eggs eat everything you eat, drink everything you drink, and take every drug you take. If you drink beer, you are giving your eggs beer. Your bodies are still developing, and the stronger you make your body, the stronger your eggs will be. Take care of them, so your future children will have the best possible chance to be strong and healthy.

Darcy and her friends spread the story, and soon all of my female students were making jokes about wallpaper and eggs. Because I wanted them to think about their behavior over the weekends, when temptation runs highest, I started reminding them on Fridays when they left my class. When the dismissal bell rang, I'd wave and say, "Have fun this weekend, girls. And take care of them there eggs." They always giggled and blushed, but I know they listened and remembered, because several girls wrote in their journals that they had been tempted to drink or take drugs at parties, but had decided not to take any risks that might affect their future children.

Drugs

Drug-abuse prevention is part of nearly every school curriculum, starting in kindergarten. Children know much more about drugs, from the way our bodies react to them, to the street value of a given dose, than most adults do. Unfortunately, young people don't often consider their mortality or frailty. Cancer, car accidents, and drug overdoses are things that happen to other people. In my experience, children tune us out when we talk to them about what drugs can do to them, but they pay close attention when we talk about why they are tempted to take drugs in the first place.

Kids know that drugs are dangerous. In fact, the danger of drugs is what attracts young people who are looking for excitement. "Just say no" sounds easy, but it is very difficult for many children to say, because they don't have the strength of character or the self-confidence to resist ridicule or rejection by their peers. Children who have long-term goals, plans for their future, exciting hobbies, strong family bonds, or membership in some kind of club or organization, are less susceptible to temptation, because they don't want to lose the things that are important to them. Students who feel lost, unloved, lonely, bored, or insecure are most likely to experiment with drugs. Instead of warning them to avoid drugs, which may only serve to make drugs seem all the more attractive, we need to help them gain confidence and hope for their future, so that they will be less inclined to take such dangerous risks. My Drug Speech takes a psychological approach to the subject.

I want you to know, up front, that if you sell drugs, I have no respect for you. If you have sold drugs, but you had the integrity to stop, then you regain my respect. By selling drugs, you are making money from other people's misery and pain, perhaps even their death. You may be creating crack-addicted babies, and you may be indirectly responsible for spreading the AIDS virus. If you use drugs, I feel sorry for you—not because you are a victim or because you are weak—nobody is stronger than drugs. I feel sorry for you because you are mentally and morally lazy. You are taking the easy way out. You take drugs because you don't like your life. You want to change your reality, but to change your reality, you have to take a good look at yourself, an honest look, and accept responsibility for your own actions and choices and behavior. Then, you have to work hard to change your life into the thing that you want it to be. It's much easier to pop a pill, light up a joint, take a hit of acid or PCP or XTC, smoke some crack, stick a needle in your arm, or chew, smoke, or swallow any of the hundreds of drugs that people are so eager to sell you. There are plenty of people who are happy to help you hurt yourself, who encourage you to feel like a victim, because they are weak themselves and it makes them feel better if you are weak, too. They don't feel so guilty.

The primary problem with using drugs is that the effect is temporary. No matter what drug you use, it wears off eventually— if it doesn't kill you. And then you come back to reality and it's just the same as you left it. It still stinks. You still hate your life. The only difference is that now you have less money and less time than you did before you took the drugs. You've given somebody else your money for nothing. And you've wasted the most valuable thing you have—your time—because your time is your life. You haven't done a thing to change your reality. It takes a strong person to take on that task, to be honest, to look yourself straight in the eye and take control of your own life.

Think of all the other things you could have been doing with your time. In just one hour, you could have listened to several wonderful songs, learned to play a musical instrument, held a baby in your arms, planted a tree, read part of a good book, enjoyed an ice cream cone, perfected your jump shot, learned to skateboard, baked a batch of cookies, helped an elderly person carry home some heavy groceries, held somebody special in your arms—you could have done a million things that would have contributed to your life and made you happier. Instead, you have nothing at all to show for your time.

The second reason I feel sorry for you if you use drugs is because you may be endangering the health of your future children. You know kids who sit in class and try and try, but can't seem to learn, and the reason some of them can't learn is because their parents abused drugs or alcohol. I'm not just talking about mothers here. The father's drug use can also affect his children. One of my roommates in the Navy gave birth to a baby who had no arms. The doctors said the baby was deformed because my friend's husband took a lot of acid when he was a kid. He stopped using acid when he grew up, but the genetic damage was already done. Maybe those doctors were wrong and acid had nothing to do with it, but nobody knows for sure. Why take that kind of risk, especially with your own baby's life? Every time you experiment with drugs, you are taking a chance with the health, and perhaps even the life, of your future children. Imagine holding your baby in your arms, looking into his eyes, and telling this helpless, innocent child that you're sorry you risked his health, but you were just "chillin' and kickin' with your friends, having a good time."

Perhaps you're thinking, "I just smoke pot. It's harmless." Think again. The latest research indicates that long-term marijuana use can cause changes in your DNA—the stuff that makes up all living things.

If you are unhappy or bored or looking for love and acceptance—try making somebody else happy and see what happens. Challenge yourself to accomplish a physical or mental goal. Instead of feeling sorry for yourself because you have no friends, try being a friend to somebody else. Look in the mirror and see who you are. Ask yourself what's missing in your life, and fig-ure out how to get what you need to be happy.

If you don't like your life, fix it. Drugs can't do that for you.

Drinking

My students often complain about the hypocrisy of adults who spend so much time telling children not to use drugs when drinking alcohol, which is a drug, is so common among adults. Instead of focusing on the fact that alcohol is a dangerous drug, I try to make my students see the issue from an economic perspective. My Drinking Speech is about money.

Lots of kids complain that adults are hypocrites because we drink alcohol, and then turn around and rag on you about using drugs. Alcohol is a drug, you tell us. You know that because you learned it in Biology or Drug Awareness or Substance Abuse classes. You are absolutely right. Alcohol is a drug, as dangerous as many illegal drugs, and the reason alco-hol is legal is simple—money. Our government makes a lot of money from sales tax on alcohol. But don't get mad at the gov-ernment. You've heard about Prohibition, unless you were sleeping in history class. Our government tried to make alcohol illegal, but the same situation developed that now exists with illegal drugs. People believed they had a right to drink, or they were addicted to alcohol, so when alcohol became illegal, people made their own and sold it on the streets for a lot of money—and they killed each other over it, just the way drug dealers kill each other today.

Alcohol is legal because it's big business. All those commercials you see where people are drinking and laughing and falling madly in love and having a wonderful time are designed for one purpose—to make you spend your money on alcohol. Advertisers aren't interested in whether you become addicted to alcohol, or whether you die from drinking too much. They just want your money.

Money may be the reason alcohol is legal, but it isn't the reason peole want to drink. People drink because alcohol is a drug and it changes their perception of reality, it makes them forget their troubles for a little while. But for many people, those little troubles are exchanged for big troubles, because alcohol is very addictive, just like any other drug. And addiction isn't always physical. Your body doesn't have to crave the drug. Addiction can be psychological. Your brain might need that feeling or release or relaxation or euphoria, or whatever you feel when you drink. It's easy to tell if you are addicted to alcohol—stop drinking. If you can't stop, you're addicted. It doesn't matter whether you drink beer or whiskey or whether you drink a six-pack per day or one drink per night or a few every Friday. If you can't stop drinking, you are physically or psychologically addicted—perhaps both. Fortunately, alcohol addiction is a problem you can fix. There are plenty of people who will help you, if you need help.

Regardless of why you drink, or how much you drink, alcohol kills your brain cells. The more you drink, the more dead brain cells. It's pretty simple. If you kill too many brain cells, you kill yourself. Unfortunately, brain cells are the only cells your body can't replace. Once they're gone, they're gone.

Aside from the fact that you're wasting money and risking addiction, the primary reason I don't think you should drink now, when you're growing up, is because you are growing up. Your bodies and brains aren't fully developed. You only get one of each in your life—one body, one brain. Give yourself a chance to grow up healthy, get some more education and experience, before you start taking risks with such valuable assets.

I used to take a glass of wine with dinner once in a while, until I had a roommate who was an alcoholic. She made me see the true nature of the drug. My friend was an intelligent, charming, beautiful young woman when she was sober. When she was drunk, she was nasty, spiteful, ugly, and pathetic. I felt sorry for her. For a year, I picked her up off the living room floor in the middle of the night. I washed the vomit out of her hair and put her to bed. I woke her up in the morning, helped her get dressed, and drove her to work. I thought I was help-ing her. Then somebody pointed out that I was helping my friend be an alcoholic. One of the hardest things I ever had to do was tell my friend I wasn't going to help her any more. Eventually, she admitted she needed help and entered a reha-bilitation program. I never saw her again. When she entered rehab, she left her old life and her old friends behind. I don't drink at all any more, because I remember what it did to my friend, and I've seen the same thing happen to other people. I don't drink because I know that alcohol is much stronger than I am.

I'm not saying that everybody who takes a drink is a drug addict. Adults have a right to drink if they want to, and I respect their right to drink. But I do think we should be honest about what drinking is. Drinking is legal drug use.

Smoking

When I was in junior high school and had smoked a few cigarettes behind the school just for fun, a woman from the American Cancer Society came to visit our classroom. She brought with her two jars—one containing a section of pink, healthy lung and the other containing a blackened, pitted piece of a smoker's lung. Those bits of lung were more effec-tive than all the literature and lectures I'd seen and heard about the evils of smoking. To this day, nearly thirty years later, I can see that sickly lung quite clearly, and it has kept me from smoking another cigarette.

My own students react just as strongly to the same pre-sentation, and I invite an anti-smoking representative into my classroom each year. In addition, I talk to my students about the economic aspects of smoking, something they don't often consider.

Here's my Anti-smoking pitch:

Do you want to know what makes me mad? It makes me absolutely furious that there are hundreds, probably thousands, of adults in this country—educated, intelligent adults—who spend their whole working day trying to think of ways to get you to start smoking. They do this when they know for a fact that smoking will harm you and possibly kill you. They don't care if you get hurt. They want you to smoke for one reason— they want you to become smokers, nicotine addicts, so that they can spend your money. They'll use your money to pay for their nice clothes, fancy cars, big houses, and exotic vacations. You'll pay for them to visit Disneyland and Paris and what do you get in return? Yellow teeth, stained fingers, terrible breath, coughing, hacking, black crap in your lungs, and less money in your wallet. That makes me mad, and it should make you mad, too.

Maybe you think smoking looks cools. I used to think so, too. When I was in school, my brother and his friends used to sneak out to the hayloft in the barn and smoke cigarettes. I wanted to be cool, and I wanted them to like me, so I smoked with them. The first few times I smoked, it tasted terrible. It made me cough and it made me dizzy. But it also gave me a rush, like spinning too fast on a merry-go-round. After a week or so, I stopped getting dizzy when I smoked, but then I found myself wanting a cigarette—I was addicted to the nicotine. Just that fast. Snap.

Nicotine is a highly addictive drug, and cigarette manufacturers add a little extra nicotine just to make sure you get addicted fast. I didn't know when I started smoking that one cigarette contains one-seventieth of a drop of nicotinic acid. One drop of nicotinic acid would kill you. So, each time you smoke, you are poisoning your body just a little bit. That's why you get a rush the first few times you smoke, or if you go without a cigarette for a long time. Your body is going, "Oh, no! She's poisoning me! What am I gonna do? Let me outta here!" Once you're addicted, you don't feel the rush, but your body still panics and it's still being poisoned, very very slowly. Cigarette makers don't want you to die quickly, because then you wouldn't be alive to give them your money, so they only put a little bit of nicotine in your cigarettes. They want you to take a long time dying.

Fortunately, somebody from the American Cancer Society came to my school a few months after I had started smoking. She showed us a piece of a normal lung in a jar. It was pink. It wasn't exactly what I'd call pretty, but it wasn't disgusting. Then she showed us a piece of a smoker's lung. It was black and had crusty little chunks of what looked like dirt hanging to it. It made me sick to see what I had been doing to myself. I was committing suicide, one cigarette at a time—and paying a lot of money to do it. Not very smart. So, I quit smoking. I had only been smoking for a couple of months, but I had smoked a pack every day. Quitting was the hardest thing I have ever done in my life. I thought it would be easy, but I have never been more wrong. I would go for hours without a cigarette and think I had managed to quit, but then the craving to smoke would hit me and I would feel like I could kill somebody for a cigarette. I would smoke a butt off the sidewalk if that's all I could find. That was the poison talking to me.

If you think you can smoke for a while and look cool, then quit when you're cool enough, look around you. See how many kids and adults are trying to quit—and failing. See how many adults are spending thousands of dollars on nicotine gum, nicotine patches, hypnotism, drugs, and other things to try to cure their addiction. Ask any adult who smokes if he or she has ever tried to quit. The answer will probably be yes. Ask if they were successful—the answer will probably be no. Most people can't quit because nicotine is a real killer. Ask yourself if you want to be like them when you grow up, because if you smoke now, you will be like them when you grow up. You'll try to quit. Maybe you'll be one of the lucky ones who can quit. And you'll try to convince your children not to smoke. I promise you will. And maybe, just maybe, you'll be really really lucky and they'll listen to you.

After we talk about smoking, I make my students an offer and a challenge. I tell them that I will give twenty-five dollars to any smoker who goes without a cigarette for a whole month. There's no contract. It's a handshake deal, and I trust them to be honest. I tell them I'm not worried about losing my money, because most people can't quit—but if they can, I will be happy to spend my money to keep them healthy. Usually, several students accept the challenge, but I've only had to pay up three times in eight years. Twice, other staff members offered to help me pay the new non-smoker. We didn't waste our money. Seventy-five dollars is a small price to pay for three healthy children.

Q & A

Questions from Teachers

When I conduct workshops for teachers or address members of educational organizations, there is always a long line of people waiting afterward to ask "one more question." Usually, they apologize for taking my time (which I don't mind at all), and they explain that they didn't ask their questions during the Q&A portion of my presentation because their questions were so different, so unusual, or so personal. I think those teachers would be surprised to find that many other teachers share the same concerns. In this chapter, I'd like to discuss some of the most frequently asked questions. Of course, I know I don't have all the answers. But I do have answers, and even if you disagree with them, they may inspire you to look at the same old situations from a fresh, new perspective.

• • •

1. Like you, I teach many students of color. I try not to take my students' belligerence personally, but I often wonder whether they would treat an African-American or Chinese or Puerto Rican teacher the way they treat me. Have you ever felt you need to apologize for being white?

I think you are right not to take your students' attitudes personally. Of course, children notice their teachers' skin color. They also notice our accents, hair textures, facial characteristics, feet size, and body odors, and they often make comments about those observations, but voicing observations is natural for children, even older children and teens. Unless they make it clear that they are concerned about the color of your skin, I would assume that they are simply acting like children. Just because a student points out that she and I look or sound different doesn't mean she doesn't accept me. It means she is paying attention to the world and articulating her thoughts.

Call me Pollyanna if you like, but you will never convince me to mistrust children, because I know from my experiences with students, from valedictorians to gang leaders, that all children have two basic needs—to be loved and accepted, and to be treated with basic human dignity and respect. If you do those two things, you will be able to teach your students. They will not automatically love you and rush to embrace you. Many of them will resist you, resent you, challenge you, and defy you—simply because you are an adult and an authority figure. But don't take it personally. It isn't personal. It's natural.

We know that children must be taught to be prejudiced. They are not as concerned about other people's skin color, religion, culture, or native languages as adults are—until we teach them to be concerned. Children mimic. Even young Nazis are usually parroting propaganda. Children who are prejudiced—whether it's anti-white, anti-black, anti-Asian, or anti-Hispanic—will make an exception for a teacher who falls into the "anti" category if that teacher approaches them from an attitude of genuine respect and caring. I believe that those students who are most defiant are usually the most frightened or insecure. Perhaps they are angry, or have had bad experiences with adults who look like you. One boy couldn"t stand me because I looked like his stepmother. And I have had African-American males, for example, who have had only unpleasant experiences with white males—police officers, store detectives, teachers, and other authority figures who punished or threatened them. Don't expect them to make an abrupt turnaround. But do expect them to give you the benefit of the doubt until they have reason not to trust you.

When I sense that my skin color is an issue in any classroom, I tell my students, "I can't help it if I glow in the dark, so cut me some slack. It isn't fair to erase somebody's face. If you decide, after you get to know me, that you don't like my politics or my personality or my sense of humor, fine, I can accept that. Or I can change those things. You don't have to like me. But it is wrong for you to decide you don't like me simply because my skin is white or my nose is crooked or because I have big feet—those are things I cannot change and that isn't fair."

You can't make your students like you, but you can make it clear that when they step into your classroom, they have made a choice and with that choice comes the responsibility for cooperating with you so that you can do your job. If any student has such a strong personal dislike for you that he or she cannot accept that responsibility, or such strong hatred towards a particular group that he or she cannot refrain from making derogatory and hurtful comments, then do yourself and all of your other students a favor and persuade the administration office to change that student's class assignment. Then get on with the program and teach those students who are willing to exert enough self-restraint to appreciate your sincerity and learn what you have to teach.

2. It sounds crazy, but it seems like I'm punished when I try to help my students, especially if they begin to achieve more than is expected of them.

You aren't crazy. Unfortunately, when you step outside the norm, even in a positive sense, you challenge other people's ideas and convictions. Many teachers have shared their stories of successes that were cut short or intentionally sabotaged. One student teacher who corresponds with me via e-mail wrote about her conversation with the principal of the school where she teaches. Given a class of "slow" students, this teacher was able to motivate the students to read a difficult book from the approved reading list at her school. When the principal found out, the teacher was told she could not teach that book to her "slow" students because it was on the list for the honors students. I suggested that she teach the standard curriculum but tell the "slow" kids that if they finished early and earned good grades on the easy book, they could read the honors-level book for extra credit. They read both books and did a good job on the associated lessons. When the principal found out, he admitted that perhaps he had underestimated the teacher's class, but he did not thank her or otherwise acknowledge her excellent teaching.

Another woman, a teacher in a Head Start program, wrote to tell me about her success in getting preschool students excited about reading. She arranged with the local librarian to open the library early on Wednesdays, just for the Head Start children. Visits were scheduled every two weeks, which would allow each of the four classes of children to visit the library once each month. Not a lot to ask. But the teacher's supervisor informed her that only one visit could be made to the library per month because library visits were considered field trips. Field trips could be scheduled only once per month, unless the students could walk. "People blame illiteracy on TV," the teacher wrote in a letter, "but kids aren't illiterate because of TV. They're illiterate because of misplaced priorities in our society."

My advice is to trust your instincts and set the highest standards for your students, but keep quiet about innovative ideas, even if they work, unless you know you have the support of other staff members and administrators. Find somebody outside the system to share your joy, and keep your success to yourself at school. My own method is to do whatever I think will motivate my students, and if I am caught in the act, I plead ignorance and apologize profusely.

3. Why bother trying so hard? Most of the kids don't want to learn, and the ones who do will learn anyway.

When I first started teaching, I confessed to one of the older teachers, a man with thirty years of experience, that I was exhausted from trying to make sure all my students learned the material I presented in class. He pointed out that I spent ten times as much energy on one or two "problem" students in a given class as I did on the thirty-five or forty students who behaved themselves and tried to learn. He suggested that it might be my ego that made me unable to accept any level of failure, and that I was cheating my students by focusing so much time and energy on people who didn't appreciate it. I swallowed my pride and took his advice. I accepted the reality that I can't save every child, that some children don't want to be saved, because they may need to fail for some personal reason that I cannot understand. I still try to save them all, but I don't ignore the ones who are working to save themselves. And I don't beat myself up for not being perfect.

Later in the same school year, the same teacher warned me, "You're going to burn yourself out in a year. Quit trying so hard. Just throw out the information. If they don't get it, screw them. Too bad. These are high school kids. In a few years, they're going to be out there on their own, at college, or working, and nobody's going to hand-feed them. It's a hard world out there and the sooner they learn that lesson, the better off they'll be."

I was too shocked to respond immediately, but the teacher read my expression correctly. "I know that's not right. I used to be young and indestructible, just like you, but the kids who don't want to learn and the administration who doesn't give a rip, and the parents who complain no matter what you do, just wore me out. I can't afford to care any more. I don't have the time or the energy."

You can do that. You can throw it out and hope they get it, pass the ones who do and fail the ones who don't. Make it easy on yourself and hard on them. Or you can really try to teach, because teaching isn't simply subject matter. If all it took was information, students could take books home or watch videotapes and learn everything they need. True teaching involves much more than knowing a subject. It involves understanding that until you address obstacles to learning, students cannot learn your lessons. Obstacles include family problems, learning disabilities, hunger, peer pressures, depression, drug/alcohol abuse, chronic illness or conditions, fear, anger, confusion, immaturity, cultural barriers. You won't be able to overcome all the obstacles, but if you try to address them and help kids learn to solve their problems or cope with them, they will relax a little, they won't feel so alone, and they will reward you by trying to learn. Beware, however. If you ask about children's lives, they will tell you. You will be given a heavy burden of their fragile hopes and dreams. Be very careful with them, and with yourself.

You can't teach all the children any more than you can save them all. You aren't there to save them all. You are there to help the ones who want to help themselves, to teach the children who want to learn. Take some advice from my cynical master teacher—give what you have to give, the best way you can, and stop worrying about whether your gift is received. And don't expect a thank-you card. Your reward comes from knowing that you have made a difference in the life of a child. If you touch only one life, you will have done enough.

4. I'm a good teacher. My students often tell me I'm the best teacher they ever had, but I sometimes feel as though the other teachers hate me. Or they think I'm crazy.

Sadly, teachers are like any other group of people. When somebody shines, instead of admiring the glow and trying to achieve their own success, some people in the group see another person's success as their own failure—similar to the concept that if somebody earns an A, somebody else has to earn an F. People who are competent and self-confident are not threatened by other people's achievements; they admire them. Try to find one other staff member who speaks your language, and develop a mutually supportive friendship. Don't overlook noncertificated staff. Library aides, secretaries, counselors, and custodians were most helpful to me. They provided moral support and did little things to make my life easier.

Don't compare yourself to other teachers. You must decide for yourself how much time, emotion, money, and energy you can afford to invest in your students. We don't all have the same capacity for handling stress or the same ability to connect with students. Take advantage of your own particular skills and talents, and don't worry whether you are doing too much or too little. If the teacher next door takes kids out to dinner, that doesn't mean you have to feel guilty if you can't afford to or don't want to. Likewise, if you enjoy introducing your students to new experiences, and don't mind spending your own money, then go, do and enjoy. Your students will appreciate you, even if nobody else does, and you will have the satisfaction of knowing that you have made a contribution to a child's education and created a fond memory for both of you to cherish in your old age.

P.S.: When I begin to feel like nobody loves me, everybody hates me, I should go eat worms, I remember the motto a veteran teacher once shared with me: *Non ilegitimus carborundum.* (Latin that roughly translates as: Don't let the "turkeys" wear you down.)

5. I'm not prejudiced and my students know it. I get along with all kinds of kids, except one group. Black girls seem to hate me; I can't get past their attitude.

Surprisingly, this comment did not come from a white teacher but from a woman of color—and I have heard other teachers say the same thing. This is not a racial issue, this is a feminist and political issue. I have experienced this situation to a mild degree and I was able, eventually, to develop a good rapport with my black female students. First, I think we must realize that black women, historically, have been on the short end of the stick, particularly in this country. Although their status has improved, it is still nowhere near being right or fair. Young black women know that if they are assaulted or raped, for example, it is distinctly possible that no real effort will be made to protect or help them. Instead of trying to convince them to give up their anger and frustration at the inequality of their position in this society, we must encourage them to harness that anger and use it for their benefit, to educate themselves, to work to better the position of women in general and black women in particular. We can introduce them to information about black women who have made significant contributions to society, black women entrepreneurs, black women who are now making history by being elected to high public office, black women who are changing history.

In my classes, I distribute excerpts from a variety of books, including passages about the possible reasons for the relatively low self-esteem of educated women, and a discussion of the ridiculous "science" of craniology—both from Gloria Steinem's book *Revolution from Within*—whereby scientists claimed that white men were superior to all women and nonwhite men because of the size of their skulls. When some women were discovered to have larger skulls, the same scientists readjusted their data to uphold their original claim. This bit of history demonstrates the foolish ignorance of prejudice and opens the door for discussion and further exploration.

My students respond with enthusiasm to Zora Neale Hurston's essay "How It Feels to Be Colored Me," which contains this surprising response to prejudice: "Sometimes I feel discriminated against, but it does not make me angry. It merely astonishes me. How *can* anyone deny themselves the pleasure of my company? It's beyond me."

However you choose to approach this problem, it's important that you accept your black female students without judging them. Don't belittle them by criticizing, even nonverbally, their slang, gestures, hairstyles, or fashions, but don't beg them to accept you or try to be "cool" by mimicking them, either. Make it clear that you respect them, empathize with their unique difficulties, but that you expect them to work hard and succeed. If, after a few weeks, you still feel strong resentment or dislike from the girls, try talking to them one at a time, not in a group. Sit down someplace private and say, "I sense that you don't like me, and I don't know why. I like you and I'm glad that you are in my class. If I have done something to insult or offend you, I wish you would tell me because I don't like to hurt people's feelings. I know how it feels to have my own feelings hurt, and I try not to do that to other people. I want my students to enjoy coming to my class."

Encourage each girl to talk, but if she refuses, thank her for taking the time to listen to you and say that you look forward to seeing her the next day. If you schedule a short personal conference with each of your "problem" girls and continue to treat them with the same courtesy and respect that you treat other students, most of them eventually will come around. If not, don't give up hope. You will have planted the seed of a thought that may grow later on. They may take your words to heart but not be able to admit it to you. I had a black student once who maintained her stony silence towards me for the entire year, until the last day of school, when she wrote me a note to tell me that I was her favorite teacher. I couldn't help wondering how she treated the teachers she disliked!

6. (This message came via e-mail.) One of my students pulled up his pants leg today and showed me that he had carved his name in his leg with a knife. I didn't know what to say. He comes from a troubled family, alcoholism and violence. He used to be a trouble-maker but a little positive acknowledgment has changed his atti-tude completely. He's screaming for help. I talked to him and offered what support I could. After he left, I went to the guidance office where I was told, "Do what you think is best." Is this what they tell our kids when they go to Guidance for help? The coun-selor said, "You're going to be burned out in five years. Slow down. Kids and parents don't change—only different faces each year." I don't really have a question, but I feel better just having talked to you about this because I know you'll understand.

Yes, I do understand, and I know how frustrating it is not to be able to help children who ask for our help, but we can't fix their lives. We can talk to them, listen to them, refer them to people who can help them—at school or in the community—and do what we can while they are in our classrooms to make them feel worthy of love and respect. A hug and a kind word or a pat on the shoulder may seem trivial to you, but they can be a major influence in a child's life. Once, I mentioned to a psychiatrist that I wondered whether children could survive such horrible childhoods, and he said that sometimes one person who cares is enough to overcome an entire dysfunctional family and years of trauma. Simply by talking to a child, reassuring him that he is a valuable and lovable person, you may provide him with a lifeline that will enable him to survive. I believe that man was right, because I have received so many letters from people who told me about one teacher who changed their lives.

As you said, it does make you feel better to talk to somebody else, somebody who will reassure you that you are not too soft for caring so much and that you shouldn't feel guilty because you can't solve every problem your students bring to you. Talking can be very therapeutic—for us and for our students.

7. Tell the truth. Aren't you afraid of some of your students?

I am afraid of the violent role models that young people admire today and the way that violence is glamorized in our society, but I am not afraid of children because they are children. I'm not afraid of the tough kids who come to school—I'm afraid of the ones who don't bother to go to school at all, who don't even make an effort to try to fit into society in some legal way. If they come to school, then I believe we have a chance to reach them.

If you work in a school district where teachers are frequently assaulted or injured by students, then I would suggest that you conduct yourself in school as you would in any other dangerous situation—keep your wits about you, don't turn your back on anybody, carry pepper spray with you, and be prepared to run. I also would campaign actively for a closed campus, with heavy security, to keep out the dangerous element. When students know there are no weapons on campus, that the administrators and teachers will protect them, that people bent on harming them will not be permitted to enter their school, that students who initiate fights will be held responsible, then they are much less prone to violent behavior.

I am not afraid of being attacked by any of my students because I give them no reason to attack me. I am straightforward and honest with them. They receive the grades they earn in my class, and they know that I will not flunk them even if I dislike their behavior or attitudes. They also know that I am available to help them if they want to pass my class. I do not embarrass, humiliate, or belittle them. If I insult someone unintentionally, I apologize in front of the class as soon as I realize what I've done. They know that I respect them, but I'm not afraid of them. I am wary of students who routinely drink alcohol or take drugs, because I can't get through the drug-induced haze to connect with the person inside. I refer them to the proper agency for help and give them a wide berth in the meantime.

Only once did I honestly believe that I had a psychotic student in my class. Believing that he was a danger to me and to the other students, I did everything I could to obtain help for that student. I also did everything I could to have the student removed from my classroom, including a visit to the district supervisor's office. If they had not removed that young man from my classroom, I would have assigned him a passing grade because his transcript does not represent any kind of truth about him or his educational progress. You may question my ethics, and I would accept your criticism, but I would also ask whether a report card grade is worth risking my safety or that of the hundreds of innocent children who spend time in my classroom.

8. In both My Posse Don't Do Homework *and* The Girls in the Back of the Class, *you mention hugging students. Aren't you afraid you'll get in trouble or be sued?*

I'm wondering whether this question is prompted by an episode in the television series *Dangerous Minds* in which Miss Johnson is suspended for hugging a student. For the record, I'd like to point out that the television series is not based on my real life, and I am not affiliated in any way with the program. Now, to answer your question.

It breaks my heart to imagine a world in which teachers cannot touch their students. Children need to be nurtured and they need human touch. Without human touch, I don't believe that is possible, and scientific research supports my belief. If we do not touch children appropriately—shake their hands to congratulate them, hug them when they are sad or discouraged, pat them on the back when they need encouragement or appreciation—then how will they know the difference between inappropriate and appropriate touching? I refuse to allow anybody to place a glass wall between my students and me. I make sure my students know that if they object to anything I do, even if it is something as insignificant as touching their hand with my own, then they are encouraged to tell me so that I will not offend them. I also make sure that they know I care about them and want them to be happy, healthy, successful adults. I don't worry about my students complaining that I touched them, because I don't touch them inappropriately. In most cases, they initiate the hugs we share.

As for parents, I contact the parents of my students, so that they don't view me as a stranger. They trust that I have their children's best interests at heart. If somebody wants to take me to court because I hugged a child, fine. Suing me wouldn't get anybody much of anything—my car is twenty years old, my savings account belongs to the IRS, and my piano is out of tune.

9. *You never seem to get tired. How do you avoid "burnout"?*

I do get tired. Sometimes I feel so exhausted that I wonder whether I can make it for one more hour. Once, I got so tired I quit teaching high school and went off to teach college. A year later, I was back in the high school classroom—older, wiser, and determined to draw the line and go home at a decent hour and forget about my students' problems. Instead of operating at warp speed for weeks, until I crashed and got sick (flu, respiratory infections, pulled muscles), eventually, I learned to pace myself. I set nonnegotiable limits for myself. No staying at school until midnight or getting up at 4:00 A.M. to grade papers. A set amount of time to be spent on lesson preparation and counseling students. I had to force myself to resume a personal life, to spend time with friends, to read books, to exercise, play music, and spend a few peaceful minutes doing nothing each day. Learning to give a little less was very difficult, but it made me a better teacher.

10. How did you do it?

The first few times I was asked that question, I was confused. How did I do what? I wondered. Eventually, I understood. "How did you do it?" means "How did you get those African-American and Hispanic kids to accept you?" My answer: I accepted them first. People who ask that question often find my answer difficult to accept. They find it hard to believe that such a simple approach could work, although I have proven time and again that it does, with students of every size, age, shape, color, and economic background. It saddens me to know that so many people think that the skin color or native language of my African-American or Hispanic or Filipino or Tongan students makes a difference. Children are children, period. They respond to honesty, respect, and affection.

I think it's interesting to note that the people who ask "How did you do it?" are always white, what I refer to as "bright white," not as an insult, but to differentiate them from the many non-English speaking light-skinned people in this world. Black people never ask me that question; neither do French or Argentinean or Mexican or Chinese or Guatemalan or Filipino or Tongan people. Children never ask, either. Why? Because those people who aren't "bright white" know what children know—that the skin color of a teacher means very little to the students sitting in the classroom. The only thing that really concerns students is how their teacher treats them. Everything else is incidental.

11. I've just changed careers to become a teacher. I'm a little nervous. Help!

Although I urge teachers to be honest and straightforward with their students, as a matter of personal integrity and self-respect, I also advocate being slightly devious at times. When you begin teaching, students will want to know if this is your first job. They may be curious and sincerely interested in your life, but more likely, they want to know if you "know the ropes" or whether they will be able to take advantage of your inexperience. So, when your students ask if this is your first teaching job, say, "This is my first year at *your* school, but you can relax because I'm an old pro." You won't be actually lying, because you haven't said you were an old pro at teaching, you only said you were an old pro. This is one of those times when being older is an advantage—students are much less apt to challenge you than they would a twenty-one-year-old recent college graduate.

Other than that, I'd suggest that you look at your classroom and your students as your business place and your employees. Their job is to come to your classroom and do the work you give them. Your job is to motivate them to try, to correct their errors with tact and diplomacy, and to produce the best possible product—happy, educated students. If you approach teaching from that perspective and take advantage of your years of experience in business, child rearing, and life in general, then you have an excellent chance of becoming an effective and well-liked teacher. You have a wealth of experiences, anecdotes, and practical lessons to share with your students, which are every bit as valuable as the lessons in their textbooks. Welcome to the most rewarding, satisfying, frustrating, and emotionally draining job on this planet. The children of this country need you.

12. If you had the power, what would you do to improve our education system?

That is my favorite question! First, I'd appoint myself Queen of Education. Then, I'd pass a law making it illegal to have more than twenty students of any age in any classroom in this country. I don't care if there aren't any statistical studies to show that smaller classes result in better learning, higher grades, happier children, and more effective (and energetic) teachers—anybody who has spent time in a classroom knows that people learn better when they have the opportunity to interact with the instructor.

Next, I'd raise teacher salaries, not to an incredibly high amount, but so that they would be comparable to salaries for licensed professionals in other occupations who have five or more years of training and education.

Third, I would pass another law, making it mandatory for students to attend school in their own communities, so that their families and neighbors would have immediate access to their school. These community schools would be limited to a maximum of 600 students and would all teach the same basic core curriculum for grades K-8: English, reading, Spanish, math, science, geography, computers, history, critical thinking, conflict resolution, ethics, and citizenship. After the eighth grade, students would attend larger schools for grades 9 to 12, although those schools would be limited to 1200 students each. High schools would offer a wide variety of elective classes, with emphasis on art, music, business management, computer science, medicine and science, and community service. All schools in this country would receive the same amount of money from the government and would have the same facilities and materials—which would eliminate the need for busing and the discrepancies in pay from one district to another. If a child happened to attend an all-black or all-white school for the first eight years, he or she would receive the same education as any other student and would be equally prepared to succeed in high school.

Don't stop me now—I'm on a roll. I'd involve students and parents in the planning and operation of their schools, although parents would not have the right to dictate curriculum. Teachers would receive annual report cards from students that would be taken seriously and addressed appropriately. Administrators would receive report cards from teachers and, if they received failing marks, would have to attend remedial classes or find other jobs. All administrators would be required to have at least five years of experience as a classroom teacher in order to become eligible for an administrative position.

Schools would be exempt from ridiculous insurance charges, so that they could be used by the entire community for after-school projects, evening and weekend recreation, continuing education courses for adults, and community celebrations. Students would be responsible for picking up trash and cleaning the bathrooms and classrooms, so that they would take pride in their schools and themselves as contributors in our society.

Finally, one of my best ideas. I would require that every senator, congressperson, and representative in this country spend two weeks teaching in public school—not giving speeches, but working from the curriculum, with the materials available. They would gain a new respect for teachers and an appreciation of what it takes to operate an effective school, and they would fall in love with our students, just as we do. We would never again have to beg for money for books and materials, and we would not have to convince people to have faith in our children.

13. Any advice for a new teacher fresh out of college?

Ask yourself whether you honestly like children, even the unattractive and obnoxious ones. If not, then please find another field, one in which you won't have the opportunity to traumatize innocent children. If you are certain that you like children, then welcome to a wonderful profession. My advice is brief:

Trust yourself. Follow your heart. Keep your sense of humor. And remember—your students may be taller than you are, but they are still children. They may act tough and fearless, but they are tender and frightened. When you walk into that classroom, know why you're there and what you want your students to learn; then relax and have some fun. Enjoy yourself. Remember, you're a teacher, one of the lucky chosen few. Where else could you earn such an extravagant salary for such easy work, enjoy such luxurious working conditions, and receive such overwhelming respect and appreciation for your efforts?

Twenty Years from Now

Your Students Will Remember You

Twenty (or forty) years from now, you may not remember your students, but they will remember you. They may not remember the lessons you taught, and they may have forgotten your face, but they will remember quite clearly the way you made them feel about themselves. They'll remember your criticisms and your compliments. Just last week, I complimented a bank teller on her beautiful handwriting. She blushed. Thinking she may have misunderstood, I repeated my comment. She looked down at her hands and said, "My second-grade teacher used to hit my knuckles with a ruler because my handwriting was so bad. I loved my teacher and I wanted her to like me, so I sat at my kitchen table every day, for months, and wrote my letters over and over."

"Well, she must have been pleased to see how beautifully your handwriting turned out," I said.

"I never did meet her standards," the teller said, "but I kept practicing, even after I left her classroom. When I was in the fourth grade, I went back and showed her how nicely I could write."

"Certainly she praised you for working so hard," I said.

The bank teller sighed and shuffled through the deposit slips on the counter. "She didn't remember me." After a moment, she forced a smile. "But that was a long time ago, wasn't it?"

Unlike other memories, time doesn't seem to diminish people's recollections of their experiences with teachers. Although age may allow people to put their childhood experiences in perspective, age doesn't necessarily dull the memory or the pain, as this letter from Diane of St. Albans, West Virginia, demonstrates:

> One instance really sticks out in my mind: My eighth-grade teacher asked us to write our opinion on a certain subject. I do not remember the subject or how I responded; however, I do remember the teacher practically snickering, the red "F" for failure and the comment, "This is not the correct answer" written at the top of the first page. When I questioned the grade, reiterating the fact that she wanted my opinion, she just laughed and said she felt I was wrong. . . . I just learned in the past three years that my opinion is valuable and I am worth something.

The Good News

For every negative letter I receive about a teacher, I receive a hundred positive ones, which confirms my belief that there are many more good teachers than bad. A couple of years ago, while visiting New York City, I had the pleasure of meeting Bill Parkhurst, a broadcast journalist and author. The conversation turned to teachers at one point, and Bill told me the most remarkable thing. As a research project for an upcoming book, he had spent a year working closely with a private detective, so that he could write accurately and realistically about the detective in his book.

"You'll be interested and surprised, I think, to know the most common reason that people hire private detectives," Bill told me. "It isn't matrimonial surveillance, as many people think. I interviewed over 150 detectives and every time I walked into an agency, one of the first things I'd hear would be somebody asking for help in locating a former teacher. People want to find their teachers and thank them."

Bill was right. I was interested and surprised to learn that so many people go to so much trouble to track down their teachers. And I was delighted, because I know that for every person who hires a detective, there must be hundreds of other people who are considering the idea—which means that teachers in this country are doing their jobs, educating and inspiring children, despite all the bad press about the failures of our schools.

Talking About Teachers: Letters from Readers

Of course, there is no way to tell what your students will remember about you, but perhaps you will see something of yourself in these letters. The following excerpts are direct quotations from the many letters I've received from readers of *My Posse Don't Do Homework* and *The Girls in the Back of the Class* who wrote about their own teachers.

Arthur, of Suffield, Connecticut, has very vivid memories of his school days. Here is a portion of his letter:

> *I remember my first-grade teacher, a woman whom I can still envision after all these many years, who taught me to read, a habit which has brightened my life for over 50 years since then. I remember a very demanding teacher from whom I took a class in Old English when I worked on my first undergraduate degree. How troublesome he was; how wise he was; what a great gift he gave me in demanding excellence. We have remained friends over the ensuing years. Many teachers stand out like bright stars in my sky.*

Bud's letter arrived from Springdale, Arkansas, on his official letterhead stationery:

My mother and father were divorced when I was about nine or ten and my mother had only an eighth-grade education. We worked very hard to survive and I can still remember vividly the stiffness of the shirts I wore made from feed sacks. It was through the help and encouragement of coaches and teachers with the love, compassion and commitment such as yours that I continued my education. I received an athletic scholarship to college and enlisted as an airman basic in the U.S. Air Force in the middle of my junior year. I then entered the flying training program and graduated with wings and a commission on the same day. I spent twenty years as a fighter pilot and four years in the Pentagon, rising to the rank of colonel. I completed my bachelor's degree under the "bootstrap program" and my master's degree at night school. I also completed the War College national security management program. I am now vice president and general manager of [an aviation company.] I am not telling you these things to brag, but to let you know that successful lives and careers often begin by warm and loving people like you.

Alex, a dockworker in Abilene, Texas, wrote this letter after he read the condensation of *The Girls in the Back of the Class* in *Reader's Digest* during his lunch break:

After I read the story, I went outside. It was a cold and dark night. I work on a loading dock from 9:00 P.M. to 7:00 A.M. I walked and walked where no one could see me and I cried and I cried hard. I had a teacher just like you in high school that did everything she could to help me. It has been six years since I last spoke to her. . . . She got me to believe in myself so good that I thought I really could do anything. So far, I've accomplished every goal that I've sent my mind to. Right now I'm in the interview process to become a probation officer.

The main reason I wanted to write to you is because I really didn't know how my teacher felt about me. Reading your story gave me some insight. Now I know that she really cared, and I wish I had just one more chance to tell her thanks. But really I wish I could hug her real tight and tell her thanks for everything. She played a very important role in forming the foundation of my life.

From Dusseldorf, Germany, Andrea wrote to tell me about a teacher who tested her and placed her in an ESL class when Andrea was in the United States as an exchange student:

That day I decided I would not like her. I still do not really know why. This teacher was just as stubborn about keeping me in that ESL program as I was trying to get out. I finally gave up, not knowing that this would save my life.

I was sure she must hate me for making all this trouble. I expected her to reject me but instead she kept asking me how I was doing and how things went. For a long time I was suspicious of her behaviour towards me since back then I could not imagine that somebody was truly interested in me and my life. I still remember the day when she offered me to talk to her. She was sitting at her desk, and when I was leaving the classroom she called to me. She looked at me and said that she would always be there if I wanted to talk. I had never heard that before. At that point I had a choice. I could take advantage of that offer or reject it. I figured I had nothing to lose since I would leave the States anyway once the school year was over so I took the risk and started to open up bit by bit.

In an environment that was filled with respect, understanding and love I was able to tell her things I had denied for a long time. By the end of the school year the teacher I had once decided not to like became the most important person in my life and she still is today. She was the first person who told me she loved me and cared about me. She always believed in me and my abilities.

Though she was on the other side of the world, she helped me get through one of the hardest times in my life. Shortly after I

returned to Germany from the U.S., I was diagnosed with can-
cer. I had a tumor at the ovary. I had surgery followed by
chemotherapy. What kept me going through this treatment
(which was hell) was the knowledge that somewhere out there
was somebody who loved me and respected me for the kind of
person I am. At times when I was about to give up she was
there in my mind and reminded me of my strength that I have
inside of me. . . . When there is somebody who loves you and
cares about you, you can handle almost everything in your life.

Though I did not expect it I got accepted at medical school here
in Dusseldorf. I have finished my first semester and I really
enjoy it. My goal right now is to become a therapist and work
with abused teenagers.

Anu, a sixteen-year-old boy who lives in Ludhiana, India,
wrote to tell me about a teacher who touched his life,
although he was in her class for only a short time:

I adored her very much but after teaching for a few months, she
went to Canada. I was really shocked but could do nothing. . . .
I have lost her, maybe forever but her sweet memories shall
remain in my heart for all the remaining days of my life. . . . I
began to think what is the magic in people like her that they
make such a long-lasting impression on the minds in such short
periods of contact.

The day our result of our 10th standard [exam] was out I stood
there with tears in my eyes and hoped that she could know that
I, an average student for others, had topped in the whole class
with 91% marks in her subject. I am writing this letter to you
because I wanted to tell her how I felt about her and express my
gratitude but I could not and I want to tell it to you because I
find you just like my good-natured, sweet, loving madam. I
hope you will accept my friendship.

Those letters make me so proud to be a teacher. But they
also scare me, just a little, because they remind me that one

day I may be the memory that people recall when they think of their school days. Actually, I am a memory already. Just today I received an e-mail message from one of my former students, Raul, who is now twenty-three years old and working in a research center at a major university. Raul wrote:

> *Hey Miss J: I received your picture with the letter you sent me. Thanks. You had some look in your face that only you know what it was about and I can only guess. You probably met your husband country dancing and he swept you off your feet. You felt like you were dancing on clouds soft and light.*
>
> *Both of you are thinking nice of me and keeping the faith. I know sometimes I do dumb things but we are all human and sometimes we make mistakes or say things we don't want to. But I know this. No matter what I do or how bad I mess up, you have always stuck by me and kept the faith that one of these days I may succeed in this life. I still recall the day you forced us to come and take those job interviews here. That was real nice and I still thank you for that. I don't think I could ever repay you for all the good you have done for me. Miss J, and Mike, you are two good people and you have a star in my book.*

I can't count the times I've told teachers: You earn a star in your heavenly crown for every day you teach children. Now I have a star in Raul's book, too. I am doubly blessed.

You Are a Star

If you are a retired teacher, there is a good chance that a former student is trying to locate you as you read this sentence. If you are currently teaching, perhaps it will make up for some of the hardships and challenges you face every day to know that right now, you are making memories and earning stars.

A FEW OF MY FAVORITE BOOKS*

Multicultural Perspectives

Coming of Age in America: A Multicultural Anthology. New York: The New Press, 1994.

Gonzalez, Ray, ed. *Mirrors Beneath the Earth: Short Fiction by Chicano Writers.* Willimantic, Conn.: Curbstone Press, 1992.

Rummel, Jack. *Malcolm X: Militant Black Leader.* New York: Chelsea House, 1989.

Shabazz, Betty. *Malcolm X on Afro-American History.* New York: Pathfinder Press, 1990.

Smith, Anna Deavere. *Twilight: Los Angeles, 1992.* New York: Doubleday, 1994.

Walker, Alice. *I Love Myself When I Am Laughing . . . And Then Again When I Am Looking Mean and Impressive* (A Zora Neale Hurston Reader). New York: The Feminist Press, 1979.

Wild Women Don't Wear No Blues: Black Women Writers on Love, Men and Sex. New York: Doubleday, 1993.

Fun and Inspiration

Anderson, Karen, ed. *Kids' Big Book of Games.* New York: Workman Publishing Co., 1990.

Big Book of Games II. Games magazine. New York: Workman Publishing, 1988.

Byrne, Robert. *The 2,548 Best Things Anybody Ever Said.* New York: Galahad Books, 1996.

How Things Work. Lincolnwood, Ill.: Publications International, 1990.

MENSA Mighty Mind Boosters. New York: Barnes & Noble Books, 1996.

Scieszka, Jon. *The True Story of the 3 Little Pigs.* New York: Viking, 1989.

Shortz, Will, ed. *Giant Book of Games.* New York: Times Books (Random House), 1991.

Essays and Short Fiction:
Good Writing that Appeals to Young People

Adams, W. Royce. *Viewpoints*. Lexington, Mass.: D.C. Heath, 1989.

Conlin, Mary Lou. *Patterns Plus: A Short Prose Reader with Argumentation*. New York: Houghton Mifflin, 1987.

Conscious Reader, The, 4th ed. New York: Macmillan, 1988.

Our Times/2:Readings from Recent Periodicals. Boston: Bedford Books (St. Martin's), 1991.

Steinem, Gloria. *Outrageous Acts and Everyday Rebellions*. New York: Henry Holt, 1995.

Sudden Fiction: American Short-Short Stories. Layton, Utah: Gibbs M. Smith, Inc., 1986.

Vesterman, William. *The College Writer's Reader*. New York: McGraw-Hill, 1988.

Individual Essays

Baker, Russell. "School vs. Education." *Viewpoints: Readings Worth Thinking and Writing About*. Lexington, Mass.: D.C. Heath, 1989.

Banks, R. Richard. "Presenting the Good News About Black College Students." *Viewpoints: Readings Worth Thinking and Writing About*. Lexington, Mass.: D.C. Heath, 1989.

Chisholm, Shirley. "I'd Rather Be Black Than Female." *Models for Writers*. New York: St. Martin's Press, 1982.

Heilbroner, Robert. "Don't Let Stereotypes Warp Your Judgments." *Models for Writers*. New York: St. Martin's Press, 1982.

Jones, Rachel L. "What's Wrong with Black English." *Viewpoints: Readings Worth Thinking and Writing About*. Lexington, Mass.: D.C Heath, 1989.

King, Martin Luther, Jr. "Ways of Meeting Oppression." *Models for Writers*. New York: St. Martin's Press, 1982.

Maynard, Joyce. "His Talk, Her Talk." *Viewpoints: Readings Worth Thinking and Writing About*. Lexington, Mass.: D.C. Heath, 1989.

Raymond, David. "On Being 17, Bright, and Unable to Read." *Models for Writers.* New York: St. Martin's Press, 1982.

Stanat, Kirby. "How to Take a Job Interview." *Viewpoints: Readings Worth Thinking and Writing About.* Lexington, Mass.: D.C. Heath, 1989.

Staples, Brent. "Night Walker." *Viewpoints: Readings Worth Thinking and Writing About.* Lexington, Mass.: D.C. Heath, 1989.

Van Oech, Roger. "To Err Is Wrong." *Viewpoints: Readings Worth Thinking and Writing About.* Lexington, Mass.: D.C. Heath, 1989.

Education and Leadership

Action in Teacher Education. Journal of the Association of Teacher Educators, Reston, Va.

Applied Management. Marine Corps Institute, Washington, D.C.: Marine Barracks (undated).

Gordon, Thomas. *T.E.T.: Teacher Effectiveness Training.* New York: David McKay Co., 1987.

Holt, John C. *How Children Fail* (revised). Reading, Mass.: Addison-Wesley, 1995.

———*How Children Learn* (revised). Reading, Mass.: Addison-Wesley, 1995.

Irlen, Helen. *Reading by the Colors: Overcoming Dyslexia and Other Reading Disabilities.* Garden City, N.Y.: Avery Publishing Group, 1991.

Leadership. Marine Corps Institute, Washington, D.C.: Marine Barracks (undated).

Rose, Mike. *Possible Lives: The Promise of Public Education in America.* New York: Houghton Mifflin, 1995.

Steinem, Gloria. *Revolution from Within.* Boston: Little, Brown, 1993.

Wallace, Betty, and William Graves. *Poisoned Apple: How Our Schools' Reliance on the "Bell Curve" Creates Frustration, Mediocrity and Failure.* New York: St. Martin's, 1993.

Psychology

Encyclopedia of Human Intelligence. Vol. 2. New York: Macmillan, 1994.

Encylopedia of Psychology. Vol. 1, 2nd ed. New York: John Wiley & Sons, 1994.

Goleman, Daniel. *Emotional Intelligence.* New York: Bantam Books, 1995.

Jeffers, Susan. *Feel the Fear and Do It Anyway.* New York: Fawcett Columbine, 1987.

Mann, Judy. *The Difference.* New York: Warner Books, 1994.

Marley, John. *Handwriting Analysis Made Easy: A Guide to Character and Human Behavior.* London: Bancroft & Co., 1967.

Pipher, Mary. *Reviving Ophelia.* New York: Ballantine Books, 1994.

Spence, Gerry. *From Freedom to Slavery.* New York: St. Martin's Press, 1993.

*Some of these books are old, but so am I, and I shop in used-book stores. If you have trouble finding these books, check with your local library or used-book store—or try the on-line bookstore Amazon, which has info on many hard-to-find books (http://www.amazon.com). Amazon is also a good source for information on the latest books, by topic or writer. For instance, you can request a list of books about education or psychology or a list of books by a given author.